SUPERNATURAL
NORTH

SUPERNATURAL NORTH

DARREN W. RITSON

AMBERLEY

To My Girls
Jayne and Abbey

First published 2009

Amberley Publishing
Cirencester Road, Chalford,
Stroud, Gloucestershire, GL6 8PE

www.amberley-books.com

British Library Cataloguing in Publication Data.
A catalogue record for this book is available from the British
Library.

ISBN 978 1 84868 277 1

Typesetting and Origination by Amberley Publishing.
Printed in Great Britain.

CONTENTS

ACKNOWLEDGEMENTS

First I would like to thank Peter Underwood, FRSA, for writing the foreword to this volume. Your kind words, advice and support over the past four years have been an enormous help and they mean a great deal to me. You are an inspiration, a true gentleman and a legend in psychical research, and I am honoured to know you. My thanks go to Peter Johnson and the Society for Psychical Research for allowing the reproduction of certain extracts from the Willington Mill case. To Mike Hallowell for being there, as always, with his support and encouragement. Many thanks must go to the very brave Marc and Marianne for allowing us to help them in their poltergeist infested home back in 2006. Thanks go to The North East Ghost Research Team and to Drew Bartley, Fiona Vipond, Lee Stephenson, Mark Winter, Paul Dixon and Ralph Keeton of the Ghosts and Hauntings Overnight Surveillance Team (G.H.O.S.T.) for sharing in my adventures. Many thanks must go to Tom Orde-Powlett from Castle Bolton for his help with the Castle Bolton chapter and to James Bolton for the use of the image of the castle; to Darren Olley, Levens Hall/Mullen Design and Muncaster Castle (Brian Sherwen) for also allowing me to use their photographs herein; to Bernard Copley and Ian Lodge of Ye Olde White Hart Pub in Hull for their use of the 'skull' image. Thanks go to Ken Goor, Leeds ghost walker and author of 'Haunted Leeds' and for sharing his information and helping me with the Leeds section of the book. Many thanks go 'Haunted Chester' for the use of certain information on their website. My thanks go to my friend and acquaintance Julliette Gregson for her much needed help with the Blackpool chapter. My thanks also go to Richard Felix and everyone else that I have spoken to, no matter who you are, during the compilation of this book. I must not forget all the landlords, landladies, property owners, members of staff, guides and officials that have allowed my overnight access to 'haunted premises' in order to carry out much needed and vital work into ghosts and hauntings: my thanks to you all. Thanks also to my partner of fourteen years Jayne Watson and our beautiful daughter Abbey May Ritson (to whom this book is dedicated). Finally my most humble respect and admiration must go to all of those individual spirits and souls that have passed over into the next world, wherever and whatever that may be. Whether or not you are really returning to our plane of existence we may never know for sure, but my thoughts and my prayers are with you all.

FOREWORD

The study of psychic phenomena has created a vast amount of literature of varying degrees of quality and I feel that it is very important not to have a fixed view either for or against paranormal activity.

Ghosts, it would seem, come in all shapes and sizes, in all weathers and in all conditions. They represent people of all ages, in all manner of occupations, or none at all, and there are reported ghosts of animals, of physical objects and of the living as well as of the dead.

I have seen perhaps three ghosts in my life and each time when I was least expecting to see anything. One was the ghost of my father, who died when I was nine years of age, on the night of his death; another was of a man I saw almost daily but did not know by name or anything about him; and the third was an unknown and unidentified face at a séance in a haunted house.

The only certain thing about ghosts is their uncertainty. It may be that when we are in a receptive and relaxed mood, and not occupied with thoughts of practical things, that ghosts, if such things exist, can manifest. I can certainly recall occasions when I and other investigators have spent the night in the most haunted room of a haunted house and, having done our best all night to tempt the ghost, given up early in the morning, deciding it was going to be an uneventful visit. Then, having collected, immobilized and packed up the machinery and apparatus carefully set up hours earlier, we settled down to rest before returning home – suddenly, without any warning, we would experience odd happenings: loud thumps, bangs, footsteps and voices – all of which we were completely unable to explain. Unfortunately, of course, on these occasions nothing is primed to record anything.

Ghosts can be so frustrating! But so absorbingly interesting too; you just never know whether the next investigation will be the really important one. Hope springs eternal in the breast of the genuine ghost hunter.

This is the seventh book from the pen of Darren W. Ritson and it includes information on the ghosts of Newcastle upon Tyne, the birthplace of the author. This was of interest to me as, some years ago now, I took part in an extended broadcast and lecture there, talking about some of the ghosts in the North Country, following the publication of my *Ghosts of North West England*. It was an engrossing experience for me and I well remember my first visit to that fine city and the welcome attention I encountered, not least by those in charge and connected with the broadcast, for I soon found myself being bombarded from all sides by first-hand stories of ghosts and ghostly activity. Another memory of Newcastle upon Tyne is signing over a hundred autographs!

At all events I was left in no doubt that the city had dozens of ghost stories associated with it – some historical and others modern. I soon discovered that many of the stories related to me were little more than legends, unauthenticated and unsupported by any testimony worthy of the name, while others relied on the sole evidence of one person or were mere hearsay, second or third hand. Having said that, I found some apparently authentic and well-substantiated stories of ghosts, and I left with a favourable impression of the city and its probable ghostly population. The author of the present volume has succeeded in discovering some fascinating and original Newcastle upon Tyne ghosts and there are even more detailed in another of his books devoted to 'Haunted Newcastle'.

Many famous and historical cases, such as the haunting of Willington Mill (actually most of the reported happenings took place in the mill house, completely detached from the mill and the residence of the mill owner, Joseph Procter), are extensively recounted. There are also reports of much less well-known cases of reported ghosts and I think it is important that instances of apparent hauntings, investigated by honest and sincere seekers of truth, should be encouraged.

With the gift of hindsight it is all too easy to suggest additional precautions that might have been taken beforehand, and while it is obviously necessary to be alert to such misleading information as being told odd things have happened at a location *after* apparent phenomena have taken place there, the collection of even trifling information is important. For if only one incident can be proved to have happened that could not have happened in normal circumstances, we are faced with monumental questions regarding our way of life and our very existence as we have always accepted them to be.

Many people will find it hard to accept some of the so-called 'facts' in this book but only the ignorant will refuse to accept the possibility of such happenings. My friend for many years, Dr Paul Tabori, used to say, 'I have never had a psychic experience but I consider it unwise to maintain therefore that they never occur or cannot happen'. This is the outlook of a responsible and open-minded person, such as the author of this book.

It is an indisputable fact that anyone who tries to conduct and carry out research into ghosts and haunted houses faces at least two great problems. Ghost hunting is immensely time-consuming and for the most part intensely boring. Ghost hunting involves sitting around, often in uncomfortable circumstances and often in the dark, for hours on end, waiting for something to happen when all too often nothing happens. Initial research and the following-up of case histories not only takes up a lot of time but are complicated by human nature; it should not be overlooked that ghost stories tend to be improved with the telling of them. Also no evidence should be taken on trust, even when presented by those who appear to be the most truthful of witnesses. Evidence needs to be sifted, checked, examined critically and then sifted again. All ghost hunters worthy of the name spend countless hours on such work and, in doing so, become authorities on the subject.

As President of The Society for Psychical Studies, a position formerly held by Professor Henry Habberley Price, Wyckham Professor of Logic at Oxford, I am frequently asked 'Do you believe in ghosts' and I am always tempted to reply in the terms of my old friend Professor C.E.M. Joad: 'Well, it all depends on what you mean by ghosts', but I prefer Price's response. He would say, 'Do you mean do people sometimes experience apparitions? The answer to that is that they most certainly do.' And he would always add the sentence that is so true and so important for ghost hunters: 'No one who examines the evidence can come to any other conclusion. Instead of disputing the facts, we must try to explain them.' Indeed we must and it is books like this one that may one day help towards a true and satisfactory explanation for ghosts and hauntings.

It is interesting to see York included with its many ghosts as well as mention of John Mitchell's admirable book. In the early 1970s I had the pleasure of addressing a large gathering of people of all ages on ghost hunting and the subject of ghosts in general at the splendid Treasurer's House; while in York I conducted the very first ghost tour of York – or anywhere else – and accompanying me on that occasion was John Mitchell. Now, of course, there are ghost tours in practically every town of any size in Britain.

Here, in *Supernatural North* (which deserves the widest possible readership) are varied investigations, some involving modern techniques and sophisticated equipment. These are elements of modern ghost hunting that may well establish the authenticity of apparent psychic phenomena; however, it has to be borne in mind that elaborate and delicate instruments may indicate activity that is caused normally, for example the movement of a bat, or wasp or some other insect. Personally I have long maintained that the reality of psychic phenomena can be just as satisfactorily established with the simplest of equipment as it can with the most sophisticated apparatus. So much depends, of course, on the quality and the integrity of the persons carrying out the investigation.

Finally we should never forget that the human mind is infinitely more complex, mysterious and fascinating than any of us can even imagine.

INTRODUCTION

In one of my earlier books, entitled *In Search of Ghosts – Real Hauntings from around Britain*, I mention the following in my introduction.

> I would like to point out that although I would *like* to say I have travelled the length and breadth of the country in search of these ghost stories and investigations, I have not! What is covered in this book does not even begin to scratch the surface of this haunted isle - not by a long shot. There are tens of thousands of haunted venues, locales, in which the ghost hunter could visit, and to cover these in one book would be almost impossible. However, as a part time ghost hunter and full time office worker, I do deem myself fortunate enough to have at least visited a relatively small, but manageable range of these haunted hot spots and investigate, report, interview, and write up all my findings and present them to you, the reader, in this book. But watch this space, with many more areas to visit, places to go and people to talk to I am sure that my ghost hunting around the UK is only just beginning.

Only just beginning! And indeed it was. Since the compilation of that particular book I have continued my quest, my travelling and my investigations around the UK – more specifically in the north of England, to which this volume is dedicated – to bring you more real ghost stories and reports from many overnight investigations that I have had the privilege of carrying out. I have dug deep into my archives at home and have released some additional material that *could* have featured in the first tome but didn't for one reason or another. What you hold in your hands now is the culmination of many years of hard work and effort, with old ghost tales that may be familiar, and some new ones too.

Again, as with *In Search of Ghosts*, I must stress that this book doesn't even begin to scratch the surface of what really lies in the north of England. There are many cities within the many counties that are littered with shades of the past and detailed books could be written on each place and, indeed, have been. To include them all in one volume would be a massive undertaking to say the least; the book would be gargantuan. It has, therefore, been my intention to write on such haunted locations and areas that I have had the opportunity of visiting for myself. Many of the locations featured herein are most certainly favourites of mine and, after you have read about them, I hope they will be favourites of yours too.

The beauty of searching for ghosts, you see, is that they can be anywhere. Its not just gaunt old castles, splendorous stately homes and ancient taverns that house the denizens of the otherworld (although, admittedly, they are great venues) but public parks, streets and new modern buildings too. In the UK we are spoilt for choice for areas to investigate and the north of England is no different. Wherever you go, you can almost guarantee that that place has a 'history' and where there is history the chances are that you will find a ghost; nowadays finding ghosts has become global.

When I first started investigating the paranormal, and reading up on it, there were no ghost hunting teams and no 'thrill nights' or 'terror evenings' in which you could buy yourself a place on, and only a very small handful of people would actually relay their experiences to you (in the strictest of confidence of course). The rest, well they kept quiet for fear of ridicule and scorn! In the last few years ghost hunters and paranormal investigators have literally taken over the planet in their quest for evidence of a world beyond our own. It is the current trend at the moment, and now almost *everyone* you speak to will boast to having seen a ghost or had a paranormal experience of some sort. At one time the mere thought of telling someone your paranormal experience would end up with you either being regarded as a witch – resulting with a punishment of certain death – or, in more recent times, being 'banged up' in a loony bin or, as previously mentioned, simply mocked. Thankfully, that doesn't take place quite as often as it once did but alas, it does still happen.

It was not the 'done thing' to relay personal experiences and, more often than not, those who experienced a ghost or a paranormal happening simply had to suffer in silence for fear of ridicule and persecution. So what has changed?

Back in 1882 Cambridge students decided to form a group to try to begin to understand alleged cases of hauntings by scientifically monitoring any on-going reports of psychic activity. The organisation was aptly named the *Society for Psychical Research* and it is still going very strong to this day. The author is one of their many members and has been for some years now, and in 2007 he was given the chance to travel to London and lecture on one of his cases. Other professional bodies dedicated to the academic study of anomalous phenomena are in existence too.

The Ghost Club of Great Britain was founded in 1862 (where the author has also had the privilege of being able to address the members at a London meeting) and is another trustworthy and respectable association dedicated to injecting science into an otherwise taboo subject. Then there is the Association for the Scientific Study of Anomalous Phenomena (ASSAP) that began its existence in 1981. The author's friend and respected colleague is (at the time of writing) the chairman of the association. It is reputable bodies and organisations like the aforementioned that have begun to make the issue of the paranormal a little more respected. Documented within their archives are many, many genuine reports of paranormal activity dating back hundreds of years.

In more recent years programmes such as *Most Haunted* and *Ghost Hunters* have brought the paranormal to the forefront of the minds of the layman resulting in thousands of teams and research groups being formed nationwide and conducting their own ghost investigations. There isn't a city in the UK that hasn't got its own ghost walks, paranormal investigation nights or ghost-hunting workshops, as it has now become big business. Entrepreneurs have jumped onto the ghost research bandwagon and have seen an opportunity to make some big money by charging extortionate prices for 'ghost nights'. However, very rarely can a serious, controlled and objective investigation take place when an alleged haunted location has been swarmed with up to two hundred people at one time (all being charged from anything up to £50 - £120 per person) by profit making ghost investigation teams.

The real ghost hunting and psychical research, however, still continues with the tenacious minority: those dedicated (and more often than not, unpaid) researchers that carry out their studies and deliver lectures on their findings outside of their normal day-to-day jobs. Year-by-year we make small but significant advances in an effort to get to the bottom of ghosts and hauntings and I truly believe that one day we *will* find out the causes of these phenomena – though probably not in my lifetime – which will result in some aspects of the paranormal becoming normal. (You heard it here first.)

During the course of my travels around the north of England, my research and the compilation of this book, I have gathered many spine-chilling accounts of ghosts and paranormal activity. I have endeavoured to keep the facts as clear-cut and to the point as possible, keeping the stories and accounts as original and as bloodcurdling as they were when they were conveyed to me. Whether you believe in the supernatural or not, it doesn't really matter as long as you enjoy a good ghost story. If you do, this book is for you. It has been packed with as many personal eye (or ear) witness ghost accounts as I could get my hands on, and they are all true!

If, by compiling my books and conducting my research, I can make people stop and think for just one minute, raise an eyebrow or possibly give someone the motivation to go and do some ghost investigating of their own, I will know my job has been done. The ritual of telling spine-chilling ghostly narratives goes back many generations, as families, school parties and groups of friends huddle around a roaring campfire in the dark, eagerly waiting in anticipation to hear the tale of the headless horseman that is said to haunt the area or perhaps the story of the human sacrifice that once took place on the very spot where they are spending the night, to slowly unfold. Trembling with fear, looking over their shoulders at every given moment, they wait for the instant the story reaches its terrifying climax (usually with a collective scream that could be heard for miles as it echoes through the night). It is a tradition that should carry on for many years to come.

As a child growing up my father often told me tales of spectres, ghosts and wraiths from where I once lived, and from that point in my life I had a serious fascination with the paranormal forever growing inside of me, never believing for one moment that I would encounter the supernatural for real. This book is about genuine supernatural encounters, real ghosts and authentic accounts from legitimate and trustworthy individuals that can testify to what happened. What a thrill it has been for me to travel around the north of England and collate, research and compile these accounts for people to enjoy, hopefully for generations to come.

CHAPTER ONE

NEWCASTLE UPON TYNE

Where better to begin a book detailing my adventures in searching for ghosts than in the city where I was born and bred, Newcastle upon Tyne. I often wonder why I never included this city (which is so close to my heart) in my first UK-based tome *In Search of Ghosts – Real Hauntings from around Britain*; after all it is a wonderfully charismatic, charming, and ancient municipality with a rich and varied history. With old side streets known as 'chares', ancient burial grounds, churches, stately homes, castles and olde world pubs, you would expect to find a ghost lurking in almost every corner.

And of course, my fellow ghost enthusiast, you would indeed be correct, as ghosts, spirits and phantoms have been frequenting 'Geordie land' for as long as I can remember, and I am thirty-six! Seriously though, since the city began its existence, when it was occupied by the Roman Empire 2,000 years ago, the city of Newcastle upon Tyne has seen it all: civil wars, marauding Scots, a great fire in 1854, floods, plagues, witchcraft, executions, crime, punishment and murders, and the list goes on and on. The city survived bombing raids from two world wars and is now famous throughout the world for its trade and industry, such as shipbuilding and steelworks, as well as its art scene and culture, nightlife and festivals.

From a one-time dirty and ancient coal-mining town to a magnificent thriving city that was in the running for the title of 'European City of Culture', Newcastle is indeed a wonderful place to live and I am so proud to call it my home. I have now become accustomed to the many ghost tales and legends this wonderful city has, so I shall relay to the reader some of my own favourite narratives.

Tucked away behind Chinatown in Newcastle city centre is Blackfriars Monastery. Blackfriars Monastery is a Dominican friary dating back to the thirteenth century and was founded by a merchant known as Sir Peter Scott. Back in the thirteenth century, Dominican friars were not allowed to own such properties and, therefore, they were often held in trust for them with Blackfriars being no exception.

Covering almost seven acres of land, as well as a number of grounds in which the friars could spend time working, Blackfriars Monastery was once a place of solitude and worship. During the nineteenth and twentieth centuries the monastery fell into disuse and bad condition. Nowadays, only the Cloisters

Blackfriars Monastery in Newcastle. Said to be haunted by a spectral monk that has been seen wandering around the area known as Friars Green.

remain of the original friary, and the stone outline of the church that once belonged there can be observed in the grassy area of the complex known as Friars Green.

On a nice day at the old friary you can unwind in these magnificent environs that are steeped with times gone by. However, when night-time falls the ambience begins to take a more ominous turn, and after the last of the shops are closed up and locked for the night, and the people have long since gone, it is said the phantom monk of Blackfriars makes his emergence as he aimlessly ambles around.

It is said that a monk from Blackfriars and a nun from the nearby Covent of St Bartholomew (in what is now Nun Street) had an illicit affair in which the nun became pregnant. When the authorities found out, it is believed (but not proven), that the nun was bricked up alive into the walls of her convent, and the monk? Well, no one knows what became of him, but it is his restless ghost that is said to haunt Blackfriars, perhaps in torment believing he was somehow responsible for the death of his lover and child.

His cowed, spectral form has been seen on numerous occasions by different people from all walks of life, during the hours of darkness and occasionally during the day. Staff in the shops that now occupy the one-time monastery have even reported seeing a hunched figure moving around on the green and have watched it disappear into thin air. Some claim to have only seen half of

The Old George Pub in the
Groat Market, Newcastle.
A wonderful olde world
drinking den that houses the
ghost of King Charles I.

the monk from the waist up. Apparently, the original ground level in Friars
Green is two to three feet below today's ground level. It is indeed a wonderful
place to go and visit and I recommend you all go there yourself sometime even
if for just an hour or so – you never know, you might even see the sad ghost of
the monk. From Blackfriars we head south through Newcastle until we reach
'the Bigg Market'.

The Old George is a fine drinking den that is nicely tucked away down an
ancient, cobbled back lane called Old George Yard and is situated to the east
of Newcastle's Cloth Market. The pub is believed to be one of the oldest pubs
in Newcastle upon Tyne, and looking at the inn from the cobble-stoned lane
outside you get the impression of a traditional-style olde world pub serving
fine, olde world ales and beers – and the impression is right, for this is exactly
what The Old George is. This fine old drinking den dates back to the early
1600s, and was once used as a coaching inn. It is also believed that there are
royal connections to the pub. King Charles I reputedly drank there back in the
mid-1600s. There is even a room at the inn named after him, and a chair he
allegedly once sat in to 'sup his ale' is still there. However, I was informed that
the chair is actually a reproduction of the original.

Stepping inside The Old George Inn is like taking a step back in time. The
past comes to life as you are welcomed with a warm and friendly feeling
of days gone by. A large open fire sits near the main entrance, the walls are

panelled and The Old George retains its ancient, low ceilings with thick, oak wooden beams. These give the inn an air of grandeur and magnificence that is still obvious to the visitor – even 400, or so, years later.

The Old George, of course, has its resident ghost. As a matter of fact, the Old George is known as one of the North East's most famous 'haunted pubs'. Perhaps it is famous because the ghost that is said to reside there is none other than King Charles I himself. Along with phantom footfalls across the wooden floors in the empty rooms, the spectre of King Charles I has reputedly been seen standing at the bar – complete with his severed head! It is interesting to add that at the time of one of his visits to The Old George pub, in 1649, he was seized, taken to Whitehall in London and beheaded. One may presume, then, that this could have been his last visit to a favourite drinking hole just before his untimely demise. Maybe that is why he chooses to haunt the very bar in which he may well have drunk his last tankard of ale.

Another well-known haunted 'toon' alehouse is The Black Boy Inn or 'Blackie Boy', as it is more commonly known, which is located in the famous Groat Market which stands opposite the Bigg Market. It is only a stone's throw away from The Old George Inn and, like The Old George, it too backs on to an old cobblestone yard. Established in 1823, the 'Blackie Boy' pub currently serves food as well as the traditional alcoholic beverages. The 'Blackie Boy' has three levels, with a long bar on the ground floor – complete with an old library – and a clock behind the bar dating back to 1923. Upstairs there is a function room that is used for parties. The third or top level is currently used for storage. The ghost, it is said, resides on the second floor.

There are a number of theories concerning who, or what, the ghost of the 'Blackie Boy' really is and why it should appear there, but in all honesty I think that no one at present knows the real facts behind the tale. During my research I spoke with the sub-manager and he informed me that he always knew the pub had a 'haunted reputation', and he'd heard strange stories from bar staff – past and present. Staff members have acknowledged seeing dark shadows darting about and an eerie sense of presence has been perceived by a few. Of course, this could be nothing more than autosuggestion on the part of anxious and wary members of staff who are well aware of the bar's reputation.

The sub-manager also told me a few stories of ghostly phenomena that are a little harder to explain, including a chilling account from one former employee. While working on the second floor, this particular individual heard what could only be described as a 'harrowing scream' followed by a malevolent voice commanding her to 'Get out, get out!'

He also admitted that he had had his own experience with the ghost of the 'Blackie Boy'. One afternoon he was on his way to the loo, whilst working up on the second floor. As he ambled across the function room towards the toilets he noticed that the door leading into the gents was open. It then crashed shut in what seemed to be an unnatural way. At first he wondered if a gust of wind, or perhaps a draught, could have been responsible. These explanations were soon ruled out when, on examination, the windows were found to be closed. Feeling quite scared, he moved back downstairs to reflect on what he had just witnessed and decided to 'pay his visit' on the first floor instead. After pondering over his encounter, he became convinced that it must have had a paranormal origin.

It was an interesting interview I carried out with the sub-manager that day and, judging by his demeanour, I got the impression he was a genuine individual and his story was true, and why wouldn't it be? This pub is well reputed to be haunted. We now meander down to Newcastle Quayside where there is yet another haunted pub (Newcastle has haunted pubs in abundance). This particular pub is probably the most famous of haunted inns (and a famous haunted building in general) in Newcastle and is also one of the oldest edifices in the city. I am, of course, referring to the Cooperage.

The Cooperage – as previously stated – is located on Newcastle's historic quayside and dates back to the 1300s. This wonderful old building was once a cooper's workshop in the nineteenth century, hence the current name of this delightful old drinking dwelling.

The beams on the outside of the building give the pub a classical Tudor look and when one steps inside the 'olde world' feel, once again, springs to life allowing the past to greet you like a warm breeze. As with other ancient taverns and inns, the Cooperage sells some of the best real ales available, making it a popular attraction for locals, quayside revellers and students. This beautiful old pub still holds its original charm, character and ambience, and some say it retains more than that. The building itself is saturated with local folklore and myth, and I must admit that when I step inside (which is also quite often) I cannot help but feel the atmosphere change, and not for the worse, I hasten to add, but there is an obvious change in the atmosphere nonetheless.

It is said that many years ago a visiting sailor was accosted by some locals (or according to some, other visiting sailors – no one knows). For whatever reason, the man was reputedly nailed to the side door of the pub that leads out onto the old stone flight of steps called Long Stairs that runs up past the Cooperage itself. It is also alleged that the original door still occupies the current door aperture, and you can still see the original nail holes. I ventured down to the Cooperage for a look one day but, regrettably, could find no trace of the abovementioned nail holes in the door.

Another, better-known spectre was reputedly seen in the 1970s on the upper floor of the inn, in what is now the function room. Rumour has it that the cleaner reported for work one morning and was eager to get on with her duties. The bar had been full of activity the night before as there has been a function on, so where better to start than at the top in the function room and work her way down? She made her way into the function room, cloth in hand, and began to clean up. During her work she became aware that someone was in the room with her, so she looked up and saw a 'white, misty cloud' floating over by one of the tables!

Shaking with fear, she stood transfixed to the spot watching this misty apparition until it began to move across the floor in her direction, all the while becoming bigger and more anthropomorphic (human shaped). Not surprisingly, she dropped her cleaning gear and ran like never before down the stairs and out of the building. She never returned.

This is by far the most well-known ghost story that is attached to the Cooperage, but there are unrelenting rumours that poltergeist-like activity occurs in the bar on the ground floor. Lights switch themselves on and off, glasses are sometimes thrown around and witnesses often mention feeling a 'sense of presence'. Perhaps it is the unfortunate sailor who was nailed to the door, who knows? Regardless of who, or what, haunts this old pub, I can safely say that the Cooperage pub has to be – without question – one of the finest haunted establishments I have ever visited during my years of research. I must also pay tribute to the friendly landlord whose hospitality I enjoyed whilst supping a pint of his finest. On leaving the Cooperage pub we head east along the Quayside, under the Tyne Bridge and along to Trinity Chare. It is here that one of Newcastle's most terrifying spectres has been seen in times gone by, and is known as 'the Quayside silky'.

The 'silky' is the traditional name for a female ghost in Newcastle that can be seen but is more often heard, due to the rustling of her silk dress or clothes. This particular ghost hasn't been seen or heard for many years now, and the area in which she haunts, although slightly changed in recent years, is still more-or-less intact. This silky is said to be a mischievous spectre that frightens the shit out of anyone that chances to encounter her. No one knows why she haunts this area but there were stories of a suicide linked to nearby Trinity House, although nothing is confirmed.

The story dates back to the early 1800s when it was said that an old local woman called Martha Wilson was found hanged in a dwelling close by. The dwelling was known as an almshouse and it was an abode that was given by Trinity House to the local poor folk in the elderly community at that time. One tale of the silky caught my attention while reading a short but fascinating book called *Dark Tales of Old Newcastle*. In it the author tells us that one dark night a keelman was on his way home after a night in the local taverns when he became aware that a woman was following him on the other side of the road. She seemed to be moving along at the same pace as he was until she reached Trinity Chare. She then disappeared up the alleyway and into the darkness.

The keelman had been aware of the tales of phantoms generally known as 'the silky' and was sceptical about them. Nevertheless he was compelled to follow her into Trinity Chare. He thought there was something distinctly odd about this woman and I guess his curiosity got the better of him. As he approached the mysterious woman from behind, she stopped and turned towards him. This halted the now terrified keelman in his tracks and a stand-off then ensued. The keelman took a short step towards the woman, and as he got closer he realised that there was no head beneath the woman's veil. Comprehending what he saw before him the keelman turned and ran out of Trinity Chare, accompanied by the harrowing shriek of her evil laughter.

Brilliant! These are the ghost stories that the author has a particular love for. Terrifying, yet allegedly true! But on many visits to Trinity Chare I have yet to encounter 'old Martha' but one lives in hope. Further along the Quayside up

The Sallyport Tower that was once part of the Newcastle City Walls is reputedly haunted by a Cavalier that looks out of one of the windows.

by the law courts, and near to the Millennium Bridge, is Broad Chare. Broad Chare, if you proceed north along it, takes you to an area known as Pandon. To your left stands All Saints' Churchyard (haunted by Jack the Beadle), and to the right, behind all the new buildings, standing majestically is the Sallyport Tower. Situated on Tower Street, which is at the west end of City Road, the Sallyport Tower was one of the seventeen towers that surrounded Newcastle as part of the defence system that was known as the city walls. This particular tower is the only one that is still more-or-less intact; one other addition that has remained at the Sallyport Tower for many, many years is, of course, the ghost of the Sallyport Cavalier.

The ghost that is said to haunt this building is said to be a soldier from the civil war of 1644. His ghost, they say, is quite often seen standing in the window merely looking out. Some say he is still defending the city he so loved, even after his sad demise into the next world. One witness that has seen the ghost said he moved in an upwardly direction as if floating towards the ceiling. It was seen in the spot where a flight of spiral stairs once stood. The ghost of the Sallyport Tower has not been seen for quite some time now, and one wonders if he is now at rest, knowing that he has fulfilled his duties as a sentry. Or perhaps he is lying dormant, waiting for the next siege of Newcastle so he can return once again and defend our noble city.

We now head back into central Newcastle where one of Newcastle's haunted theatres stands, the Tyne Theatre on Westgate Road. They say some ghosts

The Tyne Theatre on Newcastle's Westgate Road. The scene of a tragic death that well and truly left its mark on the building.

haunt places due to the tragic events that occurred to them in life and believe the author when I say there are no more tragic circumstances than in this case. It was back in my early school days when I first heard about the ghost of the Tyne Theatre during a trip to the premises. A member of staff told the school party about a man that once worked there and was killed while standing by the stage. The unfortunate victim was literally in the wrong place at the wrong time. His life came to an abrupt ending when he was hit on the head with a cannonball that was used to create the sound of thunder; you see it was kept in a box high above the stage and used as a prop during performances.

The ball had somehow made its way through the wooden receptacle, probably due to ware and tear, and had fallen through it. It plummeted down to earth, gathering momentum until it hit this poor fellow square on the top of his head, killing him outright. Since that dreadful event there has been a terrible sense of sadness… and a presence felt at the theatre. His ghost is said to haunt the stage area where he died, as well as in other parts of the theatre where he worked. It is also believed that this chap (before and *after* he died) is said to have had a favourite seat within the theatre stalls and his spectre has been spotted sitting in it from time to time. Another spectre, known as the Grey Lady, is also said to haunt the theatre. Although exact details of her demise and why she haunts there are rather vague; some say she is the ghost of a woman that was jilted by her lover and threw herself to her death from the gallery, others say she fell by accident; know one knows for sure.

I could go on forever and a day reciting the ghost stories of this wonderful old town that we Geordies call 'home' as there are indeed so many of them, too many to include in this particular tome I am afraid to say. But fear not, there is some good news... the present author *has* indeed compiled and devoted a whole book on 'Haunted Newcastle', putting just about *every* well known ghost story (and not so well known ones) under one cover. The book is simply entitled *Haunted Newcastle* and was released in early 2009.

CHAPTER TWO

NORTH TYNESIDE

North Tyneside is one of the many metropolitan boroughs that make up the north-east of England. It lies between the historic borders of Newcastle upon Tyne to the west, and historic Northumberland to the north. Semi-cocooned by the River Tyne (which is to the south) and the North Sea (to the east), North Tyneside is, by far, one of the finest regions in which to live and work, and I should know as I have been based there since 2002. The borough was formed back in 1974 after a number of other boroughs (namely Wallsend, Tynemouth and Whitley Bay) merged together along with smaller districts such as Longbenton and Seaton Valley – which was originally in Northumberland – to become one large locality, North Tyneside.

There are many reasons why North Tyneside compares to the other respective regions here in the North East. Not only is it adorned with some of the finest visitor attractions the North East has to offer, it is rich in history, diverse within its culture and was once home to some of the world's most eminent people such as the late Arthur Stanley Jefferson, who was better known as the silver screen comedy actor Stan Laurel. Arthur Stanley Jefferson was born in 1890 in Ulverston in Cumbria and spent five years of his childhood (from 1897-1902) living at No. 8 Dockwray Square in North Shields. In the centre of Dockwray Square stands a twelve-foot high statue of 'Stan laurel' that was erected in 1989 in his memory. Out of general interest it is worth adding that the long, steep and straight flight of stairs that head down to the Fish Quay from nearby Tyne Street are the stairs that are said to have been Stan Laurels inspiration for the famous piano scene from the 1931 Laurel and Hardy classic film *The Music Box*.

North Tyneside also lays claim to being home to the internationally renowned and world-class shipbuilding firm Swan Hunter. Swan Hunter have been building ships for almost 150 years and since its founding it has assembled more than 1,500 ships of various kinds, along with over 400 naval vessels. The RMS *Carpathia* was built there in 1902 and played a key role in rescuing many of the passengers from the ill-fated *Titanic* that sank in the Atlantic Ocean on her maiden voyage in the night of 14 April 1912. The RMS *Mauretania* was also built there in 1906 and at the time it was world renowned for being an upmarket ocean liner; it also had the 'claim to fame' of crossing the Atlantic Ocean in record time. In more recent years Swan Hunter was

The statue dedicated to Arthur Stanley Jefferson (Stan Laurel), who spent five years of his childhood (from 1897-1902) living at No. 8 Dockwray Square in North Shields.

responsible for the construction of the HMS *Ark Royal*, and HMS *Illustrious* but, unfortunately, nothing lasts forever.

The shipbuilding at Swan Hunter came to a sad end in 2006 when it built its last ship, the *Lyme Bay*. The banks of the Tyne at Wallsend were once festooned with magnificent shipyard cranes making Tyneside's industrial skyline just as awe inspiring as any other, but in 2008 work began to dismantle them. Still, the legacy of Swan Hunter and North East shipbuilding lives on, but a gaunt and vacant emptiness is left behind in its wake where the one time king of North East industrialisation once stood.

In the grounds of Swan Hunter, near to Buddle Street lie the magnificent ruins of the Segedunum Roman Fort. This is where Emperor Hadrian's great Roman Wall came to an end, giving Wallsend its eventual name. From Bowness on Solway in Cumbria to North Tyneside, the Roman Wall (built AD 122) stretches almost seventy-five miles (eighty Roman miles) across the north of England, effectively cutting off what was once the Roman Empire from the rest of the island. The wall's primary objective was to thwart the armed forces of the ancient Scots and Picts and to advance the prominence of Roman life. This would, of course, have been beneficial to their economic stability, simultaneously defending the northern frontier in what was the Roman province of Britannia.

The North East railway pioneer George Stephenson was born in Wylam in Northumberland back in 1781 and lived at his 'birth cottage' (which still stands) until he was twenty-three years old. On 16 October 1803 Robert Stephenson was born in Willington Quay and the following year, when Robert was aged one, the family set up home in what is now known as Dial Cottage or George Stephenson's Cottage in West Moor, North Tyneside. At the rear of this cottage – which is now a museum dedicated to Stephenson's work – are the workshops where the world famous Rocket locomotive was designed and built.

North Tyneside also boasts the gateway to Europe with the international ferry terminal at Royal Quays standing alongside one of the world's premier water parks, Wet N' Wild. But where does 'the paranormal' fit it to all of this? Well, for the best part of my life I have been fascinated with ghosts and hauntings and for over six years now I have been investigating scores of haunted houses, pubs, clubs, castles, stately homes, manor houses, museums and other such locales, and writing up my 'spooky adventures' for all to read. In all honesty, it really is a 'labour of love' and I cannot imagine my life without these tales of phantoms, shades of the past, ethereal echoes and troublesome poltergeists. The accounts told within these pages are some of the best North Tyneside has to offer and I have great optimism that they will be relayed for hundreds of years to come.

Our first port of call is at the site of the old mill house at Willington Quay. Standing near the River Tyne beneath the Willington viaduct between Wallsend and Rosehill is the Bridon Rope factory. It was on this site back in 1835, when one of the North's most bizarre hauntings began in a mill house that was owned by a certain Mr Joseph Procter who was, incidentally, a respected, god-fearing man and a well known Quaker. This case was meticulously documented after Joseph Procter made a considerable diary of the day-to-day paranormal events that occurred at their home. His son, Mr Edmond Procter, edited his father's diary in 1892 and sent the manuscripts to the Society for Psychical Research (SPR) in order to leave to posterity an authentic account of these very strange happenings.

Due to the many versions of the story of Willington Mill, I have sought permission from the Society for Psychical Research to reproduce certain extracts from the dairies of Joseph Procter in order to relay the facts as they happened. I am indebted to the SPR for their assistance and their permission to reproduce the extracts herein. It must be stressed that the sections that follow do not relay the full story, but give a good idea of the type of phenomena that was witnessed at the mill house at Willington. The comprehensive and multifaceted dairies of Joseph Procter make astonishing reading, and would, of course, make excellent material for a book itself; to reproduce these diaries here in their entirety is simply not an option. To begin with I have reproduced Edmund Procter's initial introduction to his father's diaries, followed by a few fascinating sections of the original diary.

The site of the old Mill House at Willington Quay, North Tyneside. From 1835-1847 the Procter family endured the most horrendous haunting at the now demolished Mill-House. Known as the Willington Mill poltergeist, this haunting is one of the best-attested and well-documented cases the north of England has ever seen.

Mr. Edmund Procter's brief introduction to the Dairy Notes

The 'Haunted House at Willington' has been a familiar legend of Tyneside for half a century, and the general public have been made acquainted with it in William Howitt's *Visits to Remarkable Places*, Catherine Crowe's *Night Side of Nature*, *The Local Historian's Table Book*, Stead's *Ghost Stories* and other publications. I was myself born in this 'haunted house', and have vivid recollections of many singular occurrences. As my parents, however, ceased to reside there when I was but a child of seven, any evidence of my own can be but of trifling value. On my father's death in 1875, a diary that he had kept almost from the outset of the disturbances, and during many years of their occurrence, was found among his papers. The publication of this diary has been delayed for two reasons: first, my mother's (Elizabeth Procter) objection to their publicity during her lifetime; secondly, because the manuscript breaks off suddenly, and I have long hoped, but in vain, to find the continuation and conclusion. To such readers as were not personally acquainted with the writer of this diary I may briefly state that he was a member of the Society of friends, belonging to a family of which had been attached members of that body from its very foundation. During many years he was an 'overseer' or 'elder' and was frequently appointed to offices of trust in church matters. Like many other Quakers, he took an active interest in the Peace Society, the Anti-Slavery Society, and other philanthropic organisations. He was also among the earliest teetotallers in the north of England.

His reading was fairly extensive, the *Quarterly* and *Edinburgh* being sandwiched with George Fox's *Journal* and the old *Examiner*, and Ebenezer Elliott taken alternately with some French author or the *British Friend*. I mention these details solely to place outsiders in a position to judge of the character and the reliability of the writer of the dairy, and will only add my own testimony that a man with a more delicate sense of what it means to speak the truth I have yet to meet. It only remains to add that throughout the narrative 'J.P' stands for my father himself and 'E.P.' for my mother. The earliest statement I can find is the following, in his own handwriting.

Mr. Joseph Procter's Dairy

Particulars relating to some unaccountable noises heard in the house of J. and E. Procter, Willington Mill, which began about three months prior to the time, viz., 1 mo. 28th, 1835, still continuing, and for which no adequate natural cause has hitherto been discovered.

About six weeks ago the nursemaid first told her mistress of the state of dread and alarm she was kept in, in consequence of noises she had heard for about two months, occurring more particularly nearly every evening when left alone to watch the child (Edmund's older brother then about two years old) to sleep in the nursery, a room on the second floor; she declared she distinctly heard a dull heavy tread on the boarded floor of the unoccupied room above, commonly pacing backwards and forwards, and, on coming over the window, giving the floor such a shake as to cause the window of the nursery to rattle violently in its frame. This disturbance generally lasted ten minutes at a time, and though she did not heed it at first, yet she was now persuaded it was supernatural, and 'it quite overset her'. The latter was indeed evident from the agitation she manifested.

The kitchen girl said that the nursemaid had called her upstairs sometimes when frightened in this manner, and that she had found her trembling much and very pale. On examining her further in reference to this improbable tale, she did not vary in her statement, but on searching the rooms above and finding nothing to cause such results, but little credit was attached to the story.

Before many days had elapsed, however, every member of the family had witnessed precisely what the girl described, and from that time to the present, nearly every day, and sometimes several times in the day, the same has been heard by one or more of the inmates, varying unimportantly in the nature of the sound. A few particular instances may here be selected, in which imagination or fear could have no influence.

On sixth day, 1st month 23rd, 1835, my wife had in the forenoon requested one of the servants to sweep out the disturbed room in the course of the day, and being herself in the nursery after dinner, heard a noise in the room like a person stirring about, which she took for granted was the maid cleaning out the chamber, when, to her surprise, she afterwards found that neither of the girls had been upstairs at all. The next day one of the maids, being in the nursery, supposed, from the noise she heard, that the other was lighting the fire in the room above, as had been desired, which proved a similar mistake to that preceding day. It may be remarked that the nursemaid first mentioned had left, and another engaged, from whom the affair was carefully concealed. A day or two after her arrival the noise was observed by her fellow servant whilst they were together in the nursery, but she apparently did not observe it herself, from her companion talking and using the rocking-chair. Later, however, the same evening, it began suddenly when she was present, and she, somewhat alarmed, inquired who or what was in the room above.

On First day, the 25th, being kept at home by indisposition, my wife was in the nursery about eleven o'clock in the forenoon, and heard on the floor above, about the centre of the room, a step as of a man with a strong shoe or boot going towards the window and returning. The same day, when we were at dinner, the maid, being with the child in the nursery, heard the same heavy tread for about five minutes; she came into the sitting room to satisfy herself that her master was there, thinking it must have been he who was upstairs. The Following day the dull sound was resumed, and up to this day the boots have not done duty again. It may be noted that frequently the room has been examined immediately after the occurrence of the noise; it has been sat in, in one instance slept in all night, and in every case nothing has been elicited. Several of our friends who have waited to hear the invisible disturber have all, with one exception, been disappointed.

My brother, John Richardson Procter, remained in the room below some time after the usual period of operation, fruitlessly, but within ten minutes of his departure the nurse was so terrified by the loudness of its onset that she ran downstairs with the child half asleep in her arms. My cousin, Mary Unthank, stayed two nights and was much in the room without being gratified. All the persons who have heard, and six have been so far privileged, are confident that the noise is within the room on the third floor, as the precise part of the floor above on which the impression is made is clearly distinguishable through the ceiling below, and the weight apparently laid on, shaking violently the window in the room below, when no other window in the house is affected, and during a dead calm, is itself a proof of this.

It seems impossible that there can be any trick in the case; there is a garret above, and the roof is inaccessible from without; the house stands alone, and during most of the time the window was built up with lath and plaster, whilst the other only communication with the outside, by the chimney, was closed by a fireboard which was so covered over with soot as to prove that not a pebble or a mouse had passed. The room is devoid of furniture, and for some time the door was nailed up. Not a rat has been seen in the house for years, nor at any time anything heard like a scratch or squeak, or running between the floor and ceiling; nor, it is conceived, could a hundred rats so shake the floor by their weight as to cause the window to rattle as it does.

The noise has been heard at every hour of the day, though oftenest in the evening, rarely in the night; has no connection with weather nor with the going of the mill, in short, it is difficult to imagine a natural cause having a shadow of pretension to belief.

Those who deem all intrusion from the world of spirits impossible in the present constitution of things will feel assured that a natural solution of the difficulty will soon be obtained on further investigation; whilst those who believe with the poet 'that millions of spiritual creatures walk the earth unseen' and that, even in modern times, amidst a thousand creations of fancy, fear, fraud or superstition, there still remain some well-attested instances in which good or evil spirits have manifested their presence by invisible tokens, will deem it possible that this may be referred to the latter class – especially when they learn that several circumstances tending to corroborate such a view are withheld from this narrative.

Additional particulars relating to unaccountable noises, etc. heard at Willington Mill, containing the most remarkable from first month 25th, to the present time, second month 18th 1835. On first day night, the 31st of the month, soon after retiring to bed, before going to sleep, my wife and I both heard ten or twelve obtuse deadened beats as of a mallet on a block of wood, apparently within two feet of the bed curtain, on one side by the crib in which the child was laid. The next night, before undressing, I had hushed the child asleep in his crib, and while leaning over it with one hand laid upon it and listening to some indistinct sounds overhead, which had just ceased. I heard a tap on the cradle leg as with a piece of steel, and distinctly felt the vibration of the wood in my hand from the blow. This might be a sudden crack not infrequent when wood is drying in, but sounded like a knock on the outside. Since this time the walking in the empty room has not been heard oftener than twice or thrice, of which this afternoon was the last time. More than once I have, on coming through the garden at night heard a sound like someone stepping down the gravel walk and have not been able to discover anyone. This step on the gravel has been heard by one or two others, but nothing seen.

On First day, 2 mo., 15th [1835], my wife and I were informed by our cousin, the Unthanks, that they understood that the house, and that room in particular in which the noises now occurred, was said to be haunted before they entered it in 1806, but that nothing that they knew of had been heard during there occupancy of 25 years. For about two months previously there had rarely been 24 hours without indications by noises, etc. not in any other way accountable of the presence of the ghostly visitant, to some or all of the inmates. A few days previously a respectable neighbour had seen a transparent white female figure in a window on the second storey of the house. On the 13th of last month [November], early in the evening, two of the children in the house, one aged about eight, the other under two years, both saw, unknown to each other, an object which could not be real, and which went into the room where the apparition was afterwards seen and disappeared there.

A near connection of the family on a visit [Edmund's mother's sister], but for whom, for obvious reasons, a lodging was obtained at the house of Thomas Mann [the foreman of the flour mill adjoining, and much respected by his employers] went out as usual to sleep about 9.30 p.m. Soon after going to her bedroom, T.M.'s wife went out of the house for some coals, and was struck with a figure in the window previously referred to [nothing being between the two houses but a kitchen garden and a road]; she called her husband, who saw the same figure passing backwards and forwards and then standing still in the window. It was very luminous and likewise transparent, and had the appearance of a priest in a white surplice. T.M. then called out the relative of the family and his own daughter. When they came the head was nearly gone and the brightness somewhat abated, but it was fully ten minutes before it disappeared by fading gradually downwards.

T.M. went down close under the window, and also went to inform the inmates of the circumstances, but finding they had locked up for the night did not accomplish it. It was a dark night, without a moon, and there was not a ray of light, nor any person anywhere near the house. The window blind was closed down, and the figure seemed to come both through it and the glass, as had the brightness been all inside of the glass the framing of the window would have intervened, which was not visible. In walking the figure seemed to enter the wall on each side. The occupier of the house [Edmund's father] slept in that room, and must have gone in shortly after the disappearance of the apparition.

The following account of Joseph Procter's diary has no year stated, but it appears to be about this time. J.C. is Edmund's aunt, Jane Carr, of Carlisle.

In the 16th of 12th mo., a little before twelve o'clock at night, J.C. and her bedfellow were disturbed by a noise similar to the winding up of a clock, apparently on the stairs where the clock stands, which continued for the space of ten minutes. When that ceased footsteps were heard in the room above, which is unoccupied, for perhaps a quarter of an hour; whilst this was going on the bed was felt to shake, and J.C. distinctly heard the sound of a sack falling on the floor. On the 31st of 1st month, about twelve o'clock at night, J.C. being quite awake was disturbed by a noise similar to a person knocking quickly and strongly five times on a piece of board in the room; when that ceased she distinctly heard the sound of a footstep close by the side of her bed.

On the night of 26th J.P. heard the sound of footsteps in the attic, and afterwards as of setting things down in the room above, from about 11.30p.m to 2a.m. A little after eleven he had heard several prolonged and peculiar whistles, which were also heard by the nurse in another room; they seemed to come from the landing; she had described it without knowing that J.P. had heard it.

On the 27th no one slept in the third storey; about eleven o'clock Jane C. and the nursemaid heard in the room above the sound of some person with strong shoes sometimes walking, sometimes running backwards and forwards, moving chairs and clashing down box lids, and sometimes thumping as with a fist. About midnight J.C. felt the bed raised up on one side as if to turn it over, giving two lifts.

2nd month 3rd. On nearly every day or night since the last entry more or less has been heard that could be referred to no other than the same cause;

amongst them the following may be noted: Joseph and Henry have been several times disturbed in their cribs during the evening; once they heard a loud shriek which seemed to come from the foot of the bed. On going up Joseph was found trembling and perspiring from the fright. Another time Joseph said his bed moved backwards and forwards; also a voice by the foot of the bed said, 'Chuck' twice; he is very inquisitive as to the origin of these noises, and says he never heard or felt anything like it whilst we lived at Shields.

2nd mo., 4th. In the afternoon of that same day Jon. D. Carr came to the house and stayed all night, sleeping alone on the second storey. Soon after going to bed he heard noises in the room above, as of a piece of wood or a balance rapidly striking each end of the floor; afterwards many beats as with a mallet, some very loud; also like a person stamping in a passion. He also heard a peculiar whistle, which he imitated so as exactly to resemble what J.P. heard some time before. He further heard a noise on the stairs and landing, and for some time felt his bed to vibrate very much; he put his hand down to the stock and felt it shaking. This suddenly ceased. He was quite awake and collected; indeed he did not sleep till two o'clock though unusually disposed to it. He said in the morning he would not live in the house for any money.

Literally hundreds more entries are catalogued within the pages of these diaries, with accounts of footsteps being heard, noises being heard – again in the room above the bedroom – thumps and bangs being heard in empty rooms, door latches being pulled back and forth by invisible hands, bedclothes being pulled off, noises and thumping reverberating around people while in their beds in the dead of night and an apparition of a queer- looking woman's head seen between the open curtains. The same head was seen on the landing coming towards one of the inmates of the house.

Hand bells were heard to ring in the upper levels of the house, although no one was up there at the time. Night after night unexplained and bewildering phenomena were experienced and reported by family and friends of the Procter's. We now resume looking at Joseph Procter's diary. I will, therefore, let Edmund Proctor continue the narrative.

A gap occurs in the diary here, but the following letter written by my father to my mother on July 4th, 1840 illustrates a striking incident of which full particulars are given by William Howitt and Mrs. Crowe. The Hero, Dr, Drury, (Edward) a practitioner then well known in Sunderland, had obtained leave to sit up all night on the stairs with a friend, during the absence of the family except my father and one servant. He had wished to bring a loaded musket and a dog with him; my father objected to firearms, but consented to the dog.

Willington. Seventh day, evening.

Dear Elizabeth... Last night Dr Drury came with T. Hudson, a shop man of Joseph Ogilvie, chemist, and no dog. After a long chat they sat on the landing; I went to my own bed; Bell in the camp room. About one o'clock I heard a most horrid shriek from E.D., slipped on my trousers and went up. He had then swooned, but came to himself again in a state of *extreme nervous excitement*, and accompanied with much coldness and faintness. Had seen the ghost, had been struck speechless as it advanced from the closet in the room over the drawing room to the landing, and then leapt up with an awful shriek and fainted. The other young man had his head laid against the easy-chair and was dozing, and as the ghost made no noise in coming up he did not wake till the yell of his friend called him to his help.

I called up Bell to make on the fires, get coffee, etc. but he continued in a shocking state of tremour for some hours, though not irrational. He had a ghastly look and started at the smallest sound – could not bear to see anything white; he had not been in the least sleepy, and was not at all frightened till the moment when the ghost met his gaze. They had both previously heard several noises, but all had been quiet for about quarter of an hour, and E.D. was thinking of getting his companion to go to bed, not expecting anything more that night… E.D. has got a shock he will not soon cast off. I go to Shields tonight and I question I come back at present.

A letter written by Dr Edward Drury was subsequently published in *The local Historian's Table Book* (M.A. Richardson, London, 1843, Vol I) giving details of the experience I have just cited from Joseph Procter's dairy. I now reproduce the full and original letter by E.D. to Mr Procter describing in detail what he saw that exciting night.

Sunderland, July 13th, 1840.

'About ten minutes to twelve we both heard a noise as if a number of people were pattering with their bare feet upon the floor; and yet, so singular was the noise that I could not minutely determine from whence it proceeded. A few minutes afterwards, we heard a noise, as if someone was knocking with his knuckles among our feet; this was immediately followed by a hollow cough from the very room from which the apparition proceeded. The only noise after this was as if a person was rustling against the wall in coming upstairs. At a quarter to one, I was told my friend that, feeling a little cold, I would like to go to bed, as we might hear the noises equally well there. He replied that he would not go to bed till daylight. I took up a note which I had accidentally dropped, and began to read it, after which I took out my watch to ascertain the time, and found that it wanted ten minutes to one. In taking my eyes from the watch they became riveted upon a closet door, which I distinctly saw open, and saw also the figure of a female attired in greyish garments, with the head inclining downwards, and one hand pressed upon the chest, as if in pain, and the other, viz., the right hand, extended towards the floor, with the index finger pointing downwards.

It advanced with an apparently cautious step across the floor towards me; immediately as it approached my friend, who was slumbering, its right hand was extended towards him; I then rushed at it, giving at the time, as Mr Procter states, a most awful yell; but instead of grasping it, I fell upon my friend, and I recollected nothing distinctly for nearly three hours afterwards. I have since learned that I was carried downstairs in agony of fear and terror. I hereby certify that the above account is strictly true and correct in every respect.

(*Signed*) 'EDW. Drury.'

I now leave the final words to the editor of the diary, Mr. Edmund Procter.

Finding life in the house no longer tolerable; fearing also for an unhappy effect, if not a permanent injury on the minds of their children should they remain longer in such a plague-ridden dwelling, they finally left it in 1847, and went to reside at Camp Villa, North Shields, social and other reasons also influencing them to take this step. My parents have both repeatedly told me that during the last night they slept in the old house, the rest of the family having preceded them to the new one, there were continuous noises during the night, boxes being apparently dragged with heavy thuds down the now carpetless stairs, non human footsteps stumped on the floors, doors were, or seemed to be, clashed, and impossible furniture corded at random or dragged hither and thither by inscrutable agency; in short, a pantomimic or spiritualistic repetition of all the noises incident to a household flitting.

A miserable night my father and mother had of it, as I have often heard from their own lips; not so much from terror at the unearthly noises, for to these they were habituated, as dread lest this wretched fanfaronade might portend the contemporary flight of the unwelcome visitors to the new abode. Fortunately for the family, this dread was not realised. So far as I know, and this I am confirmed by my elder brother and sisters, the eight years' residence in the new home was absolutely free from all forms of the annoyances and uncomfortable knockings, the stealthy steps and the uncouth mutterings that for ten or eleven years had disturbed the even tenor of a quiet Quaker family in the old house at Willington Mill.

Some may think the whole affair altogether a very paltry story. I admit it is not a very picturesque 'ghost'; but whatever its merit it is at least authentic, and that is rather an important feature in a ghost. The truth has been without extenuation or reverse, and if the recital points to the conclusion that the spirit or spirits, or whatever you choose to call them, belonged to the residuum of the spirit world, I hope my family may not be held responsible'.

[*Signed*] Edmund Proctor, Newcastle-on-Tyne, October 1892.

The haunting of Willington Mill is an outstanding true account of poltergeist activity, to say the least, and is one of the best-attested cases of this kind that the north of England has probably ever seen (until 2006). However, it is not the only ghostly legend that is connected to North Tyneside, and the borough is awash with tales of hauntings and spectres, as we shall see when we visit a few more places of interest. We head off now to the north-east coast and the

The gatehouse to the ruined Tynemouth Castle and Priory. Haunted by a hooded monk that is said to be seen on misty mornings looking out to sea from the cliff tops. Who he is, or why he haunts, no one knows.

mouth of the River Tyne where we have the appropriately named Tynemouth. Here stands the gaunt and romantic ruin that is Tynemouth Castle and Priory. Tynemouth Priory stands on a small neck of land that overlooks the North Sea. Once it was a seventh-century Anglican monastery and it is also said to be the alleged burial place of Oswin, the king of Northumbria. After its destruction, following the Viking invasion, the Benedictine monks acquired the land and subsequently built a Priory. This was around 1090. Tynemouth Priory was one of the finest and most well defended settlements in the whole of the North East and played an important part during the Scottish invasions. In the mid-1500s the land was surrendered to King Henry VIII and the remaining monks that resided at the priory were subsequently removed.

It is said that one of these monks still remains to this day and can be seen in the ruins looking out from the headland on misty mornings. Why he haunts here, no one is really sure. Perhaps he loved the priory so much he simply just wanted to stay. I had heard that in recent years the priory had been subject to all sorts of strange goings on, so I decided to pay the wonderful ruin – which is now in the hands of English Heritage – a visit. I took with me one of the North East's finest mediums to see if she could pick up anything spiritual.

Upon our arrival we were greeted by the English Heritage staff, who welcomed us in with open arms and smiles upon their faces, and it wasn't long before we ventured among the ruins. Being the ghost hunter I decided to try a spot of pendulum dowsing in the main entrance area of the gatehouse. I didn't have a suitable pendulum with me so I used a gold ring that was suspended from a necklace. I had never been one for using such methods during my ghost hunting work but had, on occasions, seen some pendulum dowsing which yielded amazing results and I figured I would give it a go. Meanwhile, my colleague was strolling around the gatehouse generally getting a feel for the place.

I stood still, held my makeshift pendulum-dowsing tool up in front of me and began to experiment with it. It slowly began to move from left to right but, being in a ruined shell of a building on the North East coast, I put the movement down to draughts and slight breezes. What happened next, however, astounded me. As I was concentrating on my mini experiment, the ring and necklace that I was using as a divination tool was suddenly pulled out of my hand with force. It proceeded to fly through the air, through a doorway and land at the feet of my colleague, who happened to be returning at that point. Was this the wind? I think not. I felt the force in which this thing was pulled from my hand and there seemed to be someone or something there with me that literally yanked it from me: perhaps we were not welcome.

We took heed of the sign – if it was a sign – and made our way to the chapel area of the site. It was here that my colleague came up with a very interesting fact. She told me that she felt as though there were monks, or perhaps just one monk, kneeling in prayer nearby. A bit obvious, I thought, as we were in a venue that is well-known to be reputedly haunted by a monk and at that particular time we were standing in the chapel. I pointed this out and was told 'No, I said *nearby*, not inside the chapel. I know this place has a monk too, but he haunts the edge of the complex as he looks over the seas, these ones are outside the chapel.' We ventured outside the chapel and meandered around. 'At these graves', she said as she pointed to a group of old and dilapidated headstones. 'There are monks kneeling at the graves', she said. 'Can you see them?' I asked. 'No, but they have been seen', she went on to say.

Later on, at the time of our exit from the premises, I decided to ask the staff about the resident ghosts of the Priory and Castle. A very enthusiastic young lady told me that they did indeed have a ghost who was seen on foggy mornings on the brow of the headland – of course, we already knew about this spectral visitor. When I asked if there were any more, we were surprised to hear about an unusual episode that had allegedly taken place a few years back. It appears that a group of monks were said to have been seen by a number of visitors in the Priory grounds, near the tall ruined tower at the end of the priory (right next to the chapel area). They were seen in a group and kneeling down next to the graves!

Another interesting story concerns my good friend Colin Nunn. He claims to have photographed a ghost, or at least an anomalous mist, while on a visit there many years ago. The visit took place before I even became acquainted with Colin and his wife Cindy, and the resulting picture prompted them into investigating the paranormal. This is how I eventually became to know Colin and Cindy Nunn, and this is their story in Colin's words:

> I took these frames at Tynemouth Priory. I wanted to get a nice, clear shot of the stone figures within. While it was a nice, clear and bright day, the light within the chamber was limited, therefore in order to ensure I had a good clear exposure I had to mess around with various settings on the camera, exposure, flash, aperture etc, and take several frames hoping at least one would be good. It was later, upon reviewing, that I notice the mist I had captured throughout the frames, which appeared in different places, vanished, and then reappeared again in several places. The only conclusion I could make was that this mist, which was not visible with the naked eye, was moving around inside the chamber. I was not smoking at the time and there was no one else in the vicinity smoking. It was a perfectly clear day with absolutely no mist or fog. My lens had recently been cleaned using a professional and expensive kit. I have no explanation for the mist or it's apparent movement and can only conclude it to be paranormal in nature. The camera used was a Fujitsu S620 zoom, 3 megapixel SLR.

A few years ago I took part in a radio show and the topic of conversation was, of course, ghosts. During the course of the show we began chatting about haunted headlands and the aforementioned Priory came up, as did old disused lighthouses and why they could be potential locations for a haunting. We discussed the most famously haunted lighthouse within the North East, which is, of course, Souter Lighthouse in Whitburn. It was opened in 1871 and now owned by the National Trust.

The ghosts that reside there are said to be that of the former lighthouse keeper, a woman named Isabella, related to the famous north-eastern heroine Grace Darling, and a bad tempered spirit, said to be that of a colliery worker from a nearby miners village that once stood close by. Staff had reported odd goings on for a while, including the opening and closing of doors and footsteps in empty corridors.

The conversations soon turned to another lighthouse just a few miles north up the coastline at Whitley Bay – St Mary's Lighthouse. Standing imposingly on a small island, with a causeway that is covered with every in-coming tide, St Mary's Lighthouse beamed out its warning lights over the North Sea for eighty-six years until it was taken out of service in 1984. In 1898 the lighthouse was built to replace the old light that stood on Tynemouth Point, the last of many smaller lights dating back over 400 years. Before the lighthouse was built there were many ships that had, inadvertently, found their way on to the craggy rocks and shores all around St Mary's Island. These were mainly schooners and sloops, fishing vessels and trawlers but occasionally there were other bigger ships that ran aground.

In 1861 a ship called *The Lovely Nelly* ran aground after being driven onto the rocks by a relentless blizzard just south of the lighthouse. Most of the crew were rescued but unfortunately the cabin boy, Tommy, died in the tragedy. In

1891 the 3,000-ton steamer, the *Gothenburg City* from Montreal, Canada, ran aground on rocks north of the island, and although no one lost their lives it was never to sail the seas again. Very strangely, research has shown me that Montreal was originally named Ville- Marie, which translates into Mary's City or City of Mary! How strange, therefore, that it should end its days on the rocks of St Mary's.

A more tragic story concerns the grounding of the *California* from Russia in January 1913 when the vessel was driven ashore due to a freak storm breaking. The captain and seven men were rescued but unfortunately eight other sailors perished in the ice-cold seas. The captain, I found out, lay seriously ill in the cottage on the island for a few weeks until his recovery. It is said you can still see the remains of this wreck today at low tide.

'But what has all of this to do with ghosts of the lighthouse?' I hear you all ask. Well, nothing really because, as far as I am aware, there are no substantiated stories of ghosts that reside at St Mary's Lighthouse. No spectral sailors have been seen on the island, and no ghost ships have been seen out at sea in this area. However, there have been unsubstantiated reports of spectral beings that have been allegedly spotted on the island, walking around aimlessly as though they were looking for something. The reports of these 'apparitions', I am afraid to say, are unreliable and until further sightings of these alleged 'mysterious figures' are reported we are forced to take them with a pinch of salt. However, there is a dark, disturbing tale regarding the other side of the causeway on the tip of the mainland. Now, it was this area of headland that I wanted to discuss on the radio show, as I had heard the story of a brutal murder that occurred nearby, with the murderer subsequently being gibbeted and left to rot in a gibbet cage overlooking St Mary's Island. There is a rock with a plaque mounted upon it situated on the spot where the gibbet post once stood. It was erected in 1989 to commemorate the 250th anniversary of the terrible deed. It reads,

On the 4th of September 1739 Michael Curry was executed for the murder of the landlord of the Three Horseshoes Inn at Hartley. His body was afterwards hung in chains from a gibbet at this spot within the sight of the scene of his crime. Ever since that gruesome event this headland has been known as Curry's Point.

What I wanted to know was this: had there been legends or ghost stories relating to Curry's Point? This was the place of brutal murder of an innocent victim, followed by the execution of a man, gibbeted right on this very spot which is a lonely and desolate headland. Considering Curry Point's history, I was not surprised to hear that after the radio show the telephones were flooded with calls from people claiming to have seen a ghost in this area.

Near to the site of the gibbet post there is a car park that is situated at the end of a long and winding dark road, leading to the lighthouse. This car park is a retreat for young courting couples that are in the habit of parking their cars under the moonlight to become more acquainted with one another. A number of individuals phoned in to the radio show to share their late night experiences, and I am not talking about the amorous kind! One disturbing account tells of a couple that had driven up to the car park area and had parked the vehicle facing the causeway and lighthouse. As they swung the car around to park, the couple saw – for a brief second in the headlights – the dark figure of a man. He was standing directly in front of the car, still as can be, and he seemed to be 'looking' at the couple. They turned out the car headlamps but, out of curiosity, switched them back on a second later to find the figure had vanished. They did not hang around after that!

Another listener called in to say that she had been scared witless after her boyfriend had nipped out of the car to pay a much-needed visit to the nearby undergrowth. Sitting in the car alone listening to some music, she became aware of a fleeting figure as it moved past her car window at close range. Becoming a little unnerved, she called out to her boyfriend who in turn called back from within the bushes. Then, just at that point, something struck the roof of the car with a tremendous 'thump' which sent the young girl into hysterics. The boyfriend came back to the car and asked her what all the fuss was about. After relaying the story she insisted they depart from the area as quickly as possible. What seemed really out of the ordinary, however, was that when the boyfriend was on his way back from the bushes, there was no sign of anybody else in the car park – they were there on their own. No other cars were parked up, and no one else was seen to be in the vicinity.

Or was there somebody else present? Could there have been another nocturnal visitor at the headland car park late that night? A spectral visitor perhaps? One thing is for certain; the people who relayed these experiences really seem to think that this could be the case. And if it is, who is it and what do they want? Could it be the ghost of Michael Curry stalking the headland where his body was once hanged and left to decay for all to see? Or is it someone that we don't yet know about? I must admit that it's a harrowing thought to say the least. Maybe one summer's night (when I buy a car!) I may take a drive down that long lonely road to Curry's Point to see if I can catch a glimpse of the ghost – if ghost it be. Watch this space: if anything occurs, you'll all be the first to know.

Built on the same site as the original (who fought in the Battle of Hastings) Hamo De La Val residence Seaton Deleval Hall was entirely rebuilt by the architect Sir John Vanbrugh in 1720. The original edifice stood as a ruin for over one hundred years before the De La Vals took up their residency. Admiral Deleval decided, in 1718, that he owed it to his wealth and dignity to rebuild the residence that he had recently acquired. The building work took eight years to complete but fate was to play a cruel hand for the admiral. Before the completion of the work he was, sadly, thrown to his death from his horse; therefore, the building of the new hall was completed by the admiral's nephew and heir, Sir Francis Blake-Deleval.

It appears that Sir Francis Blake-Deleval was cursed, as a prophet (or their family seer) is said to have warned him that in the next generation there would be no heir to carry on the family name. He had eight sons and five daughters, and by the time of his death, in 1771, they were all dead. His brother (Sir John) then stepped into the breach and became the first Lord Deleval until he died in 1808. The last two remaining family members (John, his son, and Edward, his younger brother) died not long after, and the hall then passed to the Astley Family of Melton Constable in Norfolk and was represented by the Marquis of Hastings.

The hall has been the seat of the Hastings' since the early 1800s and they never had good fortune with the house either. A great fire ripped through the great hall on January 3, 1882 and caused considerable damage, and for the next one hundred years or so it once again lay abandoned. In the early 1860s the house was partly restored with more renovation being carried out in the late 1950s, but despite this restoration the house remained unoccupied until the 1980s. Edward Henry Deleval Astley moved into the, now restored, west wing and he lived there until his death in 2007. The hall is regarded as Sir John Vanbrugh's finest work, and one of Northumberland's greatest and most romantic houses. It is also considered by most people to be one of the most important historic houses in Britain.

At the time of writing Seaton Deleval Hall is being sought after by the National Trust. It seems the current owner (the present Lord Hastings) has decided that after the death of his father he is going to explore new and exciting options for the hall, with a possible acquisition by the National Trust being one prospect. Who knows, by the time you come to read these words, the destiny of the great house may have been decided and I for one certainly hope it goes to the National Trust.

I would now like to tell the reader about my own strange experience while visiting Seaton Deleval Hall. In early 2002, on a red-hot summer's afternoon, during a day out partaking in another of my passions – photography – I called in at the hall to rest for a while. I had been out and about cycling for the best part of the day, with my camera in tow. Although it was blistering hot, my route from Seaton Sluice to the hall was marred somewhat, due to very strong winds. These were, typically, blowing in the opposite direction to where I was going, thus making my journey a lot more difficult, to say the least.

It seemed to take forever and a day to reach my destination, but my perseverance paid off when I at last reached the drive gates to the great edifice. I was, at last, able to dismount my bike and as I did I fell to the grass with my legs burning with the build up of lactic acid. Cycling against the wind is very hard work! With the wind still blowing furiously, I sat up and opened my bag to retrieve my camera. I stood up to take a step back whilst at the same time trying to catch my breath, and stopped to admire what was standing, majestically in front of me.

I took a few pictures from the road and began to slowly walk up the long gravel drive that leads to the hall entrance and estate office. No one else was there during my short visit, which was odd as it was such a nice day. One would expect to have seen a few tourists or locals meandering around but I didn't. As I came closer to the building I felt an eerie coldness envelope me, and a sense of apprehension came over all too quickly. I became aware of the

Seaton Deleval Hall is one of Northumberland's greatest and most romantic houses. It is home to the ghost of the White Lady who has reputedly been seen staring out from one of the windows. Photograph by Mark Winter.

feeling that I was being watched from one of the windows, but from which one I did not know. As I looked up at the windows, eyeballing each pane in the hope I would spot someone, the image of a woman in a white dress suddenly entered my mind – don't ask me why but that was the thought I had despite not having actually seen anybody.

I left my bike outside the office and popped in for a chat with the on-site warden and office attendant. We chatted about the hall for a while and, of course, the subject of ghosts came up. I asked the warden if there were ghosts at the hall (I suspected but knew nothing about them at this particular time), and was informed – to my utter amazement – that the hall was haunted by a woman that was known as the 'White Lady' who was reputed to be seen looking out from one of the windows! Well, you could have knocked me down with a feather. I explained what I had just experienced while standing in the courtyard area and the warden didn't look surprised at all. In fact he told me that this strange feeling of being watched from a window occurs more often that not. However, he also specified that the experience of being watched is all that is usually reported, and the thought of a woman in a white dress accompanying this experience had never previously been reported.

In retrospect, I wonder how I could have experienced what I did. Had I 'picked up' on the ghost of the hall? In my first book *Ghost Hunter, True Life Encounters from the North East* I explore the theory that everyone is born

The commemorative stone marker standing on the exact spot where Michael Curry was gibbeted for the murder of the landlord of a nearby public house. St Mary's Lighthouse can be seen in the background.

psychic and has the ability to sense these things, albeit on a subconscious level. Had I tuned in for a brief moment? Or had I already known about the alleged ghost of the hall and being there triggered a long lost memory? I guess I will never know.

Joyce Freeman, a colleague of mine from work, tells me that as a young girl she went to Astley High School, not far from Seaton Deleval Hall. She told me that it was common knowledge amongst the students at that time that the nearby hall was reputed to be haunted. In fact, during their dinner hour, she and her friends would visit the hall grounds and do a bit of their own 'ghost hunting', as it were. She also informed me that the ghost was that of a woman dressed in white and was seen to be standing at one of the windows looking out. She explained that this was the ghost of Lady De La Val, thought to be waiting for her long-lost love who went to war and, tragically, never returned.

A sighting of the white lady occurred on a crisp night in the early 1990s when a group of would-be adventurers visited the site after dark. Although the gates to the hall were closed and locked they all reported seeing a grey/white figure looking out of one of the upper windows. She is said to have turned around slowly and then retreated from the window. Subsequent queries showed that no one was in the hall that night as it was closed and locked up.

It is interesting to add that the stretch of road (known as 'The Avenue') that runs along from Seaton Sluice to Seaton Deleval village is also reputed to be haunted. It is said that many years ago Lord Deleval fell off his horse and broke his neck while galloping home one misty night. Indeed, on foggy evenings the galloping of his trusty steed has been heard as it thunders down the road towards the Deleval house. As Charles G. Harper said in his *Haunted Houses* (1924 revised edition), 'Monumental is Seaton Deleval, and full of eerie thrills, for the visitor'.

CHAPTER THREE

THE SOUTH SHIELDS POLTERGEIST

'*Borley Rectory* was never haunted; Harry Price made it all up.' 'The *Enfield Poltergeist* had serious flaws in the case from beginning to end.'

Isn't it ironic how phrases similar to that mentioned above have been said about the most prolific and well attested cases of poltergeist activity, and by those close-minded individuals that unequivocally refuse to even consider the fact that they could be real. Not only that, those that level such comments were never actually there when the paranormal activity was taking place! But they must be right, mustn't they, because they said so!

Somehow, these narrow-minded people whom the principal experients (the actual infested homeowners) and the investigators have never actually met, seem to know them inside out. They have concluded that they are born liars, incompetent, deluded, in it for the money, poor investigators, they have been fooled, they have over active imaginations and so on, and although the vast majority of these accusing individuals have probably *never* done a day's research in their lives, they repeatedly advise the investigators where they went wrong, and how they could have done a better job.

One wonders how they know all these things. Are they psychic? They must be, because they think they have all the answers, which of course is a contradiction in terms, as they argue the fact that psychic activity (to which category the poltergeist phenomenon falls under) is utter claptrap! I am of course being a tad facetious but I am afraid that is what really happens.

The author of this book and his colleague Mike Hallowell, were subjected to the aforementioned criticisms and *ad hominem* attacks after we investigated a poltergeist case and published our findings.

'The *Poltergeist* phenomena were all misinterpreted and the two leading investigators were uneducated goons that got it all wrong'.

Just one of the many comments we received from silly people that have never met us! I despair sometimes, I really do. To put a fine point on it, there is a phrase that goes, 'they wouldn't know a real one if it slapped them in the face'. Well, I am telling you this case and the footage we released to the national newspapers *was* real. Yes, we know it *could* have been faked, we also know other phenomena witnessed and recorded at South Shields *could* also be faked or reproduced in some way, we have never denied this fact. The individuals who have went out of their way to try to disparage our work by means of disdainfully reproducing the phenomena that we ascertained genuinely, have proved nothing except the fact that they themselves are the masters of fakery! (We found this was normally the paranormal investigators *and* so-called friends who didn't get this big case).

What we have said before, and what I am saying to you all now, is that our footage and evidence, and our case full stop, is not faked. Neither are we lying, money-makers, or poor investigators who have misinterpreted each and every occurrence over the space of nearly 12 months. Has it not occurred that there are some people out there who *are* honest and have their dignity intact?

I was there and I saw it happen, were you? The story being spread across the national tabloids, as it was, was informing the nation that the poltergeist phenomenon (or at least our case) was indeed real. This polt was literally slapping those closed minded cynics in the face and still, they didn't realise it. When will they learn to open up their closed minds? Perhaps when *they* cry for help when a poltergeist decides to pick on them.

Don't get me wrong, we expected our critics and we welcomed feedback from people. We responded to bona fide questions and queries that have been put forward in a friendly and civilised manner and *only* the questions that were put forward in a friendly and civilised manner. Some of the other downright vicious attacks were on our nature and character and are even too coarse to re-print here. They have also nearly landed a few individuals in legal hot water! And why? Because we dare to tell people about what we experienced, that's all. A suffering family at their wits end called us in to help, so we did.

I think now, at the end of the day we don't have anything to prove. We wanted to tell the world about our case so we did. At first, and deep down, I perhaps wanted to convert a sceptic or two (and maybe I have), but now I don't give a rat's ass if people don't believe it. I think the closed minded, jealous and arrogant know-it-alls are the ones with the problem, so if you think our case is fake, then you go out and provide evidence of it, and I don't mean by reproducing our footage because quite frankly, that doesn't prove shit! Ok, rant over. Let me tell you a little about the case.

There is certainly more to this world than we know at present, and that I can say with total conviction. I have seen apparitions and ghosts – whatever they really are – and I have had the opportunity of investigating a 'real vicious and unusually long poltergeist infestation' back in 2006 (as stated above). A book was subsequently written about the case by Mike Hallowell and myself, and is called *The South Shields Poltergeist – One Family's Fight Against an Invisible Intruder*. Documenting the entire affair, this book is the story of what happened after we visited the home of a troubled couple and experienced for ourselves, the bizarre antics of this psychic psychopath. We saw things that any decent psychical researcher, or the ghost hunter wannabe for that matter, could ever wish to see during these rare and often-sadistic visitations – that would also explain a lot of the unjust criticism we received, which was probably borne out of jealousy.

What Mike and I saw (and literally dozens of other bewildered onlookers) throughout this intense investigation, changed our way of thinking and it has

The author (left) with colleagues Mike Hallowell (centre) and the famous Enfield Poltergeist investigator Guy Lyon Playfair, at a lecture for the Incorporated Society for Psychical Research (SPR) in London. Mike and I lectured about the South Shields Poltergeist case after being invited down by the SPR in 2007. © WraithScape Paranormal.

forced us to realise that reality is certainly not what we thought it was. I will give you an example: can you imagine, for one minute, watching a child's toy car appear in front of your very eyes in the top corner of a room, before it drops to the floor with a crash?

'Impossible' I hear you say. NO! It isn't, I saw this happen! I never thought I would see paranormal phenomena displayed at this level but I did. A coin was seen to pass through a door from an empty landing area in the home. Pretty interesting, until you find out that the door was actually *closed* and the coin came *through* it! Matter through matter, it does happen and it happened at South Shields on a number of occasions. It was also documented in the Enfield case in 1977-78.

Knives, toys, ice cubes and other household objects were thrown around by unseen hands and on many occasions the investigators were showered with coins from nowhere. We were told by the poltergeist, via a message board (or was it a doodle board, I can't quite remember), to 'go now' and 'stop it now'. We refused, simply because we promised the family from the outset we would not, under any circumstances, cut and run or leave them in the lurch. After all, no one else was prepared to help.

Many paranormal investigators and researchers dream of getting their big case, where they are given a good opportunity to study and examine the form of some of the most bewildering enigmas there are to study. A haunting, a UFO sighting, a Bigfoot case or whatever their chosen field of research is. In the beginning of summer 2006 that dream became a reality for Mike Hallowell and myself, when I was approached by a colleague at work who informed me that 'her friend's daughter had a ghost'. After making contact with the family I was able to determine that they were genuinely frightened by something that may need our attention.

Over the space of the next month or so, I kept in touch with the family and offered what advice and assistance I could whenever they phoned up to tell me what strange events had been happening at the house. I then asked the homeowner if she could make a diary of what was happening, noting the occurrences, and the time of occurrences – and more importantly, who witnessed them! They agreed to compile the day-to-day diary and it was these notes that would ultimately play a huge part in helping Mike and I figure out just what was going on.

One day in July 2006, I got a telephone call from the homeowner, and she was very, very distraught. Apparently the ghost – or whatever it was – had been causing absolute havoc in her home. Objects were being thrown around, doors were opening and slamming closed on their own, thumps, bangs and raps were reverberating around the house, taps were being turned on, their possessions were disappearing and re-appearing and a young child, whom she lived with, began to see 'people' in the house. It was quite obvious to me that she was now terrified, and although with the advice I had previously given her she had tolerated this unwanted presence up to this point, she now wanted me to visit her house. I agreed to visit and arrangements were made for my trip. In the meantime I asked her to bear with it, be brave and keep taking the notes. She agreed.

This is where my good friend Mike Hallowell comes in. Mike is an authority on the paranormal in northern England and has been investigating and writing about this subject for over thirty-five years. There was really no one else to ask. I telephoned Mike to let him know about the case and expressed that I thought that if this was indeed genuine, it may actually be a live poltergeist at work. I asked Mike if he would assist me with the case and he agreed to accompany me on my first visit to the house. A few days went by, and the day of our visit soon came. On our way to the house Mike and I discussed the case and I told Mike all about what had been happening at this family home over the past few months. We both agreed it sounded too good to be true because in a lot of cases like this investigators turn up to the properties and absolutely nothing happens. We both agreed it would be nice to witness something paranormal for ourselves as a way of confirmation for us on our first visit, but the chances were very low. In fact, we expected nothing at all to happen but still hoped for some low-level poltergeist activity.

Little did we know what was waiting for us. That day our lives took a very dramatic turn, and it was to be a day that Mike and I would never forget. We arrived at the house and introduced ourselves and were shown to the living room where the owners, Marianne and Marc (pseudonyms), offered us a cup of tea.

We had a friendly chat with Marianne and Marc and this give Mike and I a chance to become better acquainted with the family. We then began to interview them thoroughly in an effort to find out exactly what was happening at this normal looking two-up, two-down terraced house. Equipment was set up (video cameras, motion sensors, tape recorders etc.) in all the rooms, and we spent time just talking to Marianne and Marc and trying to reassure them in any way we could, all the while hoping to experience some of the odd occurrences that had been plaguing this family for nigh on six months.

It wasn't until four long hours into our first visit on that baking-hot summer's afternoon, after many trips up and down the stairs, visiting all the rooms and monitoring the house, that we were *astounded* to see what we would later term as 'The South Shields Poltergeist' at work. We were all standing in the child's bedroom (Robert, also a pseudonym) when from out of nowhere came a yellow plastic nut. It flew across the room with speed, bounced of a wooden cupboard door and hit Marianne on the backside. She shrieked in pain as we all stood there dumbfounded.

Later in the same room, while discussing what had happened earlier on, a child's toy slid off the drawers and landed in the metal bin with a crash. Although Marc was standing close by, I could see that it wasn't him that had dropped the toy into the bin. He jumped with a start too and the look of fear upon both Marc and Marianne's faces said it all. We were becoming convinced that something really odd was indeed going on at this house.

Other incidents occurred too during the latter part of our first visit. Another yellow nut flew off the chest of drawers and across the room before landing on a large cardboard box. A rubber ball appeared from nowhere on Robert's bed and was hot to the touch. The night-light that had been plugged in on the landing stairwell was found unplugged and on the landing floor. Creaking and knocking was heard in Robert's bedroom during a designated period of time up there, and sound recordings of knocks, bumps, movement, pinging, thumps, shuffling of footsteps were recorded on tape. There was also a noise that sounded like glass marbles moving on wooden surfaces, guitar strings, coins spinning, a bloop, bloop, bloop noise, and coughing. The aforementioned phenomena were discussed at serious length between Mike and I and, although we were almost convinced it was genuine, there was a slight nagging feeling that we may have been duped or tricked in some way. Fraud (an ugly word) has to be at the forefront of any investigator's mind in cases like this and it was (to a certain extent) in ours.

But we had seen and heard objects being moved and thrown around when there was only the four of us in the house – in the room. We had our eyes fixed on the couple, watching their every move just in case something like this did occur and it was not them. This was the beginning of something special for us, and we now knew that we could have an active poltergeist. Little did we know that, in the coming months, what had seemed like a friendly, mischievous soul, or perhaps a playful poltergeist that threw around toy cars and plastic nuts, would turn into a ferocious, malevolent and terrifying entity that would turn against the family with a vengeance. It would come to terrorise Marc, Marianne and Robert, almost to the point of nervous breakdown.

Over the next seven months we made hundreds of visits and stayed over at the house many times, trying to help the family in any way we could and all the time documenting everything that occurred there. The strength and the ability of this 'thing' grew bigger as the days went by, as did its desire to frighten, terrorise and intimidate. It seemed to feed on the family's fear, and by this point, they had become almost complete wrecks! Just when Marc, Marianne, Mike and I thought it could not get any worse, 'it' turned on Marc with such viciousness and force that we were left wondering just what we were really dealing with.

From the outset, we promised that we would stay with the family and help them through this infestation no matter how tough it became – for them and for us! We would not cut and run, desert them at their hour of need – no, we were there for the duration! The poltergeist was getting extremely violent and we now knew that this entity intended to cause physical harm in whatever way it could. It had even started to throw carving knives at people. On one occasion, I actually found a large silver kitchen knife lying in situ on Robert's bedroom floor, and it was certainly not there previously so where had it come from? On another occasion, when Mike entered the empty house one day, he was greeted with a carving knife as it flew across the kitchen, bounced off the TV perched high on a shelf, and then fell to the floor. As mentioned earlier on, the poltergeist had also left messages on a doodle board for Mike and I to 'go now' and 'stop it now'. Mike and I were not going anywhere. The gloves, so to speak, had come off.

Things were now getting really serious at the house in Lock Street (Pseudonym). Just when we thought the poltergeist activity might have reached its peak, things always took a turn for the worse. I guess Mike and I underestimated the power of this bastard and it certainly wasn't going to go without a fight. One night, Marc was lying in bed with Marianne when he felt a burning sensation on his torso. He took off his shirt to have a look and it was at this point when the polt had decided to take its terror campaign that one step further. As they both stood there looking at his body the polt literally ripped Marc's torso to pieces. From nowhere, cuts and welts appeared across the chest, side and stomach of Marc until his body looked like something from a 'slasher' movie. Marc and Marianne were of course absolutely terrified, so immediately phoned Mike. Mike came down in a taxi to see what was going on.

When Mike arrived he found the family in a frantic state and offered what help he could. He took photographs of Marc's wounds, calmed the family down and proceeded to ask what had happened. As it transpired, Marc was to be viciously attacked again on that night, and Mike was there to capture it all on film! Now I must say at this point the film that Mike took that night has been heavily criticised by so- called investigators and sceptics! The film of these cuts appearing is of a low quality and is a tad grainy. This was due to the lighting conditions in the room at the time of the attack. Furthermore, the machine Mike used to film these cuts was from a digital stills camera with a 'video clip facility' and therefore *any* filmed footage would not be as sharp, or as good quality as, say, my video camera.

I live in North Tyneside, which, of course, is on the other side of the River Tyne to Mike and because the attacks occurred through the night it was Mike that the family contacted as he lives nearby. Being half- asleep, he grabbed his bag, which fortunately had his camera inside, and rushed to the aid of Marianne and Marc not knowing for one minute, of course, what was to happen.

I mention earlier that the film of these cuts appearing is of a low quality and is rather grainy to say the least, due to the lighting conditions. What deeply puzzles Mike and I, is why the graininess of the film is criticised and not the actual cuts appearing on Marc's torso. You see, I have, of course, seen this footage too and it is clear (or at least it should be to anyone with a decent working pair of eyes) that cuts and welts do appear on the torso in a way they certainly should not. The footage, albeit not 100 per cent clear, is still very much watchable! Another piece of strange footage was released at the same time as the 'cuts footage', only this time it was crystal clear. This piece of footage is showing a bottle of water being balanced on its edge, obviously defying the laws of physics. This time the critics ridicule the phenomena itself and not the quality of the film. It also must be pointed out that both short clips were filmed using the same camera and on the same night, indicating that the lighting conditions in the rooms in the house were very much at different levels.

We can't win, can we? Not that it matters though. But for the record, more poltergeist attacks with scratches and welts appearing paranormally were witnessed and filmed on another night by over eleven individuals, four of whom had their video cameras and filmed it all as it occurred. In total, Marc was attacked in this way by the poltergeist on no more than five occasions and on four of them we managed to film it.

Another terrifying aspect of this particular case came when the poltergeist began utilising the telephones in the house (both on the incoming calls only landline, and the mobiles) to instil fear into the couple. At first the messages were tame in nature but they soon took a sinister turn. Mike and I were present on one day when the telephone rang at the house. Marianne picked up the phone to answer it and was greeted by an automated voice message. It is common nowadays (but was rather new at the time) to send text messages to normal household telephone lines, but rather than read a message on a screen (as you would with a mobile) the message is converted into a robotic style voice that relays the message to you.

This message simply said 'Hi, Hi, Hi, Hi, Hi'. We worked out that the phone that had sent the message belonged to Marc, but it was sitting in the middle of the dinning table when the message was sent. We also knew that he had not been anywhere near the table at that time, but thinking there could have be

Genuine poltergeist activity. A bottle of mineral water stands on its edge in an amazing show of poltergeist behaviour. Photographed and filmed by Mike Hallowell during the South Shields Poltergeist case in 2006, this footage has caused much controversy and debate throughout the paranormal world. © WraithScape Paranormal.

something fishy going on, we decided everyone should place their telephones (including the wireless landline) on to the middle of the table. We were all sitting chatting when the landline rang again. This time another message came through and it simply said 'Hello, Hello'. One more message came through moments later, which simply said 'Sorry'. Remember, the phone it was coming from was sat on the table in front of us.

Marianne began to receive text messages on her mobile phone, from the poltergeist! At first the messages were not threatening but frightening nonetheless. Then they became worse. One text message said 'the bitch will die today'. Another came through saying 'going to die today going to get you'. We explained and assured Marianne that the poltergeist was simply trying to instil fear in her (it succeeded) and that the texts were nothing more than empty threats. On her way to her mother's, after fleeing the house, she received a number of other text messages. While speaking on the phone to Mike expressing her concerns about the poltergeist following her to her mother's, a text message came through. 'Please donwt go. I will com with you bich'. After listening to the message, she explained to Mike that she was now frightened

Messages left for the author and his colleague Mike Hallowell during the South Shields case. Clearly the polt didn't want the investigators to help. We declined its kind offer and saw the case through to the end with the distraught and troubled family. © WraithScape Paranormal.

to go to sleep. Then another message came through. 'I can get you when you awake and I'll come for you when you're asleep bich.'

It was as though the poltergeist was listening in on their conversation. This was the point in the investigation where I thought to myself, 'just what the fuck are we really dealing with here?' I must admit this was the first time I became seriously concerned, or frightened if you will. However, I had no intention of deserting the family and neither did Mike. We promised we would stay with them and see it through. Being seasoned investigators we knew it was only a matter of time before the poltergeist left the family for good: this is what poltergeists do. They come, they create havoc and fear, and then they go, usually in the space of a few months from beginning to end. This one was different, however, and it stuck around for almost a year in total but, of course, we did not realise it would at the time. We promised full and ongoing support to the family and this is exactly what we did, right up until the evil bastard burned itself out.

The thought often crossed our minds just how long this torment would go on for, and sometimes we even thought it was never going to go away. After a total of almost twelve months of living hell for the family, seven months for Mike and I, the poltergeist, at last, was brought to its knees but only for one month before it came back to wreak havoc for one more terrifying week. This one-week was the very last period of suffering for the family, for after this period the poltergeist activity at this house ceased forever. The terrifying, nasty and gruelling encounter with a vicious poltergeist had come to an end, and the family, at last, began to live a normal life once more.

The South Shields Poltergeist case was indeed an extraordinary infestation in which certain paranormal phenomena, or typical poltergeist symptoms, matched and correlated with many other classic poltergeist cases. A vast array of phenomena at South Shields has been reported in poltergeist cases for centuries. The raps and bangs, the throwing around of household objects, accompanying apparitions, the materialisation of coins and money, moving furniture, written messages that were left for the family and for Mike and I, and lots more. We even experienced a new phenomenon from the poltergeist as it sent death threats and intimidating messages via mobile phones, even when SIM cards and batteries were removed from them! Whatever the poltergeist is, it seems it can move with the times and adapt to using modern technology.

Just about everything that occurred in that twelve month period when this poltergeist was at work has been documented. We have hundreds of still photographs of displaced objects, of which many were moved and displaced while we were at the house. We have EVP and dictation device recordings, which include anomalous voices, ghostly footfalls and shuffling of feet as well as a host of other strange sound recordings. We have hours of videotaped footage catching the poltergeist at work. On it you can hear many objects being violently thrown around the house.

We have over seventeen different independent witness testimonies – twenty-two if you include the family in question – that have supplied signed statements bearing witness to what they experienced at this house. It could have been more but two or three of the other witnesses unfortunately declined to provide statements out of fear.

Both Mike and I feel this is one of the best-documented cases of poltergeist infestation since the Enfield poltergeist in 1977-78. The entire affair can be read in our book that was written about the case; but be warned, it is long, complicated and has many unexpected twists and turns. It is a true and riveting story of one family's fight against an invisible intruder and a case that Mike and I will never forget.

Subsequently, through the case, both Mike and I have travelled the country lecturing on the South Shields Poltergeist and the poltergeist phenomenon in general. We have been invited to conduct talks and lectures with some of the leading academic research associations into psychical research such as the Incorporated Society for Psychical Research, and the Ghost Club of Great Britain. Further invitations to 'lecture' have come from the renowned Harry Price, experts and authors of the *Borley Rectory Companion*, Paul Adams and Eddie Brazil, and from the Head of Psychology at Northumbria University, Dr Nick Neave, to lecture at the university to his first year psychology students as part of their 'parapsychology module'.

Indeed, Guy Lyon Playfair, BA, elected member of the SPR committee, one of the world's leading poltergeist researchers and the author of *This House is*

Haunted, An Investigation into the Enfield Poltergeist, penned the introduction to our book. The *South Shields Poltergeist* book is a positive contribution to active psychical research; it is a story that will ultimately go down in poltergeist research history. It is a permanent reminder of what Mike and I had to deal with in 2006, and it is a testament to the resolve and courage that was shown from one normal, everyday family in South Tyneside.

CHAPTER FOUR

PRESTON HALL MUSEUM, STOCKTON ON TEES

In late 2007 fellow researcher Mike Hallowell and myself were contacted by a local charity, the Butterwick Children's Hospice, based in the Stockton area of the north-east of England. We were asked if we were prepared to give up our time to attend one of their many charity ghost investigations as guest speakers. The event was to take place in February of 2008 and at that time in my life, Mike and I were carrying out talks all over the country regarding the paranormal. Our Book, *The South Shields Poltergeist, One family's Fight Against an Invisible Intruder,* was due for release in March of 2008 and it was this case and book that we were delivering the lectures on.

We agreed to appear for the Butterwick charity and help out with the investigation in general. We were then told by the event organiser Diane Williamson that Richard Felix from Living TV's *Most Haunted* was also making an appearance that night and we would be sharing the stage with him. I was overjoyed as I had always been an admirer of Richard Felix – even before his *Most Haunted* days – and I had always wanted to meet with him. In 2002, Richard had toured the UK in his quest for ghosts and had produced his own video collection documenting his adventures. It is called the *Ghost Tour of Great Britain - 2002*, and he organised the videos by the UK counties and areas. I owned *North East Ghosts, Derbyshire Ghosts, Yorkshire Ghosts* and many more and found them really enjoyable.

You see, in my eyes Richard was one of the few people with an interest, or passion, in something and had decided to get off his backside and do something with it. Out of his own pocket, he travelled the country doing what he loved to do and made something of his life. It is for this reason that I respect Richard Felix and rate him as one of the UK's finest ghost hunters and this was also why I was so looking forward to meeting him. Even before he became the Most Haunted historian, I had wanted to meet him and chat to him about the paranormal.

A few weeks prior to the event we were asked if we could visit the venue in question, the Preston Hall Museum, and check the place over. Preston Hall Museum is a Grade II listed building that is located just north of Eaglescliffe in Stockton on Tees in 100 acres of land known as Preston Park. The Hall itself was built in 1825 by David Burton Fowler and was sold by Matthew Fowler in 1882 to a local shipbuilder called Sir Robert Ropner or, to name him in full,

Sir Emil Hugo Oscar Robert Ropner. Sir Robert Ropner was a Conservative member of parliament and was named after his father, who came to England from Magdeburg in Prussia in the late 1800s. In 1904 Robert Ropner Jnr (as he was known) was given the title of 1st Baronet of Preston Hall and died aged eighty-five in February 1924. The Ropner family resided at Preston Hall until 1937 and ten years later it fell into the hands of the Stockton on Tees district council. In 1953 it was opened to the public as a museum. The museum includes many wonderful paintings, including the Dice Players by Georges de la Tour; period rooms; a wonderful old toy collection; an armoury, including some remarkable muskets and crossbows; and an incredible old-fashioned 1800s style street with an old cobbled road, old lamp posts, authentic shops and even a police house.

Diane Williamson from the Butterwick Hospice had asked Mike and I for advice on how to go about running the investigation properly and efficiently, and our pre-investigation visit was essentially to plan ahead for the night. Upon our arrival we had a tour of the buildings and we were told what areas we were allowed to investigate, and what areas were out of bounds. On this pre-investigation visit Jay Brown from Northern Ghost Investigators (NGI) also joined us. Jay and his team were attending the investigation to keep the paying charity ghost hunters in check and to generally make sure the night vigils ran smoothly.

During the tour of the building we were given some history of the ghosts and were told who the staff believe haunted the premises. The ghosts included a woman known as the Grey Lady, seen walking along the corridor on the upper level of the building. She has also been seen by staff members as she floats down the main stairwell near the building's reception area and continues into the main lobby before disappearing into thin air. Outside in the car park there is believed to be a ghost of a man dressed in black, and on occasions he is seen wearing a tri-corn hat. Believed to be a highwayman, this spectral being is said to be a harmless but unnerving apparition and has been seen countless times by the museum staff. Other presences are said to reside in the building including a woman and her dog, seen in the dungeon area of the building, now a display area for some of their ancient artefacts, and a sense of being watched by an invisible presence has also been felt in the toy gallery.

Up until this point in time, this particular building had never before been investigated by anyone and the ghost hunting event that we carried out there was to be the very first. Because of this (and Richard's appearance) it made local news with reporters from a selection of the North East's tabloids being in attendance.

During my first visit to the museum, prior to the investigation, I made it my business to track down a few of the people that experienced paranormal activity. There were lots of staff on during our visit and it wasn't hard to find my first witness, so to speak. On reception there was a middle-aged gentleman who told me he had been working there for about five years and had indeed experienced some strange goings on during his employment. On one of these occasions, not long after he had started the job, he had actually seen the spectral

The author (centre) with medium Ralph Keeton (left), and paranormal historian and ghost hunter Richard Felix at Preston Hall Museum in Stockton on Tees.

woman that haunts the upper corridor. Not being aware of the resident ghost, he thought she was just another member of staff, not realising until later on that the woman he saw along the corridor – from a distance and from the rear – was wearing odd clothing and not their uniform. It was only when he discovered that there was no woman in the museum at that particular time (as it was closed to the public) that he realised that he may have experienced something odd.

Another staff member told me that on many occasions she had been in the area known as the toy gallery when it suddenly became ice-cold for no reason. A weird sense of presence would then fill the room and she would get a sense of being watched. I was told that others have experienced the same sensations in there too, and no one knows why this happens or what it could be. So, we could safely assume the building was indeed haunted. After spending a few hours getting to know the place and mapping out the locations for the big night, we said our goodbyes to the staff and made our way home.

The night of the charity investigation (22 Feb 2008) soon came along, and upon our arrival at the venue I was very pleased to see Ralph Keeton who is a very good friend of Richard Felix and of the author. I had worked with Ralph on many occasions with another North East paranormal research team and found him to be an extraordinary psychic medium. Would-be ghost hunters turned up in their droves to see Richard, Mike and I do our talks and presentations before the main event.

Richard began the evening by delighting the 250 plus audience with some of his past paranormal experiences, his life as a ghost hunter and his theories on ghosts, poltergeists, and unexplained phenomena. We waited patiently at the back of the hall for Richard to finish off and it was soon our turn to take the stage. After one hour Richard answered many questions from the audience and then we were on. We spoke for just over thirty minutes and showed a DVD presentation. This was the first 'public showing' of the famous scratch footage we had filmed during the South Shields Poltergeist case in 2006. After our talk, we were approached by Richard Felix, and many members of the public that were attending the ghost hunt and we were told just how incredible the DVD footage and our talk was. It appears our talk and presentation went down very well with most of the people attending despite the few hiccups that occurred earlier on which will be discussed later.

However, since the 'ghost night', Mike and I have found certain comments on websites that could be deemed as libellous. It appears our talk wasn't appreciated by all present on the night which is fair enough, we accept that. People are entitled to their opinions and their beliefs and I reiterate they are welcome to hold any views they wish. What is sad, however, is the fact that these particular views were aired in a rather nasty fashion and without our knowledge. The people (or person) in question also had *every* opportunity to air these comments on the night, and more respectably, to our faces. They chose to sit there all night and say nothing to us and then posted the remarks on a website that in all likelihood they thought, or they maybe hoped, we wouldn't see. Still, we expected actions and comments like these and by gosh we got our critics when the South Shields Poltergeist case made national news in the *Daily Mail* and the *Sun* newspapers. It really was (and still is) a mind-blowing case that rocked the *real* paranormal world, and with interest coming from professional bodies such as the 'Incorporated Society for Psychical Research and the Ghost Club of Great Britain', to name a few, I guess a few negative comments from the general public, or even wannabe ghost hunters that wouldn't know a real polt if it trashed their own house, really doesn't make much of a difference to either Mike or myself.

It was now time to crack on with the evening and the guests were split into teams. Jay Brown and N.G.I. were there to act as team leaders for the charity fundraisers and in total there were about four or five groups of eager ghost enthusiasts ready to stake out the venue through the night. Mike and I, accompanied by fellow investigator Mark Winter, were 'vigil observers' so we could float in-between the groups and work with whomever we wanted, whenever we wanted. On other charity investigations we had attended with Butterwick, we had done the same sort of thing in order to get a bigger picture of the entire evening. A write up was then prepared and an article was published in the *Shields Gazette* that Mike Hallowell writes his 'WraithScape' column for, and on the official WraithScape website dedicated to our work with the paranormal. This was the idea for tonight's investigation too.

If I have to be honest not a great deal of objective paranormal phenomena was documented, which was to be expected. It goes without saying that a ghost vigil with over 250 people on it would not yield bone-fide results due to the fact that controlled conditions would be nigh on impossible. Having said that, it was only meant to be a charity fundraiser in the first place, with would-be ghost hunters doing for the first time what Richard Felix, Jay Brown, Mike Hallowell and I do more or less all the time.

The evening went well and everyone had a great time in their vigil locations in search of the denizens of Preston Hall. Mike and I worked our way through the groups and spent time in all of the most paranormally active areas of the museum. Being 'vigil observers' and generally floating from team to team, we often found ourselves in areas of the building where no other team was working at that time, and managed to get some quiet vigils under our belts, only to no avail.

During one designated period of time throughout the course of the vigils, I managed to grab a lengthy chat with Richard Felix and found his enthusiasm for our poltergeist case, and the paranormal in general, to be nothing short of exemplary. His passion and his eagerness to learn more about ghosts and poltergeists is second to none and that certainly showed during our discussions. We chatted about the great Harry Price and Borley Rectory, and he regaled me with stories about when he spent the night in Borley in search of the phantom nun on 28 July 2006. He never saw the nun but informed me he saw a badger, something we both laughed about. Talking with Richard like this really was a great opportunity for the author and, as mentioned, it was something I had always wanted to do.

Before we knew it, the end of the night had come around and it was time to close down and finish the one and only ghost night ever to be held at Preston Hall Museum. The evening went rather well, to say the least, and I believe everyone present had a really good night. It was certainly an honour and a privilege to be asked by the Butterwick Children's Hospice to attend this charity night as a guest speaker with Mike, and Richard Felix. To share the stage with him at such a venue was indeed something I will not forget in a hurry, combined with the fact that I was able to spend some time overnight in such a magnificent locale that is reputed to be haunted. Not many people will get the chance to do this at Preston Hall Museum, as this investigation was (as mentioned earlier on), a one off.

I must now tell you, the reader, all about the wonderful work of the Butterwick Hospice. It really is a worthwhile cause and a great charity. The Butterwick Children's Hospice is a charity that provides care and support free of charge to children with life limiting illnesses from birth to eighteen years of age, and supports their families. It provides day respite, end of life care, family support and bereavement care to families from Teesside, County Durham, North Yorkshire and Weardale. Skilled and experienced professionals staff the Butterwick Children's Hospice along with trained volunteers, and they work in partnership with families and other professionals involved in each child's care. At the Butterwick Hospice, the focus is on each and every child enjoying their stay there while family members take a break from their round the clock caring responsibilities. In order to provide their free service to these families, they need to raise a staggering amount of money each year, something like £800,000, and the ghost hunt night at Preston Hall was just one of many events the fundraisers like Diane Williamson organise. To be involved in this particular operation in the way Mike and I were was indeed an honour and a privilege. If any readers would like to donate funds to the charity, or perhaps help out in some other way, they can be contacted via their website or can be reached on 01642-607742.

I will leave you with my good friend Mike Hallowell's take on the evening we spent at Preston Hall Museum. It is at this point where the hiccups I mentioned earlier on in the chapter are talked about.

Darren and I often get called upon to take part in ghost-hunting events, which are organised to raise money for well-deserving charities. At one such event we were asked to give a talk about our investigation into the notorious South Shields Poltergeist case, which we eventually went on to write a book about. To be honest, everything that could have gone wrong before the event did. We just managed to get there on time, only to find that our hour-long presentation had been cut down to thirty minutes, which necessitated some impromptu improvisation before we went on stage. The equipment we'd been promised for our film presentation didn't materialise, and our DVD ended up being shown from a laptop computer, which for some reason distorted the film. This later led to some totally unwarranted criticism from someone in the audience who was completely unaware of the facts, but everyone else we spoke to seemed perfectly happy with the presentation. Well, you can't please all of the people all of the time, as they say. Afterwards we took part in the ghost-hunt, the point of which, we hoped, was to scare members of the public witless!

Preston Hall Museum is a majestic building with a multitude of winding passages and corridors, all of which add to the spooky ambience of the place after the fall of darkness. As things turned out, the event proved to be extremely interesting for a number of reasons.

Amateur ghost-hunters often support charity events like this. Many are well meaning, but some, perhaps understandably, have a tendency to get a little too excited by phenomena, which have an all-too-rational explanation. For instance, a number of people on the night took photographs of 'orbs', spherical light objects which, in reality, are nothing more than reflections from dust particles or water vapour. Orbs have become big business in the world of paranormal research since the advent of digital cameras, and many amateur ghost-hunters are convinced that they are the spirits of the dead. It's true that, in some cultures (such as those of some Native American tribes), the spirits of the dead are believed to return to the world of the living as balls of light, but these should not be confused with digital orbs. The Native American versions are truly spooky and can be seen with the naked eye. The 'orbs' captured by digital cameras are never visible to the naked eye – at least in my experience – because they don't really exist in the first place. When a number of people at the Preston Hall Museum event showed us the orbs they'd captured with their digital cameras Darren and I were tempted to reveal the brutal truth to them – namely that there was nothing paranormal in their pictures at all. However, it was a charity event and we didn't want to spoil the atmosphere. Most of them were doing their level best to raise money for a good cause, and we didn't want to put a dampener on things.

A number of the amateur ghost-hunters behaved very professionally, however, and I still correspond with some of them to this day. One lady became quite excited at the fact that her EMF meter kept going off the scale every time she waved it over my torso. So did I, until I realised that it was reacting to the heart pacemaker which I have inserted in my chest! Ah, well. There is a street of period-style shops at the museum, and they're so well constructed that its hard not to believe that you haven't skipped back in time a couple of generations when you're ambling over the cobbles. At the end of the evening a local spiritualist medium approached Darren, Mark (our friend and colleague) and I, and began to tell us some very obscure (but stunningly accurate) details about an acquaintance of ours. To be honest we were gob-smacked. There was no way she could have known the things she did by conventional means. She set the seal on a very productive evening which, despite the earlier setbacks, raised a good deal of money for the charity concerned and gave many members of the public a first-hand experience at amateur ghost-hunting.

Of course, amateur ghost-hunts can never be compared with professional investigations, which are a completely different kettle of fish, as they say. It's simply not fair to take members of the public or hobbyists into an allegedly haunted location and expect them to rise to the challenge in the same way. Don't get me wrong; I'm not knocking amateur ghost-hunting groups – I've belonged to a couple myself in the past and they do a really good job when it comes to raising the public consciousness regarding the paranormal. Some of their members go on to become veteran, seasoned researchers even if they never lose their amateur status, whilst you'll always get one or two who can be a bit irritating by pontificating on every supernatural topic under the sun and portraying themselves as the next Harry Price or Maurice Grosse. It takes all sorts, I suppose. I wish the charities that organise such nights all the very best, as well as the sensible, amateur ghost-hunters who are an asset to our profession. Preston Hall Museum is decidedly haunted and well worth a visit if you get the chance.

CHAPTER FIVE

AN ANONYMOUS PUB, CO. DURHAM

Due to the distressing nature of some of the events discussed in this in-depth haunting study and at the request of the principal experients, both the names of the experients and the public house concerned have been removed and are subsequently kept anonymous.

The author understands that in a book of haunted locales it will be frustrating for the reader not to be able to identify the building concerned and perhaps visit it. However, the protection of the family concerned must remain paramount, and I do not wish the events to precipitate a negative psychological effect upon the new, current tenants. Although the location and the names of the experients must therefore be withheld, I trust that this will not diminish the value of the account unduly. I wish to assure readers that every incident and event related hereafter is completely true and accurate in every detail.

The pub has long been said to be haunted by an old man – usually seen in the lounge. One former landlord who approached the spectre was astonished to see him vanish in an instant. The ghost has made his presence known at the inn by tinkering with light switches and bar fittings. Those who have set eyes upon him describe the ghost as wearing a white shirt, black waistcoat and flat cap. But who is he? Could he be, as some claim, a farmer who may have dwelt there in times past? Possibly, but witnesses who recall the building when it served as a farmhouse have told researchers that they never once heard of a ghost haunting the property.

One inclement February night, Mike Hallowell and I, and the North East Ghost Research Team arrived to begin a series of investigations into the alleged haunting at the pub. The family who lived on the premises at that time had expressed a wish to remain anonymous due to the nature of the events that occurred there. It appears the pub's trade had been slightly sluggish and, in an effort to boost trade, the (then) tenants decided to organise a 'psychic night'. This involved a number of psychics, mediums and Tarot card readers gathering one evening to prognosticate regarding the futures of the pub's patrons. All in all, the event seems to have been a success, but, in regards to the haunting at the pub, this is also when the trouble began.

Although the family had indeed witnessed the odd strange occurrence within the pub and surrounding grounds prior the 'psychic night', they seemed quite at ease and happy with their 'resident ghost'. However, when the psychics visited the pub one clairvoyant informed the owner that the spirit that resided there was in actual fact quite disruptive and hell-bent on literally killing the landlord. The psychic seemingly picked up on the fact that the landlord had been plagued with illness and infections during the preceding months and his health was slowly deteriorating. This was indeed true, although nothing had been said to the psychic about this previously. The psychic then went on to say that if the family did not leave the pub immediately, the spirit allegedly haunting the premises would 'continue its grudge and its campaign to rid the earth of this man'. Pretty harrowing stuff, to say the least.

Now the reader will understand why the author was asked to keep the experients' identities anonymous. This, combined with the fact that the landlord and landlady did not want to trade on the building's past and alleged haunting in any way, indicated a very high level of sincerity and an honest, legitimate belief in the reality of the ghosts that were said to reside within. To the author, this case had 'authenticity' written all over it!

On the night of the first investigation, the researchers arrived at the pub at about 11.00pm. Mike and I subsequently had a chat with the landlord and landlady. Our primary objective was to find out exactly what had been going on and listen to the first-hand accounts and experiences regarding what had been witnessed at that particular establishment. We were quite amazed at what we were told.

I began the interview by asking the publicans what experiences they had had, since moving into the inn. 'A number of things have happened which we find rather odd', the landlord told me. 'The first night we moved into the pub we were all awoken from our sleep to the sound of about five or six tremendously loud bangs coming from downstairs in the lounge. They sounded quite metallic, like metal on metal. I even put my hand on the bedroom wall and you could feel the vibrations, they were that intense. We looked downstairs in the lounge area and no explanation could be found. We also checked outside, and all was quiet.' 'Interesting', I said, but before I got a chance to enquire further, the landlady came forward and said, 'I was in bed one night and woke up to find the bed literally shaking while I was on it. It has only happened once, and it is not the first odd experience that has happened to me while being here.'

She went on to tell me that one day she was getting on with her pub duties when suddenly she felt compelled to move out of the way to let someone get past her while she was in one of the corridors. This unidentified person came from the rear and touched her shoulder as she moved to let this person past. Only no one passed her and she found herself in the corridor alone! She had been physically touched and had sensed the presence of someone. Whom? She could not say.

We were also informed of doors in the corridor downstairs that often slammed shut through the night, keeping the occupants awake. No rational explanations for these sounds have ever been found. Other phenomena were reported to Mike and I during the interview, which had been experienced first-hand by this family and their staff. These included bulbs exploding in the bar, the bar staff being touched by invisible hands, glasses being thrown off the shelves and the family dogs becoming agitated at about 03.00am most mornings for no apparent reason. One chilling account concerns the daughter of the landlord and landlady who was also present at the interview. She went on to explain:

> One day I left the pub to go home as I don't actually live here with my parents, and when I crossed the car park I had the urge to look around me. When I did I could clearly see the figure of a man dressed in a black cloak standing outside the pub on the conservatory stairs. He also had on black shoes and a black hood or hat over his head. There was something otherworldly about him and I just sensed this was not right. I turned away for one second to see where I was going and when I looked back to see this man... he was gone! There is nowhere he could have gone in the time it took me to turn around. This experience has had a profound effect on me. I was sceptical at that point but now I am not sure, as this sighting is rather hard to explain. I know what I saw!

The occurrences outlined above are first-hand accounts obtained from the family. They subsequently found out, not long after moving in, that the locals also believed the pub to be haunted. Locals visiting the pub have often asked the owners if they had 'seen the ghost yet?' The locals believe the ghost is that of a man who once lived in the pub many years ago when, as stated previously, it was actually an old farmhouse that had been built around the year 1900.

Mike and I were also informed on the night of the investigation that, before the present occupants moved in, the ghost of a man had been seen sitting at the end of the counter in the bar area. Another apparition had also been observed sitting down in the lounge area, behind the tables, 'minding his own business'. Along with the apparition seen on the conservatory stairs, could these three spectres be one and the same? Or are they different ghosts altogether? And are these ghosts responsible for the other activity that has been witnessed there? These are some of the questions we hoped we could answer, after first establishing for ourselves if something odd was indeed going on.

After the pre-investigation interview we conducted a careful and comprehensive 'baseline test' and left no stone unturned. We had a large number of locations to cover so we got to work quickly. Downstairs in the main bar area and lounge the temperature read between twenty and twenty-two degrees, which was quite normal. The conservatory area was a lot colder and read between fifteen and sixteen degrees, but was indicative of nothing paranormal. EMF sweeps showed no readings unless one stood near the bar where a rather diminutive reading showed. This was due to the presence of the beer pumps and, of course, the electronic till. There were extractor fans on the walls in both the lounge and the bar area which made a clicking and whirring noise every now and again, and the door into the kitchen naturally swings upon its hinges to a certain degree and creaks while doing so. We also traced a slight draught from along the corridor to a door that leads outside. This accounted for the swinging door! There were no creaky floorboards, or other draughts coming in from the windows or doors, except for the aforementioned draught we had just located. The cellar temperature read between twelve and fifteen degrees but when the huge fans are in operation this is quite normal, and EMF sweeps were pointless due to all the wires and machinery.

Upstairs, in the private living quarters, the team was allowed access into the main bedroom and living room, as these were the areas where strange phenomena had seemingly taken place in the past. The baseline survey in that location showed both rooms to be at a steady temperature of twenty-three to twenty-four degrees with no EMF anomalies detected. The corridors between these two rooms had very squeaky floorboards and, once again, no draughts coming from the windows. That completed the baseline survey, and the team then had readings to compare should anything otherworldly happen.

The team then split into two groups to investigate the private living areas. These locations were chosen first as the landlady could not stay with us throughout the night and needed some sleep for the next day's work. Mike and I figured that we could investigate those areas first and concentrate on the actual bar later on. The first location was the main bedroom, where I headed the first team. Mike and his group staked out the adjacent living room. My vigil proved rather fruitless, to say the least, with nothing at all being recorded. However, the pub landlord, who was with Mike, saw red flashing lights in the corner of the living room. Mike proceeded to take some photographs of the area and later, whilst examining the photograph, was surprised to find an unusual black, speckled mist obscuring the corner of the room. Analysis on Mike's laptop computer during the break could not determine what it was and further photographs taken in the same area showed no anomalies. The landlord then told the investigators that it was in that very corner of the room where other phenomena had occurred in the past!

Later the teams swapped locations for a while, and my team stationed themselves in the living room. Apart from one or two creaks and cracking noises, followed by two loud thumps as though something was in the corridor, nothing else happened. Both my team and Mike's stationed in the master bedroom with the door closed, heard these thumps emanating from within the corridor. We found these occurrences very interesting.

During our first break Mike downloaded the photograph he took in the living area so we could scrutinise it. I also took a photo of Mike and the pub landlord as they viewed the first picture on the laptop. I took another picture to document what was happening at that particular time (as I normally do), and was taken aback to see that this time I had caught a faint, fine white mist on my camera. The mist was in an area where no one was smoking and near the spot where the apparition of a man had been seen sitting behind a table in the lounge.

The next experiment, carried out after the break in the cellar, involved leaving a 'locked-off' video camera trained on a trigger object – a wooden crucifix. The crucifix was placed on a sheet of white paper and a line was drawn around it before the team vacated the room. If the trigger object moved, the movement would be caught on film. The investigators also left EVP recorders and dictaphones running too, in the hope they would be able to record other sound anomalies. It was in this location where the visiting psychic had said the disruptive spirit that pesters the landlord resided. Hopes were high, and the researchers were not disappointed with the results. Although the trigger object did not move, the investigators managed to pick up some very strange sound recordings coming from within the unoccupied room. If one listens carefully to the recordings made, one can hear the sound of male voice talking. This occurs at regular intervals throughout the recording and at times it is very distinctive. Bangs and crashes are also heard coming from within the cellar, although nothing in there was actually disturbed. A more sinister EVP came in the form of a guttural breath or sigh that sounded so clear it felt like whatever or whoever it was had breathed right into the EVP machine!

During the 'lock-off' period when the cellar was deserted, all present at the investigation were situated in the bar area waiting, watching, listening and hoping that some paranormal activity would take place. This proved rather fruitless, to say the least. However, Mike Hallowell, while in the conservatory area, was almost certain he had photographed a face at the window, complete with upper torso, looking in from outside. If I have to be honest, I think the picture is indeed a good one, but one can't help thinking that this is maybe a classic case of pareidolia. Mike is not sure. We looked outside nonetheless to see if anybody was hanging around, and found no one there. At one point during the investigation, Mike sat quietly in the ladies' toilets, as he'd been informed that, on previous occasions, witnesses had seen 'shadowy footsteps' walking past the bottom of the cubicle doors. Mike made some audio recordings at this point, and later, on analysis, found that on one of them a woman can be distinctly heard sobbing for several seconds!

By 5.00am, and after another short stint of EVP lock-off experiments, the team decided to call it a night – or rather, an early morning. It had not been a bad investigation and some decent results had been obtained.

What with the mist photographs, the EVP recordings and the loud thumps heard during the investigation upstairs I think we can safely say something odd was going on at that particular location, but exactly what I cannot say at this present time.

Was there a vicious ghost there that wanted to kill the landlord? Mike and I don't think so. Are the apparitions that have been seen in the past one and the same person? That is something we will try to determine if we get another opportunity to investigate the premises. After all, it takes longer than a few hours to begin to understand what may be going on in a complicated case such as this. After that night's investigation was concluded, a provisional arrangement was made to carry out some further research on the premises. However, three days before the second investigation was due to be carried out, Mike and I were informed that the family had decided to flee the premises. To this day, they have not been able to return, but hope to do so in the near future.

CHAPTER SIX

THE GOLDEN LION HOTEL, CO. DURHAM

The Golden Lion Hotel and Pub is one of Seaham's most ancient public houses. Not much is recorded in regards to the actual history of the tavern itself, but what is known is that the hangman and executioner from Durham Gaol, Albert Pierpoint (or Pierrepoint) stayed there on a regular basis while 'up on his business'. It is also thought to have been a school of some sort where children learnt lessons and spent a great deal of time. Ghost children have actually been seen flitting around there by the owner over the years, and when enquiries were carried out on the building, sure enough, it was found to have been a school.

The owner told the author that 'there is just something about this old building...it terrifies me and I hate being the last one in at night and having to lock up by myself'. A friend of the pub owner, who is a psychic medium, has visited the building on a number of occasions and has frequently picked up on the presence of two spirit children that run around and play in the upper corridors of the pub. He said they are 'brother and sister, and one is older and also a little taller than the other'. He also claimed that one spectral child has a neck injury due to falling down a flight of stairs and that this could be the result of one of their untimely deaths. Along with the children, he claims there is a ghost of a male adult too. He is believed to be a teacher, perhaps, or at least someone who had some authority over the children at the school.

Interestingly enough, when we arrived at the premises at 08.00pm on the night of our first investigation (20 November 2005) our (then) team psychic Suzanne Hitchinson clarified exactly what this medium had picked up. She sensed the two children *and* the male presence in the exact same area in which the medium had, in the past, picked them up. Suzanne did not know this prior to her visit, as these testimonies were those of the owner and his colleague. It was this medium who asked Suzanne to see if she could detect where in the building they were. This seemed like a test to satisfy his curiosity: either he wanted clarification for himself that he was indeed right, or he thought that Suzanne was 'just another investigator' claiming to possess mediumistic abilities. She was correct in every detail.

I then carried out a thorough baseline test and inspection of the building, checking for draughts, creaky floorboards and taking room temperatures and EMF readings. No EMF anomalies were detected, although one or

The derelict old building that was once the thriving Golden Lion Pub in Seaham, Co Durham. Two terrifying nights were spent there by the author in which a woman was heard sobbing, and a pint glass was thrown and smashed in the empty bar.

two explainable readings were noted due to loose wiring, the lighting etc. Apart from that everything seemed normal. Before splitting into groups the investigators set up some locked off spiritual interaction experiments, including trigger objects, in the hope that they would be moved by any of the spirits of the pub.

We placed a crucifix in a doorway and another in a room where the children and male figure had been picked up. We then left some motion sensors in that same area, and a flour tray with a crucifix in near the cellar in the bar. It is interesting to add that, before our investigation, a few things were seen, heard and 'picked up' by some of the investigators. I thought I saw a silhouette move from left to right at the bottom of the long passageway whilst being in there with Suzanne. I held up my camera to take a photograph, looked down the corridor and that is when I saw it. It happened in a split second, and although I took one photograph, nothing appeared on the picture. I guess it all happened too quickly.

Another investigator told me that he felt as though he was being watched when he climbed up into the attic space to look around. Suzanne also sensed the abuse of a woman in what we called the living room. She said this woman met her end violently after a rape. She was murdered.

By 11.00pm it was time to start the actual investigation. We split into three teams of three; my team went into the upstairs area of the building first, with Suzanne and a guest.

At 11.10pm a guest in my group said he felt there was something in the room with him, although he quite clearly stated that he didn't want this to be the case! Suzanne then heard footfalls, swiftly followed by a sigh or breath. We did not hear this. Suzanne then picked up the name William, and the surnames Bennett and Hardy. Then, Suzanne and the guest heard a dull but a definite ringing sound, but I, again, heard nothing. On venturing into the living room area Suzanne sensed 'the vile taste of having an abscess in my mouth'. She also sensed the name Simon.

The vigil came to an end and we then ventured back down the stairs to the main bar area for a break. It was now 11.30pm. I was then informed that the two other groups that were investigating other parts of the building had indeed heard and recorded strange noises and anomalous recordings on their equipment. Tests proved that the noises did not originate from any of the other groups.

We then reconvened at 11.30pm and headed back off to the upper floors to conduct a number of séances. Three were held in all, with the third, taking place in the living room, providing the best results. Although a long-drawn-out scrape of a floorboard was heard, and a sudden knocking noise was recorded during the first séance, these would prove to be insignificant compared to what occurred during the final séance.

We all headed off to the living room area on the upper levels of the pub and formed a ring. The séance began with team psychic Suzanne Hitchinson 'calling out to the atmosphere' to see if she could get any response. Nothing happened at first and all was quiet, then from out of the darkness and the deathly silence came a crystal-clear, long, guttural breath that was heard by all present.

Following this, the sound of a short and distinct 'sniff' was heard by one of the investigators. Some light anomalies were caught on night-vision video cameras, and when Suzanne sensed 'a shift of energy' behind two of the investigators, the EMF meter showed a very strange reading of about five to six milligauss, which in paranormal terms could be quite significant. The sound of a child laughing was also heard along with that of a woman sobbing, and I actually heard this! No explanation could be found for this anomalous noise. This was really interesting, as Suzanne had sensed 'a woman's anguish' in this very room earlier on! Could the investigators have heard the cry of a sad and distraught ghost?

At that point in the evening, all the guests had gone home leaving just the investigation team to continue with the evening's work. We split into two teams again and my group stayed in the main bar while the others investigated the 'snug' area. The 'snug' vigil was quiet, to say the least, but the vigil in the bar proved interesting. Whilst down in the cellar area cum dance floor I felt a sharp tug on my shirtsleeve, and again all present heard the sound of a breath. It did not emanate from any of the investigators present. The best was yet to come, though. Whilst I was down there investigating alone, I went absolutely ice cold and almost froze to the bone. I felt a little unnerved and weary, but proceeded to take a photograph anyway and caught the most amazing mist anomaly I have ever seen. It must be stressed that I held the camera out at arm's length and refrained from breathing until I had taken the photo, due to the 'breath factor', which is where breathing out can cause vapour to gather in front of the lens and flash, making what seems to be a ghostly mist appear on the photograph. However, further 'breath tests' proved that it could not be – and was not – breath! I might also add that I saw this mist with my naked eye, and when the flash-gun went off I was lucky enough to catch it on camera.

Looking at this incredible photograph from an outsider or sceptic's view, one could suggest it might be simply cigarette smoke. Not true, I can assure you, as no one is allowed to smoke while in these vigil conditions for this exact reason.

When one looks at the mist itself, it takes the shape of a facial profile, as if I had caught the spirit or ghost as it was walking in front of me. However, pareidolia springs to mind and cannot be ignored. Many pictures of alleged ghosts in windows, window reflections, or even of faces in fogs and mists are simply patterns in the image that look like faces and certain shapes. Patterns in wallpaper and in curtains, when viewed at night provide exactly the same sort of effect. It is well known that the first things the brain will look for and register in such instances are faces. I am not saying that this picture is of a ghost with a face, but I am merely pointing out it that it certainly looks like it. That aside, the mist is still anomalous and cannot be explained by any normal means.

After a short break the team ventured back to the living room where they attempted one last séance. One or two more breaths were clearly heard, along with distant bangings, emanating from within the building, exactly where we don't know. The investigation was now well into the early hours of the morning, and it was decided to wrap things up before the team members all became too tired. It had been a very interesting investigation, to say the least. Many phenomena were recorded and observed by both investigators and the guests in the earlier stages of the investigation. Packing up our equipment we were discussing the events and expressing just how interesting the night was. It was around 05.00am when we vacated the premises, off home to sleep before analysing sound recordings and compiling a full report from the investigation notes – an investigator's work is never done!

Almost three years later, on September 26 2008 the G.H.O.S.T. team arrived to conduct another investigation. The pub, I am sad to report, was (at the time of writing) in a terrible state of disrepair and a fire had gutted part of the building. Repairs were made to some of the fire-damaged areas but it simply wasn't enough for the owners to keep the pub up and running. Trade began to slow down, punters drank elsewhere and eventually the pub itself became a ghost. From around the beginning of 2007 the pub was completely abandoned by the owners although they kept ownership of the property. Battered by the north-east winds and howling storms that come in from the ice-cold North Sea, the pub stood corroding and derelict. It was literally rotting on the spot.

By the time you read these words the chances are the pub will have been completely demolished. The night of September 26 2008 may well have been our very last chance to encounter the ghosts of the Golden Lion Pub. Once that demolition ball begins to swing, and the walls of the Golden Lion come tumbling down, the residing ghosts may well be forced from their old dwelling, never to walk the long eerie passageways and rooms again.

At 10.30pm team member Mark Winter picked me up, and from my abode in North Tyneside we made our way along the northeast coastline to Sunderland. We arrived at the venue at 11.00pm where we were met by the rest of the team. We reconvened at the back of the premises, fighting our way over rubble and rubbish to make our way in to the pub. It felt really strange knowing the building was completely empty and in total darkness. The electricity supply had been cut off prior to our investigation so due care was taken after entering the building.

Fiona pushed the door open and it made such an eerie and elongated creak, it was like something out of a horror film. Inside we were greeted by the darkness. Darkness like I had never experienced before. A foreboding feeling came over the team as they pushed their way in to the main snug bar area to set up camp for the night. Thoughts came flooding back from the first investigation when the sound of sobbing was heard in a room upstairs and for some unknown reason – we couldn't work out why – we all had a bad feeling about this investigation. The stench of burnt and rotten wood filled the nostrils giving the whole place a sick and musty oppression.

We settled down in the snug and began to form a game plan for the night's investigation. Torches and lamps were set up and left in order to provide some much needed light and a pre-investigation cup of coffee was drank before we set about conducting our usual baseline tests. The baselines consisted of the usual experiments including the room temperatures and EMF sweeps. Trigger objects were set up in various locations throughout the premises. Because the building was derelict and no electricity was connected, we felt the EMF meter would have some significance. Also it must be noted that because the building was in a state of ruin, we paid particular attention to which windows were broken and which were not.

This was to enable us to determine where any 'draughts' or alleged 'ghostly breezes' would come from. I noticed that although there were two windows broken around the front (one boarded up), no windows had been 'put out' on the upper levels. This, in hindsight, was one of the best observations I could have made, and you will understand why later on in this report.

Some of the windows were slightly open, and draughts were indeed a bit of a problem; the floors (what there were of them) were also very squeaky in certain areas. However, once we had locked ourselves in for the night, we were pretty confident that if anything of a paranormal nature occurred, or anything that *seemed* to be of a paranormal nature occurred, we would be able to get to the bottom of it. That said, we were ready to begin.

It was decided that Drew Bartley and myself would stay and investigate the snug area of the pub, while Fiona Vipond and Mark Winter would investigate upstairs.

It was 12.37am when the vigils began. Just as we were heading off to our locations I was talking into my dictaphone, documenting what was happening when suddenly I heard a voice coming from the bottom of the stairs. I could not determine who or what it was, neither could I determine what it said. It happened that quickly. On looking around for anyone there we found no one, but, of course, we knew we wouldn't. Drew called out to the atmosphere in the hope of getting some sort of response only to no avail. After five minutes or so we heard a distinct 'thump' but again, we could not determine where it came from. We then headed off to our respective vigil locations.

As Fiona and Mark reached the bottom of the stairwell, Mark called out, 'Did you hear that?' It appears as he reached the doorway he heard what he could only describe as a 'grrr' noise, or a growl. Drew said that was the same sort of noise he had heard earlier on. Fiona exclaimed, 'I tell you what, I don't normally get scared but... I think I am going to be hanging on to Mark tonight'.

The building was beginning to show its true colours and it was having an effect on some of the team. We made our retreat back into the snug area and began our vigil. I began to take some digital and some 35mm stills to see if I could snap anything out of the ordinary. Drew began to call out to the atmosphere and felt a draught on his arm. A second later he felt it again. After taking a quick look around we determined the draught may have been coming in from a window that was slightly open. Upon trying to close the window we could not, it seemed to be stuck fast.

At 12.50am I felt a cold breeze across my arm but the same conclusion was reached. It was more than likely from the gap in the open window. Any more breezes felt from this point would be ignored. Drew then mentioned he heard a few knocks coming from somewhere nearby, but he couldn't say where. We decided to sit down on the chairs and sit in silence to see if we could hear, or maybe 'sense' anything. After a while, and after having had no luck, Drew began to call out once more to see if he could pick up any voice recordings on the EVP machine. At this point the video camera was situated in the middle of the floor pointing at the trigger object, the crucifix.

At 01.05am we decided to try a séance. We sat opposite one another and held hands. I called out for a while at the same time we filmed the proceedings. Nothing happened at all. Drew then mentioned earlier on in this vigil he was standing in the middle of the floor looking into the room behind the arch in the wall. He claimed to see a 'flash of light, in which there was a human face'. This was in the right hand corner of the base room and about three quarters of the way up the wall. Although he told me that it seemed real, he admitted it could have been his eyes playing tricks on him in the darkness. I must admit, it did sound rather cheesy, for want of a better word! It was now 01.15 and time for our first break. Fiona and Mark came downstairs and joined us and reported the following.

At about 01.00am we heard a distinct breath coming from along the corridor, and then experienced the 'pulsing' phenomenon that is so often experienced on paranormal investigations.

For those not aware of the pulsing phenomenon, let the author enlighten you. 'Pulsing' is when an investigator is in a relatively dark location. When your eyes become accustomed to the dark, you can pin point where things are, just. Pulsing occurs when you are looking into the darkened room and you become aware that the room becomes even darker until you are thrown back into 'jet black' conditions. Then, the room slowly becomes lighter again to the point where you can find your way around in the darkness once more.

This happens quite often on investigations and, as we are fully aware, it could be a trick of the light (or dark), we are not yet sure. We have carried out other investigations when this oddity has occurred. One occasion at the Coroners Court building in Newcastle upon Tyne, a doorway that was dimly lit up by the distant outside lighting, slowly became darker and darker until the doorway could be seen no more. You could understand thinking it may well have been a trick of the light, had not three individuals all experienced it at the same time. Can the dark play the same trick on three different individuals? You decide.

As I began to tape Fiona prior to her reporting what happened in her vigil, I made a very peculiar sound recording. It was not heard at the time, and was only discovered when I was compiling my notes for this chapter. You can hear the author speaking into the dictation machine, speaking the words 'Right, for the benefit of the tape, it is one twenty-eight'. Just after the words 'it is' are spoken and before 'one twenty-eight' is said, an anomalous noise is heard. I cannot really describe it accurately but will have a go nonetheless. It sounds like a loud breath type of noise expelling two consecutive sounds. The first sounds like 'oooh', swiftly followed by a long drawn out 'hay', 'Ooh hay' or 'oohway'! On the tape, the sound passes rather quickly, in a split second or two, and is really close to the microphone. The conversation carries on as normal indicating no sound of this nature was heard at the time.

Although I have used these words to describe the noise recording, I do not feel they do it any justice. Listening to the recording would, but that would be rather difficult unless you personally know me. What I can say is that it sounds rather harrowing! One could describe it as a breath.

It was now time for our second vigil location where Drew and I would investigate the upper levels of the pub, and Mark and Fiona would investigate the snug area. Drew and I left the room and pulled the snug door closed behind us. I had already started to make my way up the stairs and was a quarter of the way up, Drew was right behind me. Suddenly, from inside the main bar area, came a terrific smash, followed by a tinkling. My first thought was that a light bulb had exploded, as the loud smash that literally echoed throughout the building was accompanied by the 'pop' noise you often get when a bulb smashes. It took Drew and I a few seconds to register just what we heard. The eerie silence that followed was soon broken by my thunderous voice exclaiming,

'WHAT THE FUCKING HELL WAS THAT?'

We shouted for Mark and Fiona, who also heard the glass explosion from where they were, and came out of the snug area. Fiona had actually thought that Drew had stood on a pint glass and hurt himself. This was not the case. We all then ventured into the bar area as this was clearly where the breaking glass had came from, but we found nothing.

Although I thought the noise came directly from inside the bar area, the notion occurred that local hooligans had been putting out the windows from the outside; this proved not to be the case as the same number of windows were broken and covered up as when we came in. Searching about outside proved no one was in the area, the streets were deserted and silent. This brings us to the glasses and bottles that were left strewn around the place after the fire had gutted the bar. They were not tidied up and were lying all over. The thought occurred that maybe a beer glass had naturally rolled off the bar and smashed upon the floor. Plausible, but highly unlikely in my view, and Mark and Fiona agreed. Drew was not so sure. After searching the bar area for intruders and making sure the building was secure we had the idea of rolling a glass off the bar to see if we could reproduce the sound of the breaking glass.

When we rolled a glass off the bar, the glass failed to smash. Then, we decided to throw the glass onto the floor, still it did not smash. Then it was thrown with considerable force and yet again, it still wouldn't smash. The thought occurred that during the fire, these drinking glasses would have heated up considerably, to the point of potential meltdown. Perhaps the re-heating of these particular charred pint pots strengthened up the glass and reinforced it, so when we threw them down they were tougher than usual?

So the question remained, what smashed the glass with such force? We couldn't break them ourselves – we tried. Drew was still adamant there was a rational explanation, but I think, in our heart of hearts, Mark, Fiona and I knew this was very likely a paranormal occurrence. To add mystery to this already baffling occurrence, the old fridge door behind the bar was found to be closed. Mark had been looking around earlier on and had found three fridges full of old booze. Deciding it would be best to leave it alone (because it was not ours to begin with, and it could also have been damaged or dirty) he left the fridge door wide open. Our tests proved that the door would have to have been closed fully with the help of a hand. In other words, the fridge door would not close on its own. Even when it was pushed the door didn't close. Then, we discovered that the crucifix trigger object that had been left on bar had moved from its original position. A certain degree of controlled pandemonium (if you know what I mean) ensued and efforts were made to work out what had happened. This episode rattled all of us and it was at this point I had decided there were a number of possibilities.

A) The fridge door was accidentally left open and the trigger object was moved after someone walked into the actual bar that it was placed on. There is a slight flaw with this explanation as Drew, Fiona and Mark can all testify to the fridge door being wide open when seen last. The trigger object was in an area where no one could have accidentally bumped it without knowing. It was situated in the middle of a tall counter and to move the trigger object you would have to have bumped into the counter with force! No one did.

B) A glass did, as you would expect, roll off the bar with such speed and force hitting the floor creating a noise that was obviously an auditory hallucination that all four investigators heard, and recorded! The consequence being that it caused a draught on the way down that naturally blew the fridge door closed. Then, the powerful flow of air from the fridge door closing created another one in a million draught in the direction of the trigger object, which then wafted the crucifix off its original position! Problem solved eh? You may sense a certain degree of sarcasm coming from the author here, and you would be correct.

C) The third alternative, and in my eyes a more clear answer (baring in mind we did attempt to find a logical explanation), is that there really was a seriously pissed off spirit in the building with us and, to make things worse, it enjoyed launching bar glasses around!

D) However, a fourth explanation could be possible. It is known for certain haunted places to experience auditoria phenomena such as hearing furniture moving, smashing crockery, thumps, or bangs and even the sound of heavy objects being dragged across the floor. When these phenomena are investigated, a lot of the time nothing is ever found to be out of place, everything being as it should. This happened at Borley Rectory quite a lot. In the adjoining cottage, the sound of a wall unit full of crockery was heard to smash to the floor during the night creating the loudest noise imaginable. When the occupants got out of bed to see what had happened they found nothing at all out of place, yet they heard the noise. Perhaps we only heard the sound of a glass breaking, even though no glass at all may have been broken on the night.

I think that by the end of the night Drew was beginning to come around to the idea that something odd was occurring in the pub. He is a clued up paranormal investigator that has seen ghosts before, and on one occasion an entity has even assaulted him. But it was another incident that occurred in the same bar later on that might have changed his mind. It happened while Drew and I were investigating at the top of the stairwell at 02.20am. We both heard a rustling coming from downstairs and again from within the bar. We went down to investigate and discovered the rustling noise could only have come from one of the many rolls of fibre glass that were stacked up in the bar area. When we grabbed the plastic and rustled it, it made an identical noise. Something had been in the bar playing around with the rolls of fibreglass.

We then had another break. After the break it was decided that we should hold a séance on the dance floor that was once the cellar. The cellar had been dug out and replaced with a pit like dance area with a flight of steps leading down into it. It was there, on the first investigation, that I took the photograph of the peculiar mist anomaly. It is also in this area where the owner of the pub and his colleagues had recently seen an apparition come up through the cellar floor. What adds mystery to this account is that two ghost doves were seen fluttering around and had accompanied the apparition that was seen by the owner and his colleagues as the main apparition came up through the floor.

At 02.51am we headed into the main bar area to conduct our séance. Myself, Mark and Fiona formed the circle while Drew filmed the proceedings. After about twenty minutes or so nothing was happening so we moved the séance up near the gutted bar area. This séance also yielded no results, which, if I have to be brutally honest, I was rather pleased about. It was now well after 03.00am and we decided to call it a night. We were all beginning to get a little tired now and it was really starting to get cold. We ventured back into the snug area, packed up our equipment and headed off out into the cold September morning.

The Golden Lion Pub investigations were second to none, and the phenomena witnessed there on both occasions really were special. Whatever happens to the Golden Lion Pub, we can safely say that it has to be one of the most haunted pubs we have ever had the privilege to investigate. No one else has been allowed to investigate the Golden Lion Pub in Seaham, and by the looks of things they never will. We have been in twice and had successful investigations. It really is such a shame that the place will be coming down because some serious research could be carried out there. Our team will endeavour to investigate the property one more time before the bulldozers come in, and if we do then you can bet your bottom dollar that the report will be featured later in this book. If the report is not featured here, in this book, our third attempt was unsuccessful.

Fear not though, for the chapter you have just read covers the ghosts of the Golden Lion in County Durham and the only investigations that were ever to be carried out there. What you hold in your hands is the first and only documentation of a wonderfully old and haunted pub that exists no more.

CHAPTER SEVEN

BERWICK UPON TWEED

Berwick upon Tweed is the most northerly of English townships and is only a mile or two from Scotland. The wonderful old market town of Berwick upon Tweed has been known to be the town that is 'too north for England, and too south for Scotland'. It is tucked away in the far north-eastern corner of Northumberland and is a place where the author has spent many a happy hour meandering around and generally soaking up its historic and ambient feel.

Many a time I have been sat on the 501 bus from Newcastle upon Tyne, thundering my way up the coastal route passing through Walkworth, Alnwick, Craster, Bamburgh and Lyndisfarne on the way, with a bag full of sandwiches and my trusty camera, eagerly awaiting my arrival at this ancient walled town. My latest visit was in the blustery autumn of October 2008, the weather was pretty good and we all had a good time. I spent a week in total, exploring the side streets and back alleys and found Berwick upon Tweed to have a lot in common with other olde world seaside villages and other historical walled towns.

They say you learn something new everyday and on Tuesday 21 October 2008 I learned that the acclaimed artist Laurence Stephen Lowry (L.S. Lowry 1887-1976) also spent many a happy hour at Berwick upon Tweed, but instead of constantly meandering around the streets of Berwick, like the author has done, L.S. Lowry painted certain areas of them. There are so many locations of Berwick upon Tweed that this famous 'matchstick men and matchstick cats and dogs' painter immortalised on canvass; there is now a Lowry trail for the visitor to Berwick. I came across dozens of side streets and other parts of the town where there are copies of his work mounted on the walls next to the very area that he painted.

It is believed that his first painting in Berwick was back in 1935 and, along with at least four other pictures, was included in his first one-man exhibition in London in 1939. In fact Lowry was so charmed with Berwick upon Tweed, he continued to visit the quaint little town for the rest of his life, and it is believed that it was Berwick upon Tweed that inspired some of his finest works of art.

Lowry was particularly interested in the way Berwick was enclosed by its magnificent town walls, as is the author. I have visited many towns across the UK such as York, London, Chester and Conwy where the town walls stand proud as a reminder of turbulent days gone by. Indeed, Newcastle upon Tyne is also a walled town and like other walled townships, Berwick upon Tweed's town walls have their fair share of history and the odd ghost attached to them. During my trip to Berwick I managed to ascertain a little information in regards to ghosts that are said to reside around the areas of the town walls and those accounts will follow soon. However, being fascinated in historic town walls in general, I discovered other non-ghostly related stories, some of which I have included herein. So if you wonder why there are some accounts without spooky stories in the following text, you now know why.

We begin our look at Berwick's ancient town walls at the most obvious starting point, the ruined castle. Berwick's railway station now stands on the site of the once mighty castle of Berwick that was once the home of Scottish and English kings. There are indeed substantial remains of the fortifications that were built by Edward I, when he rebuilt and strengthened the castle after the English captured Berwick in 1296. This is shown in the sixteenth-century water tower by the river. Berwick Castle was built by the Scottish King David I early in the 1100s. It grew to be an impressive edifice with walls fifty feet (fifteen meters) high, and twelve feet (four meters) thick. It dominated Berwick town and the River Tweed from a natural rock outcrop with steep valleys on either side; it was in a superior location. Both Berwick and its magnificent castle were the focus for many conflicts between the English and Scottish kingdoms, and it is said that between 1296 and 1482 Berwick castle changed hands no less than thirteen times. The castle's strong position made it very difficult to attack, so different strategies and approaches were needed to capture it. Armies would often lay siege to capture the castle resulting in the bloodshed of many Scots and English soldiers. On other occasions it was thought that a more peaceful means was employed, and guards were bribed in an effort to take the castle.

In 1318 King Edward II laid siege to the castle and his men attempted to weaken the defences by undermining the castle walls with a portable wooden shelter called a 'sow'. This sow was used as a shelter as they worked under the walls. But the Scots were one step ahead. They had somehow become aware of the sow and subsequently devised a great machine that dropped massive bricks and rocks upon it while the English were sheltered underneath. The bricks and rocks subsequently shattered the wooden sow killing the English and ultimately preventing them from capturing the castle, this time.

The man that devised the 'rock dropper' was called John Crabbe, a pirate based in Aberdeen and eventually captured by the English in 1332. The English gave him an alternative: he could either work with the English army, as he had skills that were simply too valuable to lose, or face imminent death. An attractive offer, he decided to work with the English and returned to Berwick in 1333, helping Edward III recapture the town. He went on to serve England in the continuing wars with Scotland and France, before dying comfortably and respectably in 1352. In the latter stages of the castle's history, the ruins were allegedly used as a quarry, providing stones for the nearby Royal Border Bridge, and the Berwick Barracks. The actual platforms and station are said to be where the castle's Great Hall once stood, and the remaining wall, known as 'the white wall', is the only standing remnant of the magnificent castle that once occupied this spot. It stretches from the railway station down the steep embankment to the River Tweed guarding a steep stairwell known locally as 'Breakneck Stairs'.

For many years now the land in and around the site of the railway station and old castle ruins have been soaked in the blood of the Scots and the English. Many a gruesome death took place on this spot, so you would expect this area to be very haunted indeed. However, there is only one ghost that is said to reside at Berwick castle, despite all the death the area has seen in bygone days. It is believed that the phantom of a Scots piper can sometimes be seen, but is more often heard, as he patrols the ruined battlements pacing back and forth, up and down the aforementioned breakneck stairs, not forgetting to mention haunting the ruined sections of the castle at the foot of the steep embankment near the river.

Of course, I had to ask the staff at Berwick train station if they had ever heard or seen the phantom piper of Berwick castle and was told 'no', although some staff had heard of the legend. I was informed, by a more mature member of staff, that the last time the piper was spotted was allegedly back in the early 1970s by an Edinburgh man passing through Berwick on business.

The Bell Tower is a section of the fortifications that is situated in north-west Berwick and is located along Northumberland Avenue. To this day it still keeps watch over Berwick's medieval walls, and it was built 700 years ago. The ruined wall further down from the Bell Tower is Lords Mount. This circular gun tower is said to have been designed by King Henry III, and it was close to where we stayed in a beautiful apartment overlooking the cliffs and Berwickshire coastline. It is here where I was told by one of the locals about strange and eerie noises that emanate from inside the old tower on stormy nights. Some say it is the screams of former Scottish soldiers, once said to be kept housed in the tower after being captured, others say it is simply the wind as it howls through the ruined shell.

The Berwick Wall, in the Castlegate area of the town, are imposing walls in central Berwick and are located near the main car parking area next to the supermarket. They are the defences that were built around Berwick between 1558-1570. They were built primarily to protect Queen Elizabeth I's Protestant England from the Catholic Scots and their allies, the French. Berwick had been a walled town for over 250 years before these new defences were started; the old walls enclosed a much bigger town including all the area leading up Castlegate as far as the railway station. These new walls cut the town in two with the huge arch gate being the only way in and out. Originally, the gate was even narrower than it is today, with the gap being only one cart wide. Wooden doors and a drawbridge over a moat that was once here, were used to keep people either in or out. At night the gates were closed and locked and no one was let in or out, which sometimes caused considerable problems. In *A History of Berwick* by Dr Fuller, that dates back to 1799, he said,

> If a person upon his first coming up to the gates quarrels with the guard, the greatest importunities will more than likely be of no avail. Even medical people

Coxon's Tower on the Berwick Walls that houses a fourteenth-century chamber that is said to be haunted by a wailing man. Personally, I think it could be the wind howling through the apertures, but who knows.

returning from the country and though exhausted by fatigue and lack of sleep are sometimes detained for a long time at the gate. On such occasions, the sentry insists that the person is using a fictitious name and he will not even look to inform himself whether it is so or not.

The guard's actions did, on occasions, have tragic consequences. When two girls were sent to get help one night for a woman that was giving birth to her child they were not allowed through the gate, and the help they so desperately needed never came. This resulted in the death of mother and child.

Coxon's Tower stands on the line of the medieval walls that were built to protect the town from naval attacks. It was originally known as the Bulwark in the sands. It has a ribbed vault and a fourteenth-century lower chamber, which can be seen if you venture down the steps. It also has an upper gun deck, which was reconstructed in 1491. From inside the walls (on the path) the tower stands at about twelve feet high. From the riverside it is about fifty feet high, as are the rest of the magnificent walls that run along by the river this way.

On a blustery and atmospheric day, we ventured down to this part of the wall that faces out into the Tweed's mouth. Autumn leaves were blowing all over the place and the trees were literally bent over at a forty-five degree angle due to the strong gusts of wind that were reported to be at speeds of over fifty miles per hour, and the sea was very choppy, to say the least. No one else was around and it was perfect weather (for me personally) to see or hear the ghosts that are said to walk in this area. I had been chatting to a shop owner not less than ten minutes before we walked the town walls in this area and he informed me that Coxon's Tower had a ghost, or so he thought. He told me that the sound of a shouting man had been heard coming from inside the tower on occasions but when people looked inside with torchlight, or called out from the steps, no one answered. Of course, no one can actually get inside the chamber as it is locked up by with an old steel gate. The thought occurred to me that the sound of the shouting man could have been the wind howling through the apertures creating this natural phenomenon but until one hears it, you can't really say for sure. Since I had my dictaphone with me on my trip to Berwick (for my research notes), I decided to leave it recording in the fourteenth-century lower chamber. If there was a ghost in there, perhaps he might oblige me with his voice, or perhaps a message. I left the machine recording for fifteen minutes in total before coming back to retrieve it. Nothing of paranormal nature was recorded during that time, but hey, I tried.

During my trip to Berwick I was also rather anxious to find out about the local battles and sieges that have taken place in abundance in these parts. The nearest battlefield to Berwick upon Tweed is that of the great battle of Halidon Hill. I called into the local tourist information centre in the hope of acquiring a leaflet or some literature about the battlefield and its history, and I ended up getting a whole lot more than what I bargained for. There, in the shop, was local man and official tourist guide, Derek Sharman, who was about to embark on a tour of Berwick with a group of eager holidaymakers. I collared him just before he was due to leave on his ninety-minute tour and attempted to glean some information from him in regards to the battle of Halidon Hill. He was very accommodating and was quite happy to tell me all about the battle.

The Battle of Halidon Hill was fought on 19 July 1333 between Edward III of England and Lord Douglass of Scotland. It was, and still is, known as the great siege at Berwick, as it was the longest and most bitterly fought battle in the Berwick area. For about twenty years or so after the Battle of Bannockburn, where Robert the Bruce defeated the English on 24 June 1314, the Scots had the upper hand, so to speak, and they were constantly marauding around England. At this time, the English had a useless king on the throne (Edward II) who did nothing whatsoever to protect the north of England. By 1333 England had a new king (Edward III) and he came north to besiege Berwick. This siege went on for three months and was the first siege in Britain that had cannons used as weapons. Towards the end of the siege the Scots sent a relief force to try to break their way through the surrounding English, by which time the English were now occupying Halidon Hill. Their position there strategically covered the northern approaches to the town and the approaches from along the Tweed valley, so the Scots literally had to break through these defences in order to break the siege. With boggy marshland and swamps at the foot of Halidon Hill the Scots found this 'siege break' particularly hard, and they were ultimately slaughtered and driven off during their attempt to retake Halidon Hill. The next day Berwick was forced to surrender, yet again

Grey skies loom over the foreboding and untoward Berwick Walls. Blustery autumnal winds blew the leaves around on this, the most perfect day for ghost hunting.

changing hands. Not only was the Battle of Halidon Hill the first of the great battles in Britain where cannons were used, it was also the battle where the longbow proved its worth too.

I then asked Derek to tell me about any of the alleged ghosts that are still said to haunt this blood soaked terrain. He told me that quite often the farmers and crofters in those areas find bits and pieces of old battle equipment on the land and old bones have been dug up from time to time. Although he didn't know of any particular ghost stories he did say 'There ought to be because there are lots of dead people there'.

Although I could not find any first-hand accounts of any alleged paranormal happenings up at Halidon Hill, I am aware of a few websites that claim it is haunted by the soldiers that fell there. Not as famously haunted as other battlefields such as nearby Flodden Field, or Marston Moor in Yorkshire, but haunted nonetheless. One website claims that the battlefield has been subjected to ghostly moans and groans of dead and dying warriors and another states that an apparition of a ghost soldier has been spotted running around aimlessly at dusk. Whether or not they are true the author doesn't know for sure, but let me remind you of what Derek Sharman said in regards to the ghosts, 'There ought to be because there are lots of dead people there'. If there are any ghost sightings that so far have been unreported, or perhaps if you go there and visit the battlefield and experience something odd for yourself, please contact me and tell me all about it. You never know, the account you have may be featured in future editions of this book.

The Berwickshire Advertiser building on Marygate, Berwick. On chatting with the staff I discovered the property is reputedly

The Berwick Advertiser building is located at 90 Marygate, Berwick, and after calling in on the off chance of discovering some ghost stories, I found, to my delight, that the building itself was reputed to be haunted. I had thought to myself that if there were any ghosts, or stories of haunting, in and around the Berwick area, then maybe the local newspaper would have printed some stories on them in the past. I got chatting with the some of the ladies behind the counter and told them that I was in search of spooky stories. I asked about any accounts that may have been printed in the past editions of the newspaper. 'There is a ghost in here', they all said. 'Really?' I replied.

At this point, a man in a uniform (who I presumed was a security guard) called Michael approached the counter and told me that he had experienced the ghost himself while he was in the building alone. He went on to say,

Upstairs there was an old work area, but it isn't there now but it *was* once part of the building, and I was told a Blacksmith used it. There used to be an old guy that once worked on these premises and he was called Joe Blythe. He had worked here for many years, and even lived on the premises. He had worked here for so long he was literally part of the fabric of the building, and when I started here over thirty years ago, he was even here then. However, not long after I began work here, Joe sadly died and it is his ghost that is said to haunt this building. His presence is often felt here by the staff and on one night while in the building alone, I am sure that I actually heard him myself.

'Brilliant, what did you hear?' I asked Michael.

'Just a voice', he went on to say.

'What did it say then?' I continued to ask.

'I don't know, if I have to be honest, it was just one of those voices you hear and you don't understand what was being said, if you know what I mean? I was in the building alone and it came from inside one of the small corridors on the upper levels.'

'So what did you make of it?' I then asked.

'Well, I was one of the most sceptical and cynical people, but I am now convinced that there is something in this. I know it was Joe, don't ask me how, I just know it was him'

I explained to Michael and the girls behind the counter that it sounded like the classical case of someone loving the building so much that they wanted to continue residing there even after passing into the next world. I then asked the girls if they had experienced anything while working in the building.

'No, but if I did I wouldn't be working here', one lady said.

Another lady came forward and explained to me that on occasion, when she was in the building with only a few other people around, strange things had occurred.

'Like what?' I asked.

She went on to say that, every now and again she had felt really cold when the heating was on full. There was no reason why she should have gone cold, and after checking the windows, she found them all to be closed. She also told me that on another occasion she heard a door close in one of the rooms upstairs followed by the sound of footsteps across the floor. This startled her somewhat because she knew there was nobody up there.

After spending some time in the building chatting with all the staff and collating my stories, I said goodbye and headed off down the main street to the magnificent town hall. The staff at the newspaper office informed me that there was an old prison housed there, so I thought I would check it out.

The town hall building stands at the foot of Marygate where the street widens to accommodate the weekly markets and the annual may fairs. It was built in the 1750s by the Guild of Berwick and was completed in 1761. It became the centre for the municipal government and remained so for over one hundred years. The building comprises the Guild Hall and town prison, which was built primarily for debtors and felons. Escapes were indeed quite

At the foot of Marygate stands the impressive Town Hall. Built in the 1750s, this magnificent building houses a small number of holding cells on the top floor that were once used as a prison, and it is believed by the locals to be haunted.

common and this was commented on by the Christian Philanthropist and prison reformer Elizabeth Fry in her 1819 report that said, 'nothing can be more defective than this small prison'. The Georgian town hall building is one of Berwick's most famous landmarks and its spire can be seen from miles away as it towers 150 feet upwards, dominating the Berwick skyline. Many of L.S. Lowry's classical paintings were of this magnificent edifice and it appears that he, like the author, was inspired by the old town hall. Out of general interest, the curfew bell still rings out for fifteen minutes from the tower every night at 08.00pm.

On my approach to the town hall I got chatting to two local people that worked in the Doolally teashop that is on the ground floor of the town hall premises. They were outside having a cigarette break so I asked them if they knew anything about the prison cells inside the building. One of the two, a young gentleman, told me that there were indeed prison cells high up on the upper levels of the building, but it was a very small prison that had only six holding cells. I asked him if it was reputed to be haunted and he told me that he had always been told by folk that the prison was haunted by some of the former prisoners.

'With Berwick being a harbour, or seaport, many folk visited Berwick and done bad things. They were kept here in these cells and often died in there.

You should speak to the caretaker as he will be able to tell you more', he went on to say.

I subsequently found out where the caretaker was and immediately quizzed him about the alleged ghosts of Berwick town hall. Michael Erriot was his name and, during a chat with him, he informed me that although he didn't believe in ghosts himself, and had no experiences of the paranormal while working at the town hall, he did confirm others have experienced strange happenings. Cell doors would be heard slamming closed, eerie footsteps and disembodied voices have been heard coming from the cell areas on the lower levels of the building. Unfortunately, the tours of the building finished in September so getting a glimpse of the old prison was out of the question. I also managed to find out that on this coming Halloween (October 31 2008) an all-night ghost hunt was arranged by a few of the Berwick locals. One wonders if anything paranormal occurred.

The Brewers Arms Pub is situated in the centre of Castlegate, on Berwick's main high street, and is reputed to house a ghost or two. I called in for a pint or two during my excursions round town to see if I could glean any information regarding the ghosts. I chatted with a friendly barmaid that told me that she 'had heard the pub was haunted' but couldn't tell me who or what haunted it. I then asked her colleague who informed me that the odd strange occurrence had been witnessed from time to time in the pub. Apparently, the activity became so annoying at one time that a team of paranormal investigators were asked to visit the pub to carry out some tests. I managed to find out who this team was and contacted one of their members, a woman called Sue. I was told by Sue that although some peculiar occurrences were documented on the night, they were largely subjective leaving the team in question with very little to go on. It was a very uneventful night.

I tried in vain to find out exactly what was happening at this pub. The most information I received from the bar staff was that things quite often flew off the shelves and a presence had been felt in various locations within the pub. Given the fact that I seemed to be getting nowhere, and fast, with this one, I moved my investigations on.

Victoria Buildings is located on Bridge Street as you come off the old bridge, and stands at the foot of the very steep West Street. In fact this building can be seen in one of Lowry's paintings called Bridge End and is on the front of the *L S Lowry in Berwick* leaflet. During my adventures around Berwick I came across the place and thought to myself 'this place must have a ghost'. There is one thing that must be pointed out to other would-be ghost hunters at this point: if one is out and about in search of ghosts, one must be wary of those that will pull one's leg or, to put it bluntly, take the piss! I came across one example here, and I left the premises not knowing for sure if the building was haunted or not.

When I opened the door and walked in two gentlemen greeted me. I said 'good morning', and then I announced that I was about to ask a strange question. I then proceeded to ask if there were any ghosts inside the building.

One gentleman said 'Oh yes, there are indeed', and the other said, 'No, of course there isn't'.

'Oh there is', the first chap asserted.

The second, at this point, shook his head and proceeded to get on with his work. I got the impression he was a total sceptic and regarded anyone that were believers as either deluded or plain stupid – I was right.

I asked the first chap to tell me about the ghosts.

'I see them every day in here, one in particular', he said.

'Can you tell me about it then?'

'Aye, every time I go down the back, to open it up, I turn the corner and I see a gentleman every morning and say good morning to him,' and he went on to say, 'it's near the old tunnel'.

'Old tunnel, that sounds interesting', I said.

'Come with me', he replied.

He proceeded to take me through the back shop, through a door and along into an old landing area where there was a magnificent old staircase leading up on to the next level. Along a passageway and halfway up the stairs was a beautiful, old stained glass window depicting a woman in yellow holding a baby. He then told me to 'come this way'.

'Mind, its pitch dark down here...be careful', he warned me.

As we turned the corner he stopped and told me it was at this corner where he says 'good morning' to one of the resident ghosts of Victoria Buildings. Further down he showed me where the tunnel entrance was that led all the way along Bridge Street to the Sandgate area of the town. I ventured into the tunnel and walked in quite a distance. I imagine this building may very well be haunted but, as I mentioned earlier on, one cannot be too sure.

I then asked this gentleman if he was indeed pulling my leg by saying there are many ghosts in here. I told him I was quite serious and I didn't want anyone to take the piss and it was then when he said, 'No, if I saw a ghost in here I wouldn't be working here'. The second guy then chipped in, 'I told you he was taking the piss'.

In all honesty I think the two chaps I spoke to (who were really nice people, albeit wind up merchants), probably think the building isn't haunted. They said they had been working there for years and had experienced nothing. Fair enough, but one has to consider the fact that people can live and work in haunted properties without experiencing any paranormal phenomena at all, they may not be 'in tune' so to speak. I have to be honest and say the building does have 'ghost' written all over it but without carrying out scientific and mediumistic tests I can't say that it is haunted. I included this account simply to highlight the fact there are people out there who will wind up researchers who inquire about such matters.

Across the road stands another old shop. The same gentleman that owns Victoria Buildings owns it, in fact he told me that he actually lives in Victoria Buildings in the old flat on the first floor. I called in to chat with this fellow, who went by the name of William Cowe, and he also told me that his Victoria Buildings housed no ghosts. I enquired about bringing in a research team to investigate the premises but was politely refused overnight access. He was a lovely old soul and told me about a few of the ghost stories from around Berwick that he had heard in times past.

One story concerned a former employee whose husband was a builder working on site in the old morgue/mortuary building that once stood along Bridge Street. One day, he suddenly became aware of a strange presence that he felt was next to him. The surrounding air went cold and a sense of anxiousness enveloped him. I was told that he knew he was in that particular area on his own, but had presumed someone, perhaps another construction worker, had come to see him. He was wrong, for when he turned around a pale and gaunt looking old man, who seemed to be wrapped up in a white blanket, faced up to him. The old man is said to have then disappeared in front of his eyes, and at this point the construction worker ran like the wind. A fascinating encounter described by his former employee, many years ago.

Although this account is third-hand (not the best attested of stories), it is nevertheless a ghost story that might have been forgotten had it not been for the author prodding and poking around. Another account was forthcoming with details so scant they are barely worth printing, but you never know, someone may read these words, contact me and maybe shed more light upon the story. It concerns the Kwik Save supermarket in the town and all I was told was that someone had had a frightening encounter in there before the premises became the supermarket. I am always happy to learn more, so if you know what happened there, or who the ghost of the Kwik Save is, please get in touch and let me know.

One of the last stories I came across at Berwick was when I paid a visit to the local library. When I was searching through some of their old files and books for ghost stories I was overjoyed to read about an apparition that was known as the Vampire of Berwick. Of course, this spectre was not a razor-sharp-toothed, blood-sucking menace like the traditional vampire but a pale, gaunt, apparitional victim of the Bubonic Plague. The story dates back to the 1700s and it is said that a very wealthy (and unfortunately unnamed) man died and was buried nearby in the churchyard.

A version of the *Historia Rerum Anglicarum* by the English Historical Society of 1856 (which is the medieval sourcebook that was translated by Joseph Stevenson, and is a history of England from 1066-1198) is said to detail the story of this man, who rose from his grave after his death and began to terrorise the townsfolk of Berwick upon Tweed. Accompanied by a howling pack of dogs, this walking corpse became known as the vampire of Berwick and was feared by all that lived there.

The people of the town were afraid to leave their houses at night for fear of running into the vampire, for it was said that the rotting stench of his decaying body could, and would, give those that smelt it an awful, deadly disease. After being petrified for so long, the townsfolk of Berwick held a meeting and decided something must be done about this 'creature'. It was decided that a group of young men would dig up the remains of the body, cut it into pieces and then burn it to cinders. This they did and, at last, the spectre ceased to haunt the town, leaving the Berwick folk in peace to get on with their lives and safe in the knowledge they could rest easy at night.

There was, however, an eerie postscript to this tale for it is said that after the body of the vampire was burned and disposed of, the group of men responsible slowly began to die horrible deaths, one by one. Some folk say it was the plague that they had caught from the corpse, but others suggest it was the dead vampire seeking his vengeance on the men that rid Berwick upon Tweed of him forever. Berwick upon Tweed is a historical gem with its ancient walls, side streets and back lanes, nooks and crannies, and wherever you may roam during your visits there, keep your eyes open and your ears to the ground for you may just run into one of the many echoes of the past that festoon this little northern town, close to the Scottish border.

CHAPTER EIGHT

CARLISLE AND CUMBRIA

From Scotland and north-east England, Carlisle is the gateway to the beautiful Lake District in Cumbria and is a direct link to the North West and Yorkshire. It lies fifty miles or so west of Newcastle upon Tyne and is only one of two cities that the magnificent Roman structure of Hadrian's Wall runs through, Newcastle upon Tyne being the second. The Romans settled here over 2,000 years ago, their base being established to serve the forts along Hadrian's Wall. Known as Luguvalium, Carlisle lies only ten miles from the Scottish border, and during the Middle Ages its proximity to Scotland meant that it became an important military stronghold. Carlisle is the largest settlement in the county of Cumbria and, like Berwick upon Tweed, it has been fought over many times and has belonged to both English and Scottish empires before these two countries became one almighty kingdom.

Today, Carlisle is a wonderful old semi-walled town and I always enjoy meandering through the old side streets visiting all the shops and attractions that Carlisle has to offer. Contrary to what most people think, I have not done that much snooping around when it comes to actual ghost hunting. There have been many occasions when the need to visit Carlisle has come about, such as passing through on my way to Workington or staying over at my friend's abode in Harraby when we fancied a good night out away from home. But, of course, that was in my younger days. More recently I have visited Carlisle on days out with my other half but as of yet never managed to do a great deal of research there.

There have been, however, a few occasions when I have been able to squeeze in a little ghost hunting and what little research I have managed to do while visiting Carlisle, I will detail in this relatively short chapter. Of course, no self respecting ghost hunter would visit Carlisle without first going to the most obvious choice of locale, which is Carlisle Castle. I am a self respecting ghost hunter, so that was where I made my beeline the first chance I was given. The history of the castle is detailed throughout the different locations within this information, and after a chat to one of the English Heritage wardens, I have gleaned the following information.

Carlisle Castle is an impressive landmark and has just as impressive and turbulent 900-year history, bearing witness to many conflicts and sieges. It is believed that an earlier castle stands on the present site of the current castle

Carlisle Castle, a magnificent bastion situated on the gateway to the Lakelands. Mary Queen of Scots was imprisoned there in 1568 but it is not her ghost that resides here. An unknown ghost of a woman wearing faded tartan can be seen walking around the keep. One sentry on duty here many years ago saw the spectre and subsequently died of fright after she disappeared into thin air.

and was of timber and earth construction. It was built by William Rufus in around 1100, and he was, in fact, at that time, the king. A century later it was rebuilt in stone by Henry I, and to this day it is believed that the towering stone keep that dominates the castle complex is the oldest surviving edifice belonging to the establishment. It is also believed that Carlisle Castle was also used as a prison. There are carvings on the walls that were said to have been etched in by prisoners that were held there by Richard III in the late 1400s. Mary Queen of Scots was also held there from May to July in 1568 in a tower that once stood in the corner of the castle's complex, and it is just another of her many prisons in the kingdom of England. Unfortunately, the Queen Mary Tower, as it was known, is long gone but remnants of its existence can still be seen inside the complex if one looks close enough.

The great fortress at Carlisle also saw its fair share of the English Civil War after it was besieged for just less than ten months in 1645. Its Royalist garrison surrendered in late 1645 after being forced to eat rats for a number of weeks. There are many things to see and do at Carlisle Castle which include visiting the Border Regiment Museum that is housed there. Located within the inner ward of the castle, this museum relates the history of Cumbria's County Infantry Regiment from 1702 to the presesnt day. Having visiting the museum on many occasions, I have to say, in all sincerity, that it has an absloultely magnificent display of military artifacts ranging from swords to cannons, old uniforms to rifles and other types of armoury, and I have not found another museum like it.

An exhibition on Charles Edward Stuart (Bonnie Prince Charlie) and the Jacobite Rebelion of 1745 is located at the top of the impressive keep along with a giant wooden model of Carlisle dating from the same year; and you certainly can't visit the castle without seeing the infamous 'licking stones' that the thirsty prisoners were forced to lick and suck on during their hostile captivity there, in their vain efforts to survive. Moisture would seep from out of the castle walls and slowly store in the small grooves of the stonework, and it was the only water that the prisoners could get.

In regards to ghosts the author is only aware of one and that is detailed in Jack Hallum's book, *Ghosts of the North*. In it he states that many years ago a woman's skeleton was found walled up in the keep, but no one knows who she was or why she was walled up there. She was dressed in a faded tartan and had expensive jewelry on. Hallum goes on to say that a sentry that was on guard there had seen the mysterious lady in the keep and lunged at her as if to challenge her. Suddenly she faded into thin air and disapeared without a trace. He is said to have died of shock only a few hours after his encounter.

The author regularly works with the acclaimed TV medium and UK exorcist Ralph Keeton, and after discovering that Ralph had been invited exclusively to investigate the castle and its alleged resident ghosts, an interview was set up with him to find out just what happened during his investigations there. He told me that 'it was a real honour that was bestowed upon me, allowed to roam free into the areas of unspoken truths'. I asked him what he picked up on during the investigation, to which he replied 'the first place I walked into I was told [by spirits] of a death and a coffin within these rooms and I have to respect the man', he said. 'I was then led to two empty rooms where I explained in detail the uses for each room, I was proved correct by the guides and historians that were attending with me. One was for a prisoner called 'Major' and the other was used for a coffin that belonged to royalty.'

'I then picked up on a spirit man that looked down on everyone and described them as peasants. After describing the man I mentioned the name James I, but I thought, 'no, It can't be'. At this point one of the attending guides said, "you have just described him and why he is here".'

I then asked him what else he had picked up on during the night's investigations. He told me the following.

> The cellars revealed more than anyone was expecting, as names were very much forthcoming and many disembodied voices were heard by all present. I explained that I could feel that it felt like there were many people packed in the room like animals, to be informed later on that 341 men *were* confined in this

The Licking Stones in Carlisle Castle. Water droplets would collect into the grooves of the stones giving the prisoners their only source of hydration.

area of the castle. They were to be hung, drawn and quartered, and these men's terror, pain and anguish that I could clearly sense, was firmly embedded into the fabric of this atmosphere and these walls, never to leave.

So, how did the investigation go as a whole? I asked Ralph. 'In all, the night proved rather interesting as we recorded some interesting and unusual facts. We were the first group ever to be allowed in to investigate the castle's ghosts and it was an honour and a privilege to be joined on the night by the Lord Mayor of Carlisle, Mrs Jacquelyne Geddes.'

It is said that a former restaurant once on English Street and only a mile or two from Carlisle Castle was haunted back in the 1960s by a large dark figure of a man, seen on a number of occasions. A man that was waiting for his friend to turn up at the restaurant for lunch observed the figure as it walked straight through a wall in the restaurant area. During a visit to Carlisle I attempted to find the particular building in question on English Street – to no avail. Maybe the restaurant has a new name, or perhaps another building occupies the site, it was, after all, in the 1960s when the haunting took place. Regardless to say my search for the English street ghost ended here.

We now travel to mainland Cumbria and to one of the best-attested ghost sightings in history. The ghost army of Souter or Souther Fell (spelt Souther but pronounced Souter) is probably equal in authenticity to the famous Roman legionaries that were seen by Harry Martindale down in the cellar of Treasurer's House in central York back in 1953. The ghosts of Souter Fell are said to date back hundreds of years, after a farmhand saw the spectral marching army for the very first time. For over sixty minutes it is said that he stood in total awe of the spectacle that came to pass in front of him. The spectral army marched from the north side of the summit and disappeared into a small gap on the side of the mountain. No one believed the farmhand's story, as the summit of the fell was full of crags and sheer drops which would essentially make it impossible to walk straight across.

Nothing more was thought about the encounter and the farmhand, and all else concerned, forgot about the entire affair until a second sighting was documented two years later. On this occasion it was observed by an entire family, and they too stood flabbergasted as they watched in total amazement as an army of warriors traversed over cliff tops and rocky terrain that was nigh on impossible to walk over normally. They too became a laughing stock when they re-told the story, just as the farmhand had two years previously.

It wasn't until eight years later in 1745 when people began to take the ghosts of Souter Fell a little more seriously, as on this occasion, they were witnessed by almost *thirty* people! By then it was decided that a watch should take place on the anniversary of the sightings, which was midsummer's eve. Everyone attending was chosen specifically to observe the phenomenon and each had their own jobs to do in order to document the event should the phantom army make their appearance, which of course they did. All those attending observed open-mouthed and rooted to the spot as, for two hours, the spectral army marched across the fell top.

After the sighting, the word got round and it wasn't long before magazines and newspapers were telling the amazing story of the phantom marchers. The observers of this phantom army were all convinced (as was the farmhand and the farmer's family) that they had indeed seen an otherworldly vision that could not be explained away. Some folk even suggested that it was a naturally occurring vision, due to marchers, existing at the present time, somehow being projected onto the cliff tops by a reflection from the sun. This natural, beautiful and mystical atmospheric phenomenon is known as a brocken spectre and maybe if it occurred only the once then, fair enough, but every year on the same day – highly unlikely! Besides, this explanation simply could not account for the crystal clarity in which the army and its horses were seen. Brocken spectres are usually cast in shadow and not in full colour with glorious detail. To quote Jack Hallam, 'one thing is indisputable; it is one of the best-authenticated ghost stories in the long history of the paranormal'.

Moving on, and we end this short, but fascinating, chapter by heading off to a railway station in Maryport that is haunted by the sounds of a young baby crying. It is believed that after the train station was opened in the nineteenth century, a murder-most-horrid took place there. A man and his wife were said to be crossing the bridge when, for no apparent reason, he grabbed his young child and threw the baby to its death onto the rail track some fifty feet below. The baby was run over by a train that was hurtling along the tracks at the time. A most heinous crime and one of the lowest order which, of course, resulted in the subsequent death sentence of the baby's father. Not long after this brutal act, people began to hear mysterious crying coming from the area in which the young baby had been killed.

It is said that some people hear the screams of the child prior to trains entering the tunnel, but I can't help thinking that the anomalous noises that can be heard just as the train enters the tunnel could in fact be some natural occurring phenomenon with the wind and the acoustics of the tunnel. I may be wrong but one thing is for sure and that is that there was indeed a brutal act carried out there and strange noises are indeed heard from time to time in this vicinity. Perhaps there really is a ghost of a young child that haunts the area after being slain in such a horrific way. There have been no recent accounts of this phantom crying but who knows? Should you ever visit the area keep your eyes open and your ears to the ground because you never know, the next time the ghost baby puts in an appearance, so to speak, it may be you who is around to witness it.

This, for the time being, concludes this small section on Cumbria in the north of England. Fear not, however, as later in the book I will delve a little further into the supernatural happenings of the upper North West when we visit places such as Levens Hall, Muncaster Castle and the old haunted inn, known to the weary traveller as the Kirkstone Pass Inn. For the time being I will leave you with the assurance that the author will most certainly be returning to Carlisle itself and indeed Cumbria as a whole to continue the mission in my hunt for phantoms, ghosts and spectres. These adventures and my findings will no doubt one day be published in yet another tome detailing my searches and my investigations. Until then, I hope you have enjoyed this small meander around the wonderful county that was once known as Cumberland.

CHAPTER NINE

SCARBOROUGH, NORTH YORKSHIRE

Scarborough, on the North Yorkshire coast, is a thriving tourist town and a place I have visited on many occasions. Popular with bikers, holidaymakers, day-trippers and the like, this old fishing town oozes a charm and character like no other. It has two magnificent bays (North and South) that are separated by a quite sizable peninsula in which the beautiful, yet gaunt, ruin of Scarborough Castle is perched. The castle is itself reputedly haunted, so we shall return to discuss this soon.

Personally, Scarborough is a special place and I have very fond memories of my visits there, both as a child and an adult. During a hot summer a few years ago I decided to take a dip in the North Bay and subsequently swam from one end to the other. Many a time I have sat on the seafront with a bag of fish and chips and munched away in the baking heat. Other occasions I have enjoyed a fine pint or two in the many pubs and inns Scarborough has and, on occasion, taken part in the fabulous ghost walks and tours that so often entertain the many thousands of visitors every year.

Out of general interest, one of the most magnificent hotels I have ever had the privilege of staying in is situated on the seafront overlooking the south bay. I am, of course, referring to the Grand Hotel. The history of this particular building is absolutely fascinating. It was built by the Hull based architect, Cuthbert Brodrick, who ironically came from a family of fishermen. It was finished in 1867, and I only learned quite recently that the hotel was built with a 'time' theme. I guess Cuthbert Brodrick was fanatical about time and about Queen Victoria, as we shall presently see. The hotel was, in fact, built in the shape of a 'V' as a tribute to Queen Victoria. There were four towers built to represent the four seasons, spring, autumn, summer and winter and it has twelve floors representing the months of the year, originally the hotel had 365 rooms to coincide with the days, and has 52 chimneys to mark the weeks of the year.

The famous writer Anne Brontë, younger sister to Charlotte (author of Jane Eyre, 1847) and Emily (author of Wuthering Heights, also in 1847), came to Scarborough in the nineteenth century after a long illness, in the hope she would make a full recovery. However, it was not to be and in 1849, aged only twenty-nine, she passed away. She is buried in St Mary's Churchyard, Scarborough, and to this day her followers visit her final resting place in their droves.

A fishing port in Scarborough's South Bay, North Yorkshire.

My last overnight visit to Scarborough was a couple of years ago now, and I stayed in a very pleasant little guesthouse at the top end of the North Bay. My visit was purely for relaxing and taking time out from my increasingly hectic schedule, but I couldn't resist doing a bit of ghost investigating while I was there. Scarborough Castle was only a five-minute walk from my accommodation, so I decided it would be there that I would start.

The castle is one of the more famous haunted locales in this wonderful north Yorkshire seaside town. It was built around 1135 by William Le Gros (later William of Newburgh) in the reign of King Henry I. Between 1158-1168, the castle was besieged and subsequently captured by Henry II and from that point on the castle became a royal castle. Henry II added the magnificent towers and its magnificent keep that, to this day, stand majestically, albeit ruined, overlooking the town. Scarborough had been subjected to many more attacks and invasions from Piers de Gaveston in the early 1300s and from the legendary Scottish King, Robert the Bruce in 1318. Is it any wonder, therefore, that the gaunt, ruined shell of this once-magnificent fortress lays claim to having a ghost?

The ghost that haunts the castle is said to be none other than the aforementioned Piers de Gaveston who held the castle for a short while before giving it up it again after a siege. He was promised that his life would be spared in doing so but on his way to stand trial he was abducted and then quickly beheaded on Blacklow Hill on 19 June 1312. The Norman keep at Scarborough Castle is where the restless, and headless, spectre of Piers de

Gaveston lurks in the shadows, looking for revenge for his untimely and horrifying demise. A motionless and silent apparition is said to lurk in the shadows and then charge at anybody who goes by, presumably in the hope of terrifying them into jumping from the keep to their deaths in the ice-cold North Sea, 350 feet below.

I asked the castle staff if he had been spotted lately and was told,

'Have you heard of anyone jumping in to sea lately?'

I laughed and said, 'I don't know, I am not from around here'.

'Well, there ain't been', came his reply.

'Do you believe the ghost exists?' I asked him.

'Nah, its more likely folklore and superstition, but you never know!' came his reply. 'Anyway, he is not seen until night time, and lurks in the dark shadows in wait, well, he once did... until the floodlights were put in. Can't hide in the shadows now.'

'Good point' I said, and then bid the chap farewell.

I spent the best part of the morning at the castle meandering around and taking in the aesthetic beauty of the locale with my camera in hand hoping Piers might just make an appearance for me but, alas, he did not. I decided to then stroll into Scarborough town centre for a spot of lunch – fish and chips, of course!

After lunch I decided to head off to find St Nicholas Street. St Nicholas Street is the scene of one of Scarborough's most famous (or infamous) spectres and any ghost hunter's visit to this wonderful seaside township isn't complete without taking a peek at St Nicholas Street. It didn't take me long to find the place as I was informed it was located a few streets east of Brunswick Shopping Centre. I jumped on a bus and made my way to the shopping centre and subsequently made my way from there, it made sense to do it this way. After walking down Somerset Terrace I crossed Vernon Road and ventured on to Falconers Road. From there I proceeded east until I reached Harcourt Place. I knew I was close by, as I had been told to look out for this street. I ventured along Harcourt Place until the road became St Nicholas Street. To the layman, well, it's just your run of the mill street with shops, hotels, and wine bars, but to the ghost hunter it's more than that, for it is on St Nicholas Street where the restless ghost of Lydia Bell, 'the ghost in the pink gown', is said to walk, near to where the old mansion house once stood.

Lydia was a pleasant young girl with a wonderful disposition. She was well liked by everyone that knew her, and she was the daughter of a respected businessman. One grim day in the summer of 1804 her lifeless body was found on the beach on the South Sands. She had apparently been strangled to death. The night before her sad end, she went out wearing her favourite pink dress after quarrelling, while on holiday, with her parents. It appears her parents did not approve of a relationship she was keeping with a young army officer stationed nearby, and had locked her in a cupboard in her room, in the hope she couldn't get out and meet up with her man. This was all to no avail as the meeting did indeed take place between Lydia and her fella.

Scarborough's South Bay viewed from Castle Hill. The magnificent Grand Hotel can be seen in the centre of the picture.

No one knows what happened next, but it was the following morning when her lifeless corpse was found on the beach. Tongues began to wag and fingers began to point, and subsequently the army officer became the prime suspect in the murder. Although it looked likely that he was the murderer, he was somehow acquitted of the crime and walked away a free man. Mysteriously, all the men who had testified against the accused all died within a year or so of the case being closed. One man is said to have actually confessed to the murder on his deathbed.

The townsfolk seemed happy with this confession but Lydia, apparently, did not! For not long after, her sad ghost made its first appearance. From that point on the ghost of Lydia Bell was frequently seen in an around the area of St Nicholas Street. Some say this is where she was murdered but no one really knows for sure. An old mansion once stood nearby that was converted into shops and letting apartments. When the conversion was taking place it is said that Lydia made a number of appearances to the on site workers. One in particular refused to go back to work after spending the night on site and encountering her.

A local artist is also said to have included a woman in a red dress in one of his paintings and when asked why he had included the 'lady in red', he said that it was the ghost that his grandfather had seen many times before and had mentioned it to him when he was a child.

I must admit the thought of running into Lydia was quite appealing but I knew deep down that I wouldn't. She was allegedly exorcised many years ago by a group of 'visiting mediums' that had decided 150 years was long enough for poor old Lydia to walk the streets of Scarborough. However, I did notice a number of young ladies wearing red dresses and gown type garments, but unfortunately they were not the old fashioned type. Shame really, because had one of them been Lydia I would have most certainly introduced myself to her, just to see what would happen.

There are plenty of fantastic old pubs and inns at Scarborough, one of my favourites of course being the Newcastle Packet, which is actually on St Nicholas Street. The pub is a fantastic Tudor style alehouse and dates back to 1890. There is a wonderful wooden beam that is located in the west wall that is part of a much older building and for this reason the pub has now been given listed status. I popped in for a pint of the landlord's finest and sat down in the corner. As I was sitting there, soaking up the ambience of the pub, when my thoughts turned to ghosts. Then, what looked like two fishermen sat down on the table next to me and gave me a nod as they made themselves comfortable.

I asked the two men if their 'local' was indeed haunted and was told 'we haven't got a clue mate'. I then proceeded to ask the barmaid who didn't know either, so I asked the landlady. She told me that although she had never experienced anything during her time there, she couldn't rule out the possibility since the pub is old and may retain one or two of its former patrons. I didn't seem to be getting anywhere with this one so I said thank you and sat back down to finish my pint.

'You been to the castle lad', came a voice.
I turned and realised the voice came from one of the fisherman.
'There is ghost up there, if that's what you are looking for', he said.
'Yeah, I know. I have been', I replied.
'What about Cloughton Hall, it's a few miles away mind but I had heard there is a ghost story connected to it', he said.
'Oh, aye, do you know anything else about it?' I asked.
'Not really lad sorry... except the ghost is supposed to be a white rabbit, that's all I know.'

I had the inclination that the white rabbit he was referring to was in actual fact a white hare. White hares are common in folklore and legends and it is said that most white hares are the spirits of distraught ladies that have been done wrong by the so-called lovers. They are said to haunt them relentlessly until they meet their demise; in some cases even causing their deaths in an act of revenge. I was very much intrigued by what this fellow had said so I decided to follow it up with a little research.

On visiting the local library in Scarborough I discovered that there was indeed a Cloughton Hall and it is located on the outskirts of Scarborough. However, I could find no records of any paranormal activity linked directly to the hall, but on looking through some of my books at home, upon my return, I did find reference to a ghostly white hare that haunts the cliff tops nearby. My inclination had been correct, as it was indeed a hare legend.

The Keep at Scarborough Castle is haunted by Piers de Gaveston who is said to lurk in the shadows and lunge toward you in the hope you will flee with fright... straight over the cliffs into the freezing sea 350 feet below.

The story goes, as told in *Ghosts of the North* by Jack Hallam, that a nurse maid in service at Cloughton Hall was on her death bed, breathing her last and very annoyed at the prospect of dying young. The doctor in attendance could do nothing for her and therefore the maid, in her despair and anger, cursed the doctor.

Days after the girl died, a ghost of a white hare was seen in and around the area, flitting about in the long grass and suddenly disappearing without a trace. Winter was drawing in and the temperatures reached below zero making the roads a very dangerous place.

The doctor, nevertheless, still had his rounds to carry out and did so with extreme care. On occasion, the local minister would accompany him on part of his rounds, so car sharing was the sensible thing to do in such treacherous conditions. Answering an emergency call one night, he and the minister set off to visit a dying villager but were involved in a terrible car crash. The doctor was killed instantaneously yet the minister survived with nothing more than a scratch. Upon asking the minister what happened, he replied by telling the investigators that the doctor had been driving along and suddenly swerved to miss a large animal that had seemingly jumped out from the hedgerow directly into the car's path. When asked what kind of animal it was the minister replied, 'it was a Hare...a large White Hare!'

Could that have been the manifestation of the maid that once worked at Cloughton Hall? Since the death of the doctor whom, of course, she had cursed, the sightings of the mystery white hare ceased altogether, adding more intrigue to the narrative.

There are many other ghost tales and legends associated with Scarborough and upon my return home I decided to consult my good friend and colleague Mike Hallowell. I knew that during my trip to Scarborough I had uncovered one or two stories and followed up a few leads, but I wanted to include a little more in the chapter in order to do justice to Scarborough.

On many occasions I had heard about a phantom horse that is said to haunt a certain area of the town. I had no idea where this ghost horse was said to haunt and subsequent research pulled up nothing or very little apart from the basic details, and these I already knew. I figured if anyone knew anything about this alleged spectral stallion then Mike would, and I was not wrong. I rang him up on my return and queried it. He told me to bide my time and he would get back to me. A day or two later he rang me up and told me he had dug out some information from his archives. He had found a photocopy of an old newspaper cutting that had been in one of the Scarborough's dailies back in the mid-eighties. Unfortunately the name of the newspaper was not copied onto the photocopy so I have no idea what paper it actually was. He scanned the news feature in and sent it to me. It is from this newspaper that I have new details in regards to the phantom horse and other tales concerning Scarborough.

It appears the black horse has allegedly been haunting Scarborough since around the year 1300. It is believed that when the ghost manifests, the skies begin to darken and a great thunderstorm ensues. Some say the ghost itself bursts out through a cloud that hovers over the road, terrifying anyone that happens to see it. Hundreds of people have allegedly seen this grim apparition over the years. However, I personally think that this ghost account is more of a folkloric tale, or an urban legend, rather than well attested haunting although, of course, I may be wrong.

A more convincing account of a haunting comes from a one-time pub known as the Three Mariners Inn. This former public house (now a museum) is situated on Quay Street and is said to be the first licensed pub in Scarborough. It is also known to be a host to a number of ghosts. Riddled with passageways and tunnels, this one-time tavern is haunted by a headless woman. Rumour has it she is not an evil ghost but more of a friendly old soul. She is said to warn the local fishermen when the weather at sea is going to be perilous. There is another ghost reputed to walk the corridors here at the Three Mariners Inn. No one knows who she is or why she is seen walking along with a loaf of bread on her head.

Quay Street itself is reputed to be haunted by another headless woman, and a phantom coach and four that has been seen galloping away – to where, no one knows.

One final narrative gleaned from Mike's information is in regards to the famous Grand Hall. We all know and love the Grand Hall in Scarborough, for it is better known for being the glitzy cabaret club Mr Boo's in the 1998 smash hit movie Little Voice, starring Jane Horrocks, Ewan McGregor and Sir Michael Caine. The Grand Hall is reputedly haunted by the ghost of a sailor who died after falling from a balcony inside. He is said to reside in an area known as the Green lounge and, by all accounts, he is alleged to be quite rude, frightening people whenever he gets the opportunity. One woman is said to have had a cup and saucer grabbed from her hands by him one day while drinking tea. Of course she saw no one at the time, which scared her somewhat, as you can imagine. It is also said that during the building's refurbishment a few years back he is said to have thrown around cutlery, cups and plates etc. as if forever in a foul mood. Perhaps he was angry with the builders making renovations? Or perhaps he is annoyed at himself for getting himself killed the way he did.

It's infuriating really, because during my visit to Scarborough I actually visited the Grand Hall and spent some time there. Being a bit of a movie buff, and enjoying Little Voice when I saw it, I decided to pay the place a visit. Had I known it was well haunted I would have asked a few questions and taken more photographs. Still, you live and you learn, don't you?

To the author's knowledge, there are many more ghost stories linked to certain venues such as hotels and pubs in and around the Scarborough area but details of these hauntings are very scant. On a return trip sometime, I plan to visit these venues and find out for myself what these ghost stories are, and find out whether or not they hold any validity. This, to me, is what ghost hunting is all about and I look forward to my inevitable return. Scarborough is a picturesque and modest industrial place with history, charm, character and aesthetic beauty. It is also a town that undoubtedly has a mixed plethora of phantoms and wraiths lurking in the shadows, just waiting to be discovered by the dedicated ghost hunter.

CHAPTER TEN

WHITBY, NORTH YORKSHIRE

Approximately fifteen miles north of Scarborough on the north-east coast lies another magnificent and olde world fishing port. Similar to Scarborough (and run by Scarborough council), it flourishes with tourists all year round and is home to one of the UK's oldest ghost walks (founded in 1972). It is a world famous industrial fishing village that is split into two sections by the River Esk. I am, of course, referring to the town of Whitby and the fishing at Whitby is said to date back to the twelfth century, making it one of the oldest villages of this kind.

Bram Stoker visited Whitby back in the 1890s and stayed in a hotel on the western side of the town overlooking the rest of this picturesque seaport. It was at the Royal Hotel where his inspiration came for his world famous creation, *Count Dracula*. From his hotel window, he could observe the famous St Mary's church and neighbouring Abbey perched high on the rocky cliff tops and, of course, the 199 stone steps that lead from the riverside down below to the Abbey.

This ancient town is also home to a legend, a master seaman and adventurer who made some remarkable achievements, including the mapping of the Pacific Islands and being the first European to sail the eastern coastline of Australia. James Cook, or Captain Cook as he is more commonly known, began his training as a seaman in Whitby. He was actually born in Marton-in-Cleveland in 1728 but has become world famous for being a 'son of Whitby'. He made his first voyage on the *Freelove,* in early 1747, transporting coal to London. His first voyage on the famous vessel the *Endeavour* was in 1769 and its primary objective was to discover a southern continent. For this trip he was promoted to Lieutenant and was given full command of the ship. The *Endeavour* was a ship built in Whitby, and when James Cook was given the post of skipper it was, essentially, the beginning of the relationship between James Cook and the town of Whitby.

Whitby really is a delightful locale that I have visited more times that I can remember. It has an abundance of ancient buildings, pubs and inns. It has many wonderful old cobble-stoned side streets and back alleyways, and is festooned with many quaint red roofed houses. It also has fantastic fish and chip shops (the reader may have become aware that the author loves fish and chips), a grandiose feel that is second to none and it is also well heeled in ghostlore.

I just love visiting places such as this and exploring the alleged ghost legends attached to them. Of course, there are the more famous ghosts, such as at the haunted Abbey, (which we will delve into soon) and the not so well-known ghosts. I like to think that I can discover new ghost stories on my travels and, so far, I don't think I have done too badly. Whitby is no different to any other place I have visited in this respect, and I have managed to chat with a number of individuals, all with stories to tell. But the best place to start – so they say – is at the beginning, so where better for the author to begin than by looking at some of the town's more well-known ghost tales?

However, let me show you something first. During my research of this chapter I discovered an old passage that was first published way back in 1828. It describes – quite nicely – the feeling at that time about Whitby town and its resident ghosts. Due to the book being now out of copyright, I have been able to reproduce the paragraphs herein.

> Apparitions both before and after death are, of course not infrequent in Whitby. Many a valuable house has stood untenanted for years on the suspicion of it being haunted; the last residents having experienced considerable alarm and anxiety; the bedclothes torn off, the china broke, and furniture demolished.
>
> Strange traditions exist of certain yards, lanes and alleys; of some terrible homicide there committed: of departed spirits which have there walked for several nights successively, deprived of their rest, desirous of being addressed by someone, but none daring.

The Whitby Repository, 1828

It is interesting how the passage mentions the bedclothes torn off, the china broken and the furniture demolished. That type of phenomena is more typically associated these days with poltergeist activity. That is not to say poltergeists were not around in the early 1800s, they were, of course. Perhaps the house in question was subjected to an infestation of poltergeists? The mention of lanes and streets is fascinating too, and this is what Whitby is famous for in the eyes of ghost hunters. It is interesting nonetheless to read such old text and we shall now take a look at some of the ghosts that dwell here at this ancient town.

The ruined shell that is Whitby Abbey stands on the edge of the cliff tops overlooking this old, wonderful and haunted whaling town. As mentioned, Whitby is associated with Bram Stokers *Dracula*, and those brave enough (or fit enough) to venture up the 199 stone stairs to the top will be rewarded with glorious views of this little old town beneath their feet, and of course the splendid ruin that is the Abbey itself. Many a time I have puffed and panted my way up the stone stairwell in a dreadful hurry to simply admire the view from the top, but not forgetting to visit the Abbey. Being a member of English Heritage and the National Trust, access to buildings such as these is free. I would recommend anyone with an interest in such historic properties or ghostlore (or both) to join these organisations for the sheer volume of ancient buildings entrusted.

Whitby Abbey is said to be haunted by St Hilda, who is said to stare down at you from one of the windows high up in the ruin, and a former nun that has supposed to have broken her vows.

It is said the Abbey was founded around AD 650-660 on top of an older Roman edifice. The Abbey is famous due to the fact that it was once the abode of the Northumbrian princess St Hilda and she became a legend and part of Whitby's folklore in her own right. It is said that she once expelled snakes and serpents from the town by cutting off their heads with a mysterious and magical whip. However, more commonly known in regards to the legends of Whitby Abbey are the spectres that are said to reside within the ruined shell of this gaunt structure.

It is believed by some that St Hilda herself still resides there at the Abbey. She is said to be one of the resident spectres, and can be observed in one of the upper windows (although there are no actual floors), wrapped up in a covering, or a blanket. She has been seen on a number of occasions with the most recent bona-fide documented sighting being around the early 1970s, or so I have been informed.

Another female spirit is also said to haunt the Abbey. She is supposed to be a former nun who broke her vows; it is said she was bricked up alive afterwards in the dungeon at Whitby, ultimately being starved to death. Rumour has it that her restless shade has been glimpsed and also heard, on occasion, pleading for compassion on a stone flight of stairs that once led to these very dungeons.

A phantom hearse-style coach and horses complete with spectral coffin is yet another terrifying apparition that has been observed to thunder across the nearby graveyard. It is said to race headlong towards the cliff tops, eventually tumbling over the cliffs into the ice-cold North Sea almost 250 feet below. It is driven by a headless horseman, and is pulled along with four horses that are also said to be headless. It is said to be a grim spectacle, should you ever have the misfortune to encounter it.

During my visit to the Abbey I enquired about the alleged ghosts to the English Heritage staff. They informed me that it had been a few years since reports had come in regarding any ghost sightings at the Abbey, but there were a few. One staff member was a total sceptic and didn't believe a word of any of it but was prepared to keep an open mind.

'In my years of working here I have not seen a thing, but you never know', he told me.

Another member of staff held opposing views. He informed me that he believed in ghosts as he had seen one for himself. This ghost was not at the Abbey, however, he saw it when he was staying with a friend in town many years ago. I attempted to glean more information from him and to find out where it was that he saw his ghost, but I got the impression he wanted to remain tight-lipped about it. All he said was that it occurred one night on the way home after an evening out and the whole encounter had 'rattled him somewhat'. I guess it must have occurred outside as he said 'it was on his way home from an evening out', perhaps along one of the many old cobbled side streets that snake their way round Whitby? I guess we will never know. Not wanting to push him any more (although I did want to pursue the lead) I then said my goodbyes and headed off.

There are interesting ghost stories that relate to the wonderful lighthouses that are located on the ends of the old harbour piers. The lighthouses were built between 1832 and 1834 and each solid sandstone lighthouse is said to house a ghost. The visitor to Whitby (should they wish) can pay a small fee and climb to the top of the western lighthouse to take in the nice views that can be seen from the top. Indeed, this is a ritual the author tends to carry out during his visits to Whitby and although it is only a small lighthouse, one never gets tired of traipsing round and round the old stone stairs in order to reach the top. On my first trip to the lighthouse, a good few years ago now, I happened to ask the toll man about the legends of the lighthouses. I knew there were ghost tales associated with them but I was not too sure exactly what they were. I was delighted when the toll man informed me of the spectral figure that is said to appear on the stairwell as visitors make the ascent to the top. He is thought to be the phantom of a local man that fell from a cliff top many years ago. Said to have only one arm, this spectre apparently frightens the living daylights out of anyone unfortunate enough to encounter it. It must be said that during my many visits to the lighthouse and treks up and down this haunted flight of stairs, I have not seen him.

When I was there I also enquired about the eastern lighthouse. I was informed that a sad tale of lost love and rivalry is responsible for the ghostly occurrences are said to have once been experienced there. It is quite a famous legend, by all accounts, and it begins with a young local lady answering to the

The two lighthouses of Whitby Harbour. The lighthouse to the right has a haunted stairwell in which a figure of a man with one arm greets you as you make your ascent. Not a friendly chap by all accounts, as he alleged to scare you witless should you bump into him. Note the Abbey on the cliff top.

name of Sylvia. Sylvia is thought to have caught the attention of two brothers called John and Peter. Sylvia, of course, played off John and Peter against one another and because they both longed for Sylvia's affections they were happy to compete for her. Her father heard of the rivalry and so put forth a challenge to the boys. Whoever could land the most fish in one day of fishing at sea could marry his beloved daughter. This challenge was issued simply because he wanted to know that the victor would be able to provide for his daughter after they were wed.

The day of the challenge came and the boys headed out to sea in their trawlers to the sound of cheering and applause from the locals that had turned out in their droves to see the challenge. The day passed slowly, and eventually the sun began to sink. The locals slowly made their way back to the eastern pier until there was no room to move. On the horizon, the silhouette of two fishing boats came into view. By now Sylvia and her father were waiting on the pier to see who would arrive with the biggest catch. As the boats drew nearer, the noise of the cheering crowd drifted out into the sea and was heard by the two boys. Getting carried away with the whole affair, the trip back to shore then became a race. John was a slightly better seaman than Peter and edged ahead in the race to which the love struck Sylvia shouted out 'COME ON PETER!'

At the very moment she made her feelings felt – obviously preferring Peter to John although never specifying this until that moment in time – John, for some unknown reason, let go of the controls of his vessel and threw himself into the ice-cold sea subsequently being dragged away by the strong current and drowned. Peter, seeing all of this, turned his boat around and went to look for his brother. He too dived into the sea in an effort to save his beloved sibling but, alas, the North Sea claimed him too. Both their battered bodies were washed up days later a few miles down the coast.

Sylvia blamed herself for the death of the two brothers and never looked at another man again. For hour after hour she would be seen standing at the end of the eastern pier looking out to sea, maybe hoping the brothers would indeed one day return home. Of course, they never did. Nowadays, and many years after the death of Sylvia, it is believed that on cold and stormy days when the wind howls around the lighthouse, you can hear the tormented cry of Sylvia as she calls out the name 'Peter'. Locals also believe that the heartbroken apparition of Sylvia can, on occasion, be seen standing at the end of the, now inaccessible, eastern pier waiting for the return of her one true love.

A trip to Whitby is not complete for the ghost hunter unless one visits the Tudor manor house that is Bagdale Hall. It is said to be the oldest building in Whitby, being built in the year 1516 for the (then) most important family in Whitby, the Conyers. The bailiff of Whitby, a man known as James Conyers, lived at the house for a period of time until his nephew Gregory took up the living there. James, as it transpires, had been appointed to sergeant-at-arms to King Henry VIII and so left Bagdale Hall to carry out his duties to the king. It was subsequently passed down from generation to generation until it came into the hands of a certain Nicholas Bushell, who was in fact the father to the infamous Browne Bushell, the man said to be the ghost that haunts Bagdale Hall to this day.

Browne Bushell married the daughter of Sir Thomas Fairfax and fought with the Parliamentarians against the Royalists in 1643. Browne Bushell re-took Scarborough after it had been surrendered to the Royalists only to hand it back to them some time later. For this act of treachery he was later tried by the House of Commons, imprisoned for three years and then executed in 1651 by beheading. After he died his ghost was allegedly seen close to where he was buried in the graveyard at Whitby, and on an old woodland dirt track known as Union Steps. This is where his headless spectre has been observed standing silently and holding his decapitated head under his arm.

His most famous haunt, however, is at his former home of Bagdale Hall. In the early twentieth century the activity reported was so terrifying that it caused great problems for all living there. It is said that he threw furniture around, stomped about the place slamming doors in his wake and often showed his headless body to the young maids, scaring them witless. Nowadays it is said that the ghost of Browne Bushell is not as active as he once used to be, but his presence can still be felt on occasions in some of the guest rooms and corridors.

Bagdale Hall is a wonderful historic hotel with six en-suite bedrooms with four-poster beds and a sense of the past that greets you like a warm breeze. I found the place to be utterly charming and, although I never came face to face with Browne Bushell, my stay there was one I will not forget for a very long time.

Our final visit to haunted locations in the old town of Whitby is in an area known as Grape Lane, which is situated just off Bridge Street, opposite Sandgate on the eastern side of the river. Located on Grape Lane is the Captain Cook memorial museum, which is a wonderful place to visit if one happens to be in the area but, more interestingly for the avid ghost hunter, there is also a harrowing spectre known to appear there from time to time. It is called 'the burning woman'.

It is said that the story dates back to around 1915 when a beautiful local woman accidentally burned herself to death. She is said to have been an assistant to one of the local bakers on Grape Lane. One day she was asked by the baker to put a tray full of bread into the hot fiery oven. Her hair was said to have been long and golden and it was this beautiful head of hair that led to her demise, for when she bent over to put the bread in the oven her hair slumped into the flames. In view of the fact that she used flammable hair oil to groom her hair and keep it shiny, her head caught fire almost instantaneously. In a state of sheer panic, she ran out of the shop onto Grape Lane, at which point her clothes were now in flames. The baker followed her and dowsed out the fire but it was too late. She had suffered serious burns and died in hospital a short time later.

The area in and around Grape Lane is said to be haunted by the screaming ghost of this woman. The spectre, when seen, is said to appear as a single flame. The flame is then said to get larger and larger until the form of the girl can be seen in it. The burning woman is then said to run down Grape Lane accompanied by the rotten stench of burning flesh and charred hair. The original bakery where her hair caught fire is also said to house a ghost. No one knows if it is indeed the unfortunate woman's presence, but those that have worked there in the past have reported feelings of a strange sense of presence accompanied by a bizarre aroma of what can only be described as scorched hair.

A wonderful and historic township with a population of only 14,000 people, Whitby really is the epitome of the traditional olde world fishing village, many thousands of which adorn the wonderful coastlines of Great Britain. Full of charm and character, and with a personality that draws in many a visitor and tourist, Whitby is rich in folklore and ghost tales, with legends in abundance. I have never been disappointed with any of my visits there, and any would-be ghost hunter with a yearning to track down denizens of the otherworld could do no better than to begin their endeavours at the birthplace of Bram Stoker's *Dracula*.

CHAPTER ELEVEN

CASTLE BOLTON,
YORKSHIRE DALES

As mentioned earlier on in this volume, the author regularly gets asked to attend charity functions as a guest speaker and this chapter covers yet another one of those instances. This time it was an event run by Diabetes UK. Appearing on the guest list tonight was *Most Haunted* star, spirit medium and world famous astrologist David Wells. Mike Hallowell and I had carried out other investigations with David Wells for Diabetes UK and we were looking forward to seeing him again at the Castle Bolton ghost hunt. Also in attendance was acclaimed psychic medium and former editor of *Vision* magazine, Diana Jarvis. She and her colleagues, York's ghost finder general Rachel Lacy and co., were there as special guests to help organise and run the night vigils. Mike and I were there to cover the event for the *Shields Gazette*, our WraithScape website and of course guest speak at the event. Our talk, on this occasion, was entitled 'Voices of the Departed' which was all about the phenomenon known as EVPs.

A spectacular medieval fortress preserved in an outstanding condition, Castle Bolton is by far one of the most awe-inspiring and atmospheric castles I have ever had the opportunity to spend the night in. It is situated in the heart of Wensleydale, near Leyburn in the Yorkshire Dales National Park, and is surrounded by many miles of incredible aesthetic beauty. The castle was completed in 1399 and its ruined disfigurements bear its demonstration to well over 600 years of history. Many sieges took place at Castle Bolton, including the civil war of 1645, and it is said that Mary Queen of Scots was held captive there in 1568 before being moved to Tutbury Castle in January 1569.

Richard Le Scrope, who was the Lord Chancellor of England and the first Lord Scrope of Bolton, built the castle and it is the direct descendant of this fellow (the present eighth Lord Bolton), who owns the magnificent edifice today. The castle, in all of its history, has never changed hands and has been held by the same family since the beginning. It was the son of Lord Bolton, Tom Orde-Powlett that the author corresponded with while preparing this chapter. As mentioned, Richard Le Scrope, Lord Chancellor to Richard II, commenced building the castle in 1379 and it was competed in 1399. The Scope family had risen to quite significant status almost a generation before under Sir Henry Le Scrope who was, at that time, Chief Justice of the King's Bench, Chief Justice of Common Pleas and father of Sir Richard. Sir Henry

The awe-inspiring Castle Bolton in the heart of the Yorkshire Dales. Another one time prison of Mary Queen of Scots that is haunted by a mysterious woman in the courtyard, presumed by some to be Mary Stuart herself. Photograph courtesy of James Bolton of the Castle Bolton estate.

had served in the entourage of the Earl of Warwick in France, and later with John of Gaunt (who is said to haunt the derelict ruins of Dunstanburgh Castle on the Northumberland coast). Sir John was knighted at the Battle of Durham and he fought in just about all the most important campaigns and battles between 1346 and 1384. Between 1371 and 1375 Sir Richard served as Lord Treasurer and was made Lord Chancellor in 1378, a post he held until 1380, whereupon his great seal was 'taken from him'.

> After the death of Edmund Mortimer, Earl of March, and of some other tenants in captive, numerous applications were made to the King for their lands, which fell to the Crown in consequence of the minority of their heirs. His Majesty, regardless of his own pecuniary necessities, having commanded the Chancellor to comply with those requests, Scrope ventured to remonstrate and urged the propriety of keeping the lands in the King's own hands for the supply of exigencies. Incensed at this behaviour, Richard sent messenger after messenger to Scrope, desiring him forthwith to return the Great Seal, but he 'refused' to deliver it up to any person other than the King himself.

There is said to be great mystery as to the origins of the Scrope wealth and it is thought that Henry and Geoffrey Le Scrope founded the great family fortune. However, there seems to be a few problems with this theory due to the fact that they did indeed secure land holdings but only on a minor scale. It is said that Henry applied for a licence to embattle his manor house at Kirby Fleetham, but his declared money from gifts and fees never amounted to more than eighty pounds per year. Richard Le Scrope, however, spent a reputed 18,000 marks on building Castle Bolton, which is about 90 million pounds in today's terms. He acquired some of his properties by lending money on the security of the land, and when people were unable to pay him back, their land and manors fell to him. Ultimately Castle Bolton was built and it took eighteen years of hard labour to do it. He spent 1,000 marks per year in the process. What we see today are the semi-ruined remnants of over 600 years of history and what a magnificent bastion it is. Described by Sir Francis Knolly as having 'the highest walls of any house he had ever seen'.

Bringing things more up to date, the castle's north-east tower collapsed in the year 1761. This was due to the many years of wear and tear and also due to the Parliamentarian militia weakening it. After a monstrous storm in 1761, with lashing rains and 100mph gale-force winds, the tower could take no more and it crumbled under the strain. It collapsed into a giant pile of debris and was never rebuilt. Luckily, no one was hurt. In 1794, the Dukes of Bolton ran out of male heirs and the estates went to a woman named Jean Mary Paulet, the natural daughter of the fifth Duke. She was married to one Thomas Orde who was, at that time, a politician and the Governor of Ireland. The name Paulet became Powlett and so the Orde-Powlett name subsequently came about. Thomas Orde-Powlett was then given the title of the first Lord Bolton in 1797.

In 1807, Thomas's son William Orde-Powlett became the second Lord Bolton, and from that point on a succession of 'Lord Bolton's' began. The castle today is owned by the eighth Lord Bolton and his son and daughter-in-law, Tom and Katie Orde-Powlett, oversee the running of the castle. The present Lord Bolton carried out much work in the 1990s with the assistance of English Heritage, and together they cleaned up the entire estate so that it was accessible to the general public. Gardens were re-created, with new additions being added such as herb and rose gardens, and a fabulous maze was also planted. These new additions give the grounds an authentic medieval feel that accompanies the magnificent three-towered structure that is Castle Bolton.

On the night of the investigation (24 November 2007), Mike Hallowell, Mark Winter, Suzanne Hitchinson and myself set out really early to make sure we arrived within plenty of time. It was a pitch dark, stormy night as we approached the castle from the long, thin road that leads to it, and we couldn't help but notice just how immense and eerie looking the castle was. It looked like something out of a horror film with its tall walls and towers stretching high into the night sky, dimly lit only by the light of the moon.

When we got out of the car we were greeted by one of the Diabetes UK charity workers. We were taken round the side of the castle, up the stone stairwell and into the side entrance. After putting our equipment down, we were shown to the main hall area where we were to do our talk.

Not long after settling in and having a nice hot cuppa we had the chance to chat with Tom Orde-Powlett, which, from my point of view, was great. We were able chat with him personally about the castle's wonderful history and its resident ghosts. Dressed in sandy coloured combat trousers tucked into his Wellington boots and a green body warmer, he had the look of a sophisticated conventional peer of the realm. He is a down-to-earth gentleman who gave up his time to speak to us and for this I must thank him. He actually reminded the author of Prince William in a strange sort of way, with his similar fair hair and cheeky, boyish looks. He subsequently told Mike and I about the ghosts seen by his family and members of staff that are said to walk the castle and grounds.

It is said, by some, that the ghost of Mary Queen of Scots glides through the large courtyard but when I asked Tom about this alleged apparition he said that he didn't believe this to be the case, although he told me that another female ghost has been seen there. He thinks that this ghost could have been mistaken for her. This is the ghost of a lady that has been seen wearing a dark coat or cloak. A woman in the village, an old caretaker and the present Lord Bolton have all claimed to have seen this ghostly form as she wanders silently through the castle before disappearing into thin air. He told me he had never heard of Mary's ghost actually residing at Castle Bolton, but that's not to say she doesn't haunt it, although it's unlikely. I think Tom is a little sceptical when it comes to ghosts, but I got the impression he is also quite open-minded about them. Mary Queen of Scots did, of course, reside at Castle Bolton for a short while as she was once held captive there, but her ghost is more often associated with, and seen at, Tutbury Castle in Staffordshire where she was moved to in 1569. Tutbury Castle was allegedly one of the prisons she most loathed – she was held captive in an abundance of places – and she was held there on four separate occasions, so it is no wonder her ghost has been seen there. She has been seen in many areas of Tutbury Castle including the great hall, the top of the south tower and walking across the grass in broad daylight. Many documented and corroborated sightings of Mary have been seen at Tutbury Castle, but none as yet (we think) in the courtyard at Castle Bolton.

There is, however, an eerie tale linked with the Mary Queen of Scots's bedchamber at Castle Bolton. In this room there is a bed that is made up of segments from the eighteenth and nineteenth centuries. It was given to the Orde-Powlett family after a succession of the preceding owners suffered from bad dreams, ill health and hallucinations after sleeping in it. We were told that two exorcisms were attempted in order to rid the bed of its demons, only to no avail. As the Orde-Powlett family were looking for furniture to deck out the castle, they brought the bed from the Isle of Man, and assembled it in the Mary Queen of Scots's bedchamber. Nothing more was thought about it until the family dogs (which I had the pleasure of meeting on the night) ran into the bed chamber and went berserk barking and growling at the bed for no known reason.

In the meantime, Diana Jarvis and her team had arrived and set up shop downstairs in the reception area ready for the fundraisers. After a while they began to pour in from outside and soon the room was packed with eager first-time ghost hunters ready to spend the night in Castle Bolton in search of its resident spooks. Before the evening began, a magnificent buffet was laid on for everyone and we all tucked in to it like there was no tomorrow. The food was eaten in the Great Hall (Great Chamber) upstairs and an abundance of free wine and Lyndisfarne Mead was shared out between everyone. Everyone was having a really good time, and the night hadn't even begun yet. Prior to the evening's festivities and ghost hunt Mike and I were shown around this magnificent fortress before it was time to take the stage. About 150 fundraisers and charity staff had turned up for this great cause, and they all seemed to be looking forward to hearing our talk and listening to some 'anomalous sound recordings' that we had made during our days of investigating the paranormal.

Our talk went really well with the audience, and I think our EVP presentation spooked them a little, yet somehow got them in the mood for the great ghost hunt that lay ahead. David Wells was next to talk and, like Richard Felix at the Preston Hall Museum ghost night, he delighted the crowd with stories of his experiences with the *Most Haunted* team. Then all present were treated to a talk from Tom regarding the castle's history and alleged ghosts. This was followed by a talk from one of the castle's groundsmen who regaled everyone present the tales of his paranormal experiences at the castle during his many years of employment there. We were told of strange and eerie footsteps reverberating around the empty rooms when only he was there to hear them. Shadows, he said, often flit around from room to room and quite often he catches glimpses of them from out of the corner of his eye, and an eerie sense of presence can be felt in dark depths of the castle. Other locations in the castle are said to have an 'eerie feeling' to them, but after many years of working there, alone on many occasions, he finds the ghosts to be quite friendly and to him 'well...its just water off a duck's back'.

After all the talks and pre-investigation festivities, Diana Jarvis and co. divided the crowd into their respective groups in order to begin 'the Castle Bolton Fright Night'. David Wells was due to work with each group while Mike and I (accompanied by Mark and Suzanne) were set to 'float' around the castle joining up with different groups and generally take notes on the investigation as a whole. Our first vigil of the evening was spent in the bowels of the castle in a chamber that was located just off the 'Threshing Room'. We accompanied Diana Jarvis and her team of ghost hunters and assisted her with her vigil. Diana was also a guest medium on the investigation so she was able to run this 'awareness' session quite effectively. A large circle was formed and a séance began. A number of alleged sprits came through during the séance and a range of 'odd' occurrences were felt and picked up on by the circle members.

I monitored the séance proceedings with my EMF meter and my digital thermometer gun and there were indeed some anomalies accruing with the environment. After a while I felt as though one of the group members was walking behind me but when I turned around to see who it was I was surprised to see no one there. I took a photograph in the area where I thought whomever had walked behind me was standing, and on development that particular photograph came out jet-black although the flash mechanism did indeed work at the time. The picture taken before and after that particular frame (in the same chamber) came out fine. After a while things quietened down for the investigators so I left the room with the North East Ghost Research Team psychic, Suzanne Hitchinson.

We then entered the Threshing Room itself, which is a huge chamber adjacent to the one we were just working in and sat down in the corner of the room. The door between the two chambers was closed tightly so the noise factor from the other investigators was reduced to the bare minimum. This room felt cold, dark and oppressive, simply because it *was* cold, dark and oppressive. An eerie sense of presence came over both Suzanne and I but we thought it might only be the imagination taking hold. I took out my EVP machine and flicked the 'record' switch. I called out to the atmosphere so see if we could get any response from the spirits of the castle, only to no avail. Just before the end of this first vigil, however, both Suzanne and I saw, in the corner of the room (near to the exit), a black shadow flit across the doorway. We both ran over to see what it was, only to find no one there. No one had left the other chamber and we were the only group down in the dank depths of Castle Bolton. What, or who, it was remains a mystery. Suzanne, eerily, then sensed a feeling of dizziness while sitting on a circular stone construction in the centre of the room. It felt as though she was 'going round and round'. However, it wasn't until later on in the investigation when we found out that that room was actually used for grinding the rye and oats. In the centre of the room was an old horse mill that the horses would have been walked around again and again as it produced the grain.

After a break, myself, Mark Winter, Mike Hallowell and Rachel Lacy ventured back down to these parts of the castle but instead of turning left as we got to the bottom of the stairs into the chambers we had just investigated, we turned right. We ventured down some steps and into an undercroft area where an abundance of rooms were joined together by a long passageway. As we moved along to the end it became clearer we were entering the ruined area of the castle. It was open to the elements and by gosh was it cold. We went through an old doorway to then find ourselves standing in the main courtyard area of the castle. This is where the magnificent portcullis is situated near the castle's main entrance.

I decided to spend some time there on my own in the hope I would run into the ghost that is thought to be Mary Stuart. However, I didn't, but it was great fun trying. How many people get a chance to stand alone at midnight in the courtyard at Castle Bolton? By now the rain had ceased falling and the stars were shining in the clear sky above. The moon was radiating its light down over the ruined tower and walls of the castle, illuminating the scene – it was bloody marvellous! The castle walls towered up into the night sky and the view I had from the centre of the courtyard was just amazing, words can't describe what I felt right at that moment. All that was needed now was a silent,

CASTLE BOLTON, YORKSHIRE DALES

floating apparition moving from one end of the courtyard to another, but it didn't happen. What did happen, however, was that when I turned around in the hope of seeing the apparition, I saw David Wells as he sneakily cut through the courtyard on his way to carry out a private reading, won by one of the fundraisers. We acknowledged one another's presence with a quick 'hello' and a nod of the head and then continued with our investigations.

After a while I re-joined the others in the undercroft area, only to be told that nothing had occurred. After spending a little more time in this area we decided to join one of the groups in an upper area of the castle. We found our way to the Great Chamber area where we had carried out our talk and found a group in there carrying out a vigil. The roaring fire was burning furiously and casting a red-orange glow across the investigators' faces, giving them a warm and cosy look. However, this was not the case as we soon found out. It appears the investigators in this room were feeling ice-cold although the fire was burning. The room temperature, it seemed, had been dropping for a while and a succession of taps and bumps had been heard by some of the investigators. We sat in with this group for a while and observed the group when they tried a séance. The séance lasted for twenty minutes or so and nothing much else was experienced. This vigil came to an end giving everyone the opportunity to warm up with a well-deserved hot cup of tea.

For our next vigil we ventured into a room named 'The Solar', another room allegedly used by Mary Queen of Scots during her captivity. This is another beautifully decked out room with a huge fireplace. David Wells joined us on this vigil for a short period of time and picked up some very interesting things indeed. He sensed the fundamental nature of the Scottish Queen and told us that she may have indeed resided in this room. He did point out, however, that it was just her essence he could feel, and not the spirit of Mary herself. It turns out he was correct.

Moving on, our last port of call was the Mary Queen of Scots bedchamber itself where Tom's pet dogs once growled at the 'haunted bed'. If I have to be honest, not a great deal happened in there during our vigil. It would have been good to get the dogs in there to see what happened but that, of course, was out of the question. It was now approaching 02.00am and the ghost night was coming to an end. After this vigil we all met up in the reception area and one by one the guest investigators and fundraisers slowly made their way out into the night to make their way home.

It had been a great evening and a lot of money was raised for yet another fantastic cause. We eventually left the castle at about 03.30am due to saying goodbye to just about everyone there. It was really good to meet up and investigate with Diana Jarvis and Rachel Lacy again and, of course, to guest speak at an event with David Wells. It had been a very worthwhile investigation at a magnificent old castle, and I would return to re-investigate it at the drop of a hat. A serious scientific investigation with only a handful of investigators and all the latest hi-tech gadgetry and CCTV is a must at Castle Bolton, and one wonders if there has ever been one carried out.

CHAPTER TWELVE

THE THURCROFT MINERS INST. SOUTH YORKSHIRE

The venue I would like to take you to now is a very haunted one. It is not often I say such things with this much conviction. However, after visiting the place on many occasions and experiencing bewildering paranormal phenomena for myself I feel I am justified in saying so. The amount of witness testimony and scientific documented evidence that I (and the Ghost and Hauntings, Overnight Surveillance Team) have accrued over the past few years is quite staggering. Considering we have only investigated the building on two occasions I think the amount of evidence speaks volumes. I would love to spend a long period of time at this venue in South Yorkshire to accumulate even more evidence to support the notion that it is haunted. Not that *we* need convincing of course.

Throughout my travels around the UK I have met the most astonishing individuals, people from all walks of life who have experienced ghosts and witnessed paranormal activity first-hand. Some people, as you can imagine, are terrified of what has happened and we try to offer our support as best we can. Others have taken it in their stride and are more than happy to share homes or properties with their guests from the other side. The good people in relation to this particular case are, I suppose, a combination of the aforementioned, as they are not scared of what is happening to them but did call in G.H.O.S.T. to observe the hauntings and try to discover some answers. A correspondence received after our team's appearance in a nationwide publication reads as follows. (I thought it would be best to publish the correspondence *exactly*, although one or two minor details have been excluded for obvious reasons.)

Subject: unexplained activity.
My name is Cheryl Booth and I am writing to you after seeing you in a paranormal magazine. I am secretary for the Thurcroft Welfare Community Hall. Thurcroft has been a mining village from the late 1800s until 1997 when the Thurcroft Colliery closed. The hall was built in 1925 to provide a place for miners and their families to socialise. The hall was once used to hold tea dances and various film nights, using the projection room, which is situated at the back of the hall on the second floor, and did so for many years. The reason for contacting you is because there have been a number of unexplained and paranormal events reported to me by guests and staff, and

there have also been a few odd experiences that I have personally witnessed. Here are a couple of examples:

1) Last week I was alone in my office sorting through some paperwork when I heard one of the doors outside my office open. I immediately went to look and there was nobody there. Due to the size of the building, you can hear people moving about and walking through the building as it amplifies the sound, but I never heard anything other than the door opening, shortly after I was picking some paperwork up off the floor and out of the corner of my eye, I saw somebody standing in the middle of the foyer, I immediately turned my head to look (thinking it was somebody who required some information or assistance) and the figure vanished.

2) Late last year we held a social night for user groups of the building. We had some music on low and halfway through the night we heard a number of 'footsteps' directly above us. First we thought it was the music so we turned it off but the noise continued. Thinking then that somebody was on the roof or had managed to get into the projection room, a number of us went to investigate (in separate locations) but there wasn't a soul in sight. About 10 people all heard these footsteps that night.

3) A member from one of the user groups was using the toilet facilities when they heard talking coming from one of the cubicles, they immediately opened the toilet door and the voices stopped! No other toilets were in use and all the doors were open.

Many more occurrences have taken place but there isn't enough room on here for them. I am not sure if this kind of building is something that you have investigated before, but if you want to have a look for yourself and hold an investigation, you are more than welcome, if only to help us understand what these incidents could be.

I have enclosed a rough drawing of the layout of the building so you can get an idea. Any information or advice you could provide us with would be much appreciated. Should you need to contact me, you can do.

Many Thanks

Cheryl Booth
Secretary
Thurcroft Welfare Community Hall
Rotherham
South Yorkshire

When we arrived to conduct the investigation I promptly interviewed everyone present that had experienced a ghostly, or unexplained, encounter. I wanted to get a bigger picture of what had been going on in order to conduct a thorough investigation. An SNU committee member, June Thompson went on to say:

Sitting in the bar room for our Sunday evening spiritualist service, the kitchen door was wedged open. As the service went on my eyes were drawn to the fire door in the kitchen which can be seen through the bar room door. I saw a shape, which resembled a human form stood there in the corner. This happened on three occasions. On another Sunday evening we held our service in the side room. It was during the summer months so the only door into the room had been left open by using a chair, before the service began. During the service the chair was moved and the door slammed closed. When the door closed the chair amazingly wedged itself behind it making it hard for us to exit the room. When we did eventually get out the room, we searched the building for a joker but found no one. The premises were empty apart from those in our meeting room, and all the exterior doors were locked!

Elaine Hollis, another SNU committee member who was present told me her accounts of what she had experienced.

'Although I can verify what June has said, as I was there too, I have also found this place to be very odd indeed. There is a certain feel to it and more often than not it feels as though you are being watched. On one occasion I walked through the main hall and into the kitchen to tend to some duties and when I returned into the hall I found three of the seats had been moved into the middle of the hall (which were all around the edge of the hall when I went in the kitchen) and were facing towards each other like in a circle. Very nerve racking indeed.'

She went on to say:

'It is rumoured that a death occurred in this building somewhere around the stage area in the main hall. Who it was though we are not certain. Also the old library room out back, which is now used as an office, is often quite cold for no reason whatsoever, even in the summer. The smell of tobacco smoke often fills the room even though this is a no smoking building, and we have never found an explanation for it.'

My last interview before the investigation began was with Chris Wood. Chris is the bar manager/odd-job man for the welfare building and is often in the building on his own through the night carrying out jobs. He tells me:

'Working through the night on your own here is really not that bad. I know ghosts exist here and I feel we have a mutual respect for each other. I often hear doors opening and closing on their own and footsteps are quite often heard reverberating around the premises during the night. At first I thought we may have intruders in the building, or perhaps someone had been locked in, but on checking for people and for a potential break-in I found nothing out of order and the building empty. After a while it just becomes second nature to ignore it. It is something you get used to.'

My interviews were complete and now I had a much better idea of what had been happening over the years at the premises. I was informed that lots of other folk also had stories to tell, and I would love to chat to them all to hear their encounters in this lovely old building. One day, maybe I will.

It was now time to carry out our preliminary baseline readings and prepare the building for the investigation to come. This baseline was rather odd as one or two anomalies were picked up during the tests. Backstage was a place that everyone agreed had a certain feel to it, and we all felt a cold draught. Upon tying to locate its source we came up with nothing, then it simply vanished! We also decided to leave a flour tray experiment in this particular area.

A flour tray, for those not familiar to ghost hunting techniques, is simply a tray full of flour that has been levelled out and has an object pushed firmly into it (usually a wooden cross in our case, depending on where we are investigating). It is then left on a sturdy or flat surface in the hope spirits, or playful ghosts will interfere with the object in the tray. If successful, we will have achieved some spiritual interaction and maybe caught the ghost in the act, so to speak.

Experiments of this nature on one of our previous investigations gave us *the* best result we ever could have wished for in regards to 'flour trays'. Not only was the flour disturbed during this investigation in County Durham, but we also the actual trigger object (a red lollipop) taken from the tray (yes, taken!) never to be seen again. This happened while the investigators were in the room, and when I personally was standing next to the flour tray. The alleged residing ghosts at this venue were two children. For this reason we use this simple and effective experiment on all our investigations.

The old library room was of interest too, as when we had ventured in there earlier on to take our readings; we recorded the temperature at a steady nineteen degrees. We needed to return a few minutes later and when we did we found the room to be a lot colder than previously recorded. The temperature *had* dropped to thirteen degrees. A six-degree drop in only a minute or two! Trigger objects were also left in this room too. The rest of the baseline tests ran quite smoothly and nothing else peculiar was reported.

We now had a basic reading of the premises for our records. During the baselines we also placed a trigger object in the projection suite on the second floor along with some motion sensors in the thin corridor that leads to the old office. Other motion sensors were placed near the newer main entrance where an apparition had been seen in the past.

We then split into groups and began the investigation. In the first group there was myself, Lee Stephenson, Chris Wood and Cheryl Booth, and our first port of call was the backstage area. The temperature measured seventeen degrees and no EMF anomalies were recorded. This area was absolutely pitch black and it took some time for our eyes to adjust. Lee, when filming with his night vision video camera caught an amazing selection of the strangest light anomalies. The peculiar thing about these is that when I ventured over to have a look through the viewfinder I asked them to discontinue and they did. When I asked for a sign for any potential spirits to show themselves in some way, the light anomalies began once more.

Cheryl then felt a cold breeze, and she told us she was beginning to feel rather apprehensive. Chris then claimed to see an orange light anomaly with his naked eye, and he told us it was coming up the corridor and floating around at the top of the room. He started to become agitated and then became emotional. Chris, who is a big strapping fellow, then began to cry uncontrollably. This is something I have never seen before on an investigation and certainly not from a sixteen stone, burly, strapping powerhouse like him!

The thought crossed my mind that there were only three explanations as to what was going on. I had decided that he was (a) either getting carried away with the whole thing and imagined it all, as no one else could see this orange light that he claimed he could see, or (b) he was making the whole thing up for whatever reason, or (c) he was a lot more psychic and in tune with the spirit world than he gave himself credit for. I am more inclined to go with the latter, simply because when he told us where to point the video camera, lo and behold we caught what looked like an orange light anomaly moving across the ceiling.

Although we could not see it with our naked eyes like Chris could, it verified to us that something very odd was going on. Chris then went on to say that his emotions were all to shot, he felt that he was sad and also felt a heavy pressure on his shoulders and back. Was he sensing some sad and tormented soul that, for whatever reason, still lingers in this area backstage? After all, we had all felt that this area had an eerie feel to it earlier on.

Group two consisted of Drew Bartley, Fiona Vipond, Elaine Hollis and June Thompson, and they investigated the bar room. A relatively quiet vigil was held in there with only one or two possible psychic or ghostly occurrences noted. The first was when June and Elaine felt as though they were being moved, followed by an unexpected breeze across the room. No trace for the draught was found, and I was told that June and Elaine suspected that this might have been the presence of their former friend, who sadly passed over into the next world. The other strange occurrence was a strobe of light being seen in the room followed by an unexplained banging noise. The entire group witnessed this and no explanation was found.

Location two and our group were due to investigate the projection suite on the second floor. It was a cold, dark and dusty environment, open to the elements due a broken window or two. We ventured up the flight of stairs, which, if they had been any steeper would have been ladders, and entered the projection suite. If anything untoward happened in there, getting out quickly would be rather hard indeed so care had to be taken. The trigger object we had placed there earlier on had not yet been moved and after trying some calling out nothing much happened at all. However, I got a bit of a fright when something prodded me in the lower back region while I was sitting on a chair. What it was for sure I cannot say.

Group two, in the meantime were investigating the kitchen area where a human figure had been seen on a number of occasions. An interesting vigil was documented in here with the sound of some unexplained knockings being heard by all. They started off quite faint and built up into quite a loud noise. The knocks also came on demand when the investigators and guests asked for them. However, they were not recorded on tape. After a break our group then investigated the bar area and group two investigated behind the stage. Not long after venturing into this location I heard the sound of what can only be described as a chair being scraped and dragged across the main hall floor. On venturing in to see if anything was out of place we found nothing.

This, to me, was quite interesting as chairs have been known to move in this area and although nothing seemed to be out of place, I did actually hear the sound of a chair being moved. I took my seat in the bar and sat in the darkness for a while. I called out to the atmosphere and took some digital stills only to no avail. As I was sitting in the darkness, the other three members of my group claimed to hear a grunt or a moan coming from directly behind me; however, I heard absolutely nothing. The rest of the vigil was rather quiet.

The other group, while backstage, sat in silence for about forty-five minutes waiting for something to happen. Just as they were about to leave the area the lavatory (which is located in this area) flushed on it own. This is something else that happens here at Thurcroft quite a lot but we were not informed of this. Upon walking into the gents, it was reported that you could hear the cistern re-filling back up. The flush mechanism is the usual silver handle type which, of course, needs to be pushed down hard in order to activate the flush. No one was in the lavatory at the time so it seemed that this happening could well have had a paranormal origin.

At the end the night it was decided that a séance should be held backstage in order to try and experience more paranormal activity. It seemed that our gut reactions to this area proved right and it was the most active area during the investigation. We took our chairs through, formed a circle and began the séance but not before setting up a whole host of video cameras on tripods to monitor the proceedings. Fiona led the séance and it lasted about thirty minutes. During the séance, one or two light anomalies were caught on tape and the usual array of feelings was reported. Feelings of being touched, draughts, coldness being felt but nothing that we could class as good objective evidence. However a sitter did report that she felt 'odd' and said her arm went ice cold. My temperature gun registered a reading of fifteen degrees on her cold arm and twenty-seven degrees on the other, so a difference of twelve degrees – extremely peculiar, to say the least! Perhaps there was indeed a presence there with us. It did seem likely.

It was now 05.30am and we packed up our equipment, loaded up the car and prepared to go home. When we were chatting in the office, Drew asked me if I thought the venue was haunted. Although I was compelled to say yes (as I thought it may well be), I said that conclusions could not be made based upon one night's investigation. The testimony of all those who I had talked to seem credible enough, and a lot of the data we accumulated on the investigation does indeed point to the direction of the building being haunted but more work and research needs to be carried out.

At this point (as it happens) we were invited to return to carry out more research, and on one cold night in February the following year we did indeed return. The same staff and community workers who had joined us the on first investigation also assisted in the second investigation. We also had guest medium Ralph Keeton and his partner Nikki Austwicke joining us on the investigation, as we needed a reputable medium to assist in the investigation. After the centre had closed for the night and all the centre users had left to go home, we locked all the doors and proceeded to carry out the baseline tests.

While the baseline tests were being carried out I re-interviewed Cheryl Booth and June Thompson and I asked them what had been occurring since our last visit.

'Well, basically it's more of the same really, chairs are still moving around on their own, and doors are opening and closing when nobody is around. Some of the cleaning ladies often tell us they see shadows flitting about and hear unexplained whistling coming from somewhere – but where? They cannot say. I also saw a full on apparition of a man who I thought was my father (still alive) and when I went to speak to him in the room I saw him walk into, there was nobody there at all, and there were no doors or other exits for a normal person to leave by!'

The baselines tests by now had been carried out and no anomalous readings were ascertained, and we were now ready to begin the second investigation. We spilt up into three groups and headed off into the locations to see if we could document any more paranormal activity. As it happened, the night turned out to be rather good. During the course of the investigation various strange occurrences were reported by the team members and guests, including breaths and disembodied sighs, light anomalies, the sound of chairs being moved in the main hall (I was in the hall at the time and, even more unusually, no chairs were found out of place). Other phenomena included lights being turned off while we were in the actual locations. Our guest medium Ralph also picked up on number of ghosts that resided there and told the staff present.

One name in particular came up and that was a certain W. Gregory. This person was picked up backstage where Chris had his emotional experience on the first investigation. The office not far from this area does indeed have a plaque on the wall with a list of people in relation to Thurcroft who had died in the Great War from 1914-1918. One William Gregory is named on the plaque. I can guarantee that Ralph did not venture into this room prior to him picking up this name, so he could not have, and did not cheat.

Another interesting occurrence happened during my first vigil when Cheryl was looking through the doors in the main hall into the room that runs by next to it. She told me she thought she saw someone walk past the windows inside the other room. Now the interesting thing about this is that one of our team investigators, Drew Bartley, saw the exact same thing while we were on a break in there later on. He was quite taken aback by the whole experience and, as much as we tried, we could not duplicate what he saw by normal means. We thought it may have been a reflection in the window by someone in the hall with us, but the tests proved this was not the case. Combined with Cheryl's sighting earlier on this incident proved very significant indeed.

I guess it must have been Drew's night, as he also saw a figure or a person quickly pop their head around a door and then withdraw it back! It was not one of the team, nor was it any of the staff or guests that were there that night. We also know there was no one in this actual room at this time. Drew described him as short, balding and quite chubby faced, just as Ralph had described one of the spirits earlier on. Again, Drew had no knowledge of this description from Ralph and was quite flabbergasted to say the least. Drew is rather sceptical and always puts other explanations forward to try and explain what has occurred, but this time he was at a loss to explain it, and it was to get better, or worse – depending on your views.

One of the last vigils of the evening saw Drew, Nikki, and Chris backstage investigating when suddenly all three, for no reason, became scared. The room's atmosphere took a turn from being warm and normal, to 'unnerving and intimidating'. Suddenly a thump was heard coming from down the empty corridor, and when all three investigators turned around to see what it was, Drew was physically assaulted. As they were looking down the corridor into the darkness wondering what the thump was, from out nowhere came a tremendous blow to the top of Drew's head. The impact was so hard that his knees buckled and the sound of the 'slap' it made on the top of his head can clearly be heard on videotape, which he had recording at the time. The three investigators screamed as they scrambled to make their getaway. A normal, quiet vigil had turned into sheer pandemonium. Later, I was told, accompanying the assault was the eerie sound of an angry and evil sounding howl that enveloped his head at the time of the attack. This howl can also be heard on the videotape.

Drew described this encounter as the most terrifying he has ever witnessed, and at the time of the attack he thought he was not going to get out of this one alive. Nikki and Chris also agree beyond all doubt that something otherworldly had happened, which indeed terrified them somewhat. This can also be heard on the videotape.

It is shocking video footage, to say the least, and watching it makes the blood run cold. One wonders now if Drew is still sceptical! After the incident when I was chatting to him, I could clearly see he was shaken, upset and very frightened indeed. This is not the Drew I know and I have never seen him like this in all my years of investigating the paranormal with him. But in true ghost-investigator style, he marched straight back into the unknown to try and find out why this entity had chosen him for attack. Ralph Keeton told the investigators that Drew was assaulted because he was just there at the wrong (or right) time, and it could have happened to anyone present that night. It was this entity's way of saying 'get out, we have had enough!'

We took heed, packed up our equipment and headed off home. This second investigation there proved to be one of the best for the team so far, especially for Drew. Our guest medium Ralph Keeton answered one or two questions that needed answering from the first investigation, for example who the ghost was backstage? And how many ghosts resided in the building altogether? Etc. but, as with most investigations, more questions had been raised than answered. One question we can answer from the first investigation is 'is this place haunted?' I can now say without a shadow of a doubt that yes, this place is haunted.

It wasn't for a year or so until the staff contacted the team again and asked if we would like to come back and re-investigate. The hauntings had been continuing and the staff and members of the association continued to take the sightings in their stride. I must admit the thought of heading back to that area backstage did not appeal to me, nor did it appeal to the rest of the team. But if questions are to be answered, and research needs to be carried out, who are we to refuse the invitation. If most psychical researchers run away at the first sign of paranormal activity, especially if it is a threatening and violent entity, then we will never get to the bottom of these matters will we?

Perhaps Drew was assaulted because we were there to probe, and experiment? It seems that June, Elaine and the rest of the staff live quite happily side-by-side whatever it is that is there. It only seemed to become violent when G.H.O.S.T. came in and started to research. Perhaps this time around it may lash out at one of the team again, if so, which one? I suggested to the team members that we go into this investigation with extreme precaution because we all know what this particular spirit could do, if it so wished.

In a way investigating potentially violent cases like these reminds me of the *South Shields Poltergeist* that I investigated in 2006 with Michael J Hallowell, which the story is summarised in this book. Being at that polt-infested domicile kept us in a constant state of vigilance, as we had no idea what may have been coming at us next. When it reached out and attacked the male householder by brutally cutting him to ribbons, it really made us think long and hard about what is *really* going on in our supernatural world. Our respect for the unknown literally doubled overnight and nothing...nothing is ever taken for granted.

Unfortunately, due to unforeseen circumstances, our third investigation there was cancelled and for one reason or another (and no fault of the author), the investigation has not yet come off. By the time this book goes to print it will be too late to feature the third (and maybe final investigation) and this is something I am most disappointed with. However, look out for future updated editions of 'The Supernatural North' because rest assured, investigation number three will have been carried out and written up fully by then. One just waits in anticipation for the return to Thurcroft Minors Institute. We all wait with baited breath and with only one question on our minds; and that is which member of G.H.O.S.T. will the entity decide to pick on next time? Watch this space.

CHAPTER THIRTEEN

YORK CITY

One can hardly write a book on the 'supernatural north' without including the city of York. It is a wonderful metropolis in the heart of Yorkshire in northern England and is allegedly the most haunted city in Great Britain. York City dates back around 2,000 years and was first occupied by the Celts. When the Roman Empire was at its height, they moved in on this particular region and founded *Eboracum*, which was the Roman name for York. The Romans moved north in AD71 from Lincolnshire to invade what was then *Brigantes* as they acknowledged the area as a superior locale for a military stronghold and Roman base. The Roman governor of Britain, *Quintus Petilius Cerealis* brought his troops here and it wasn't long before new roads, and a civilian township was erected, and soon Eboracum was the leading city in the Roman Empire.

The Romans occupied Eboracum until the fifth century with their headquarters being situated where the magnificent York Minster now stands. Ruins of their headquarters still remain beneath the Minster and one can see them during visits there. The Anglo-Saxons then arrived after the departure of the Roman Empire and Eboracum became *Eoferwic*. The mighty King Edwin of Northumbria ruled Eoferwic until the Vikings arrived in 866 subsequently re-naming this up-and-coming and now prospering city, *Jorvik*.

The Normans were next to arrive in York, which saw the inception of William the Conqueror (the Duke of Normandy) in 1069, which of course was only three years after his famous victory in the battle of Hastings in October 1066 (the Norman conquest) when he defeated King Harold who had originally invaded England from Norway. Hell bent on destruction and eradication, he caused major damage in York. In time however, the city began to re-build itself and it wasn't long before the Minster was re-built, churches and abbeys were erected, and hospitals and monasteries were made and it became a fine trading city, which made a lot of money and prospered through its business and importing.

Each and every period of time has left its mark on what is now the city of York and if one has a roving eye for detail and knowledge of history, it is not hard to find the remnants of the Middle Ages, Tudor, Elizabethan, Stuart, Georgian, Victorian, and the Edwardian period, some is easy to spot, and yet some is well hidden away in what is now a modern day and hi-tech city.

York Minster towering above 'the haunted city'. Photograph by Darren Olley.

While the aged buildings, edifices and magnificent structures reveal the cities turbulent times of yore, there are also the shades of the past in the form of the citizens that once lived, worked, fought and died here.

These are the ghosts of York and there are so many documented cases here. Apparitions, spectres, ghouls, wraiths and shades of the past have been seen all over this ancient township, so much so it has been considered to be the most haunted city in the UK. A lot of other UK cities also claim to be 'the most haunted' city, but I truly believe that York may well be the true holder of this esteemed title. But, if York is *not* the most haunted city in the UK, then it has to be the most *renowned* haunted city in the UK, for it is there at York stands the impressive *Treasurer's House*, where the most famous ghost sighting in history was recorded and documented.

It was way back in 1953 when the apprentice Plumber, Harry Martindale was working in the cellar of Treasurer's House. He was at the time, an 18-year-old working alone and drilling holes in the ceiling for some new central heating pipes. Simply getting on with his work, he suddenly became aware of the sound of a trumpet being played that *seemed* to be coming from way off in the distance, he thought nothing of it. As he then continued to work he heard the sound of the trumpet being blown again but this time it seemed a lot louder. Suddenly, out of the cellar wall, which he was leaning against at the

The Treasurer's House in York is perhaps the scene of the most famous ghost sighting in history. As well as the world famous Roman Soldiers in the cellar, there are a number of other ghosts residing there, leading people to believe this could be the most haunted house in York.

time with a ladder, came a Roman soldier. The soldier's head covering was at Harry's waist height so he was ultimately looking down upon him. He then immediately leaped down from his ladder and recoiled into the dark corner of the cellar where he then watched in awe, as another twenty or so Roman soldiers (along with a horse) walked *through* the cellar wall.

Curled up in the corner and absolutely scared stiff, he observed this amazing spectacle for goodness knows how long until the last soldier had came through the wall and disappeared through the opposite wall. The sound of the trumpet now becoming quieter as the phantom army of Roman legionnaires became further away. Then, when he saw his moment, he then ran out of the cellar in utter disbelief and sat at the top of the stairs, shaking and trying and come to terms with what he had just witnessed. It is thought that the curator of Treasurer's House saw him and simply said, 'By the look on your face, you have seen the Roman soldiers'.

This account turned out to be one of the most authenticated and genuine ghost sightings that has been ever reported, and still is to this day. There were certain things that Harry noticed about these small and scruffy Romans that no one had known at this point in time. It was only when more research had been carried out, and new things were discovered about the Roman Legions of York did people begin to take Harry's sighting more seriously. One such discovery was the old Roman road called *Via Decumana* that ran under Treasurer's House where Harry had seen the Roman ghosts. Harry reported that he could only see the Romans from the knees up. It was later discovered that *Via Decumana*, the Roman road, ran 18 inches under the cellar floor. The Romans were walking on the original level of the road.

I have visited Treasurer's House many times during my visits to York and always wanted to see the cellars where Harry saw the Roman ghosts. Unfortunately, they were never open to the public, which was a shame. However on the day of another of my visits there a few years ago, I was informed that the cellar was opening for public tours. To my sheer delight I was also informed that the first ever tour down the haunted cellar was that very afternoon. As you can imagine, I was delighted and I immediately paid my fees for my tour. Not only was I going to get to see this actual famous cellar, I was going to be one of the *first* members of the public to be allowed down there since Harry's sighting in 1953.

Before my tour, I spent some time looking around Treasurer's House and took some time out in the beautiful garden out front. When it was time for the tour down the cellars, I was pleasantly surprised to find out that there were only four of us booked in for the first visit.

Our guide met us and we made our way down stairs and through the door that leads to a long passageway with a slanting passageway. The ceiling became lower and the passage became narrower as we ventured further down towards the cellar entrance.

We reached the entrance of the cellar, and I made sure I was the first to step in. Of course I asked permission from the other three group members (one being my partner, Jayne) if I could have the honour of stepping inside the cellars first, they all respectfully agreed. Being the first member of the public to be allowed into these famously haunted cellars didn't mean much to the others on this tour, but it did to me. I walked into the cellar and onto a wooden platform that decked the floor for the new visitors to stand on which would protect the old Roman road underneath from wear and tear during these new tours.

The actual wall where the ghost soldiers had marched through all those years ago was clearly visible to see and it was a very poignant moment in time for me. In total, we were down in the cellar for about half an hour as the guide regaled the famous ghost story to us and it is something I will never forget. The only thing missing that day was Harry Martindale himself. The house guide later told me that he had actually been in to Treasurer's House not less than one week ago. I was disappointed to say the least, as I would have relished the great opportunity to hear this remarkable story from the very man that witnessed it all those years ago.

During my stay in York I also wanted to go in search of the legendary highwayman that is Dick Turpin. I subsequently visited the condemned cell where he spent his last night before he was executed on the Tyburn near York's racecourse on 7 April 1739. The condemned cell is housed at the York Castle Dungeons, which are now part of the York castle museum in which there are

400 years of history on display there. The dungeons are indeed a menacing place, and you can't help think that they may indeed still house some of the prisoners of the past in the forms of spectral beings. The ghost of Dick Turpin himself is said to reside at his condemned cell, which is partly my reason for visiting. The York Castle Museum is actually housed in York city's old prison buildings, and the museum gives the visitor, a fascinating look at prison life 200 years ago.

The museum includes a genuine old cobbled Victorian street, and while chatting with the some of the staff, I was informed of a ghost or two that resides there at the museum. There is, I was told, a spectral woman in black who has been seen sitting next to one of the old fireplaces. This lady has been seen by a number of different witnesses on a number of different occasions. The sound of another spectral lady that can be heard engaged in beautiful song has also been witnessed when staff is on the premises. No traces can be found of anyone when they have a look around to see who it may be. The voice fades away to nothing just when they think they have located it. Then there are the old cellblocks in which I touched upon earlier. It is said in here the sound of doors slamming closed have often been heard along with the tormented cries and snivelling and whimpering of those condemned to death.

On my trail for Dick Turpin, I also visited the site in which he drew his last breath at Tyburn and then subsequently sought out his final resting place, (resting, if he is!) which is located opposite St George's church in a small area of land barely recognisable as a graveyard. There he is buried in a rather large plot of land, large because it *believed* by some that he is buried with his trusty steed 'Black Bess'. This of course, is a fallacy, as 'Black Bess' never actually came to York. Turpin's first and last visit to York was for his trail and execution. The grounds in which he is buried is right in the middle of a private housing estate. It was here at the local pub, where we decided to go for a drink and have our lunch. The pub we chose to visit for our lunch housed no ghosts, I asked, but it did serve a mean roast chicken dinner and damn good pint of ale. But there are many haunted inns and taverns in York that are frequented by the shades of the past and one particular pub, the Black Swan in Peasholme, was a pub that was definitely on my agenda for a visit.

It is York's oldest drinking establishment and it is a beautiful medieval timber framed building. It has a fantastic interior dating from the seventeenth century, although other certain parts date back to the early 1400s. Originally, it was a home to the Bowes family in which William Bowes became Lord Mayor of York in 1417. When I first stepped inside I was taken aback by the ambience and the charm that the pub retains. It really is an olde world pub that is stereotypical of the British haunted inn. I approached the barman, that also happened to be the [then] owner, and ordered myself a pint and asked almost immediately if there was any chance of spending the night at the pub with a research team. I felt strangely confident that my request would be accepted but I was wrong. I was politely refused and subsequently told that the ghosts there are to be left alone and not disturbed. I respected the decision he gave me and asked if it was acceptable to have a look around after I had drunk my ale.

The Black Swan, York. Built in 1417 as a house for the Bowes family and haunted by three ghosts. A woman, a man, and a phantom pair of legs!

'No need to look around' he said, 'One of our resident ghosts sits right there in the bar in that seat next to the fireplace; she sits staring into the fire, but you can't see her face as it is covered with her long black hair'. (Subsequent research has shown the woman in question actually has long blonde hair).

When I asked whom the ghost may have been I was told that no one actually knew. I went over to the chair with my pint and sat down. It was nice to be sat in an olde world pub with a pint of the landlords finest; trying to soak up the general atmosphere that pub has, hoping that the mystery ghost lady makes an appearance. There was no one else in the pub at that time (apart from my partner, Jayne) so we sat there together and enjoyed our own company.

'We also have a ghost of a man in a suit and hat who wonders the rooms upstairs'. The landlord went on to say.

'And a pair of ghostly legs has been seen on the upper levels too'.

'Not uncommon' I said. 'I have heard of other ghosts similar to this, where the upper torso has only been seen, or like your ghost here, just the legs. It is not as uncommon as one may think. In fact, there was an account of a ghost pair of legs that actually protected, and took a very distraught woman to safety back in the mid 1970s.' I told him.

'It was on the city walls near the approach of Micklegate Bar, when a woman was suddenly overcome with terror for no apparent reason. Frozen to the spot, it is said the lower section of what was probably a Dominican monk (as his black gown and brown sandals were identified by the witness, who was an historian) appeared from nowhere. A voice was then heard saying something like 'come with me'. She did, and as she moved away from the scene her feelings of terror subsided. The ghostly legs then disappeared as quickly as they came'.

'Do you know I have lived in York for many, many years and I have never heard of that one.' The landlord told me.

It's always good to chat to people when 'out and about' and for me personally, getting to places like these, if only for an hour or so to find out who haunts, and why etc., is the epitome of ghost hunting. Visiting venues, asking the questions, and keeping lookout for the resident spectres during these visits really is

The Golden Fleece in York is said to be the most haunted inn within York's historic walls. The author spent a night alone in the 'Minster Suite' and slept through undisturbed until morning.

ghost hunting at its best. Granted, overnight scientific investigations are most enjoyable too and the author has carried out many of them, but you can't beat 'site visits' when on your travels, and the collation of first hand accounts from those that have actually witnessed these ghosts. I saw off my pint, said thank you to the landlord for the time he had given me, and headed off up the road to another of York's famous public houses, the Golden Fleece.

The Golden Fleece is reputed to be *the* most haunted pub in York, and reputedly the most haunted pub in the whole of the UK, but some people would indeed beg to differ. Other contenders for the most haunted pub in the UK include the famous Marsden Grotto cave bar that is situated in the limestone cliffs at South Shields, The Mermaid Inn at East Sussex, The George and Dragon Hotel in West Wycombe, The Devils Stone Inn, in Devon, and the Ostrich Inn at Berkshire to name a few. The Golden Fleece stands opposite York's most distinguished and charming side street, the Shambles and is said to date back to 1503.

During my visit the owners informed me that there is an abundance of ghosts that are said to haunt the pub. A female dressed in Victorian garb believed to be that of Lady Alice Peckett. Her husband John was a one time Lord Mayor of York and a former owner of the building. Her ghost has reputedly been seen dozens of times as she walks through one of the walls inside the premises. Another ghost said to be that of a Canadian airman, is said to reside on the upper levels the building and it is thought that this fellow fell to his death there during the Second World War. The ghost of a playful young boy is also said to haunt the pub and he is reported to tug and pull the trouser legs of people in the pub. More harrowingly, disembodied voices and laughter have been heard literally scaring the witnesses and patrons half to death, and poltergeist-like activity has been reported downstairs in the bar. I was also informed that at the main bar area, staff and patrons alike have felt the sensation of having their throats squeezed by an invisible force, and this is in the area where a former landlord is said to have hung himself from the rafters.

Quite an array of ghosts it seems, so maybe it is after all, a good contender for being the most haunted pub in the UK. My curiosity ultimately got the better of me and in March 2009 I decided to return to York and spend a night or two in the Golden Fleece's most haunted rooms, just to see if anything would happen. In all honesty I spent the night in the Minster Suite (on my own) with absolutely nothing happening at all. My colleagues, Darren and Julie, spent their night in the Shambles room, again, with nothing of a paranormal nature being reported. Video cameras were set up, EVPs were left recording only to no avail. Of course, just because we didn't experience anything on that particular night doesn't mean to say the rooms are not haunted, I am quite sure they are, however, no ghosts came forth whilst we were in residence there. Despite this fact we had a very enjoyable weekend in York. Many haunted pubs and other places of 'ghostly interest' were visited with an abundance of ghost stories collated and pictures taken.

York is reputed to house 140 ghosts in total within its historic walls and there are many, many books detailing them. However, I deemed it unpractical to even attempt to include them all in this volume so I have summarised some of the ghost stories that I have managed investigate with some of the venues I have visited during my adventures in this amazing city.

The York Arms pub in High Petergate (next to the Minster) was *once* reputed to be the most haunted pub in York until the Golden Fleece took this accolade. I was told by a friend of mine, who is a native of York, that it was haunted by the ghost of a lady that appeared in the gent's toilets, and that the pub suffered horrendous poltergeist-like activity. Former landlord Barry Grayson said quite often pictures and ornaments would often fly off the shelves in the bar when no one was near them. When asked if it concerned him at all, he said it was 'water of a ducks back'. It didn't bother him in the least.

The gaunt and atmospheric ruin of St Mary's Abbey that is located in the Yorkshire Museum Gardens (that lies to the west of the Minster) is reputedly haunted by a spectral monk who has been seen from time to time as he aimlessly meanders around the place. I was lucky enough to be staying in a hotel that was just around the corner from this one time Benedictine Abbey, so on a nice summers evening at dusk, I made my way around to the ruins in

The York Museum next to St Mary's Abbey was subject to spooky goings on which led the hauntings being the most well known in York at that time. A vigil was held overnight in which a book was thrown onto the floor by unseen hands. Photograph by Darren Olley.

the hope I would catch a glimpse of this elusive phantom. Of course I knew my chances of running in to him were rather slim, but I thought I would at least have a go nonetheless. I took my camera and my EVP machine for my vigil, and attempted to make some sound recordings as I enjoyed the summer evening.

I was all alone in these wonderful and peaceful surroundings and I enjoyed every last tranquil minute of it. The birds were singing in the trees filling the warm night air with beautiful evening song, and rabbits and squirrels came out from the bushes and undergrowth and scampered around the place without a care in the world. In all honesty I felt at one with nature, it was a beautiful experience that I only wished I could have shared with Jayne. She had decided not to venture around to the ruins with me, just in case we actually bumped into the ghost monk. However my short vigil there that evening proved rather fruitless as no anomalous EVP recordings were made, no pictures of ghosts were taken, and no sightings were made. Still, it was a most enjoyable experience and something I would very much like to do again.

As previously stated, the ruins of the Abbey are situated in the gardens of the York Museum, which is also reputed to house a ghost. It is said that one night a certain George Thomas, who was the [then] caretaker, was in the building and was doing his rounds after closing time when he stumbled across a visitor who had not yet left the building. George thought to himself; perhaps the visitor presumed the building was still open and was enjoying his visit to the museum. George then decided that he must inform the gentleman that the museum was now actually closed and began to walk over to speak to him. As he got to within five feet of the man, the would-be visitor began do disintegrate before his very eyes and disappear into thin air.

Other sightings of the ghost were subsequently documented which led to the haunting being one of the most well known in York at that time. Notable members of the *Incorporated Society for Psychical Research* (Eric J. Dingwall and Trevor H. Hall) investigated this case and wrote it up in their book 'Four Modern Ghosts' which the author has in his cherished book collection. A vigil at the museum was undertaken by a number of distinguished individuals where upon a book was reported to have been thrown from one of the shelves. It is interesting to note that the individual that donated this particular book, one Alderman Edward Wooler (who had been dead for many years) fitted the description perfectly of the spectral visitor, so it was assumed at this time that this man was the ghost. After showing the caretaker a photograph of the late Mr Wooler, it is said that he positively identified him as the disintegrating spectral visitor that he seen in the library. An absolutely fascinating narrative, don't you think?

Clifford's Tower is a nickname for York Castle after 'Roger de Clifford' was hanged by chains upon the walls of the tower for opposing Edward II in 1322. It is another of the cities better known haunted locations and stands opposite the York Castle Museum that was touched upon earlier on in this chapter. The original wooden construction that was built there prior to the stone one that we see today, was built by William the Conqueror in 1068 and was replaced 100 years later. It was in 1190 when the infamous massacre of the Jews took place. It is said that during riots in a troubled and turbulent York, a thousand Jews took refuge inside the tower. It was then burnt to the ground resulting in the gruesome deaths of everyone inside. By all accounts, this circular stone structure is now haunted by apparitional blood that is said to seep from the stones and drip slowly down the interior walls. It is also thought that Roger de Clifford himself also haunts this edifice, as many visitors who go there, experience a feeling of being 'ill at ease' as a horrible sense of foreboding overcomes them.

It is a fabulous little visitor attraction and the views from the top walkway high on the top of the tower offer spectacular scenery from all directions. Out of general interest, the guide, there informed me during my visit that the hillock that this very construction sits upon was the very hill that the *Grand Old Duke of York* marched his 10,000 men up and down again in the famous nursery rhyme.

In regards to ghost sightings or paranormal happenings, I was informed there hadn't been any for a while, although paranormal teams do come in from time to time and photograph 'light orbs'. However, upon chatting to my work colleague from York that was mentioned earlier on in the chapter, he told me that he and his friends had their own terrifying experience while playing at the castle back in 1985 when he was only 18 years old. Sitting at the top of the hill at the foot of the castle with their backs against the big wooden door one night, they were all suddenly surprised to hear a tremendous bang and simultaneously, they were all thrown forwards with a jolt. I was told that it was as though someone or something *inside* the locked and empty tower had battered the door they were sitting against ultimately throwing them forwards.

My first question was 'were they drunk?' and the reply I was given was an unequivocal 'no'. I then asked if anyone could have been inside the locked up tower and I was adamantly informed that there was no one there. The castle had closed for the night and had locked its doors, besides; they all called out to see if anyone was inside the tower and got no reply whatsoever. Considering the reputation of Clifford's Tower, and the fact that *three* individuals all experienced something odd that night, they concluded they must have had a paranormal experience. Maybe they did, maybe they didn't, but whatever happened at Clifford's Tower that night was certainly a frightening account for those involved and one wonders if this has occurred to anyone else. I would love to hear from anyone else that has experienced anything similar to this.

I was informed that the magnificent Kings Manor, which has been a royal home, an abbot's house, a school for young ladies, assembly rooms and a school for the blind, is one of York's historic buildings and is reputed to be haunted by a number of ghosts. It was here at Kings Manor, during one of my trips to York where we started on one of the many ghost walks that York has to offer the visitor. Actually, we took part in all of the different ghosts walks with this particular walk being the first. There were only five or six people on this ghost walk, which I felt was quite odd. Normally there are literally dozens of 'ghost walkers' blocking up the side streets and touring the ancient cobbled lanes as they are regaled terrifying stories of the dead by tour guides that are dressed to the hilt with large black hat, cloaks and sticks.

Perhaps it was the *lack* of over dramatised narratives and gimmicks that usually come with these ghost tours which resulted in this particular ghost walk not being as popular as the rest. Most people love the 'scare factor' and the potential 'thrills' that one may get while on a ghost walk. Not this one, this ghost walk was informative, straight to the point, and comes with no element of 'cheese' whatsoever. It was in fact a damn good tour to which I would recommend to any serious ghost enthusiast.

Back to the Kings manor then, and it is said that are many alleged ghosts that reside in this old historic edifice. One being a phantom monk in black that has been seen in various parts of the building over the years, and a woman dressed in Tudor style clothing that is believed by the locals to be Anne Boleyn although nothing is certain. We were told that on one particular occasion a woman that was working in the manor one day suddenly screamed, and then fainted. When she came around it is reported that she said one of the cupboard doors flew open and before she knew it, a woman had glided out from the aperture towards her and then proceeded to walk straight through her. She was described as the woman with Tudor style garb.

Another tale concerns a failed siege of the manor in 1644. It is said that a number of Roundhead soldiers had died during the siege of the manor and it is their moans and groans that have been heard echoing around the area next to the inner courtyard. Perhaps their groans of anguish and pain were somehow recorded into the surrounding atmosphere and it is these 'psychic recordings' that have been heard recently. The *stone tape* or *psychic recording* is a very familiar concept these days that could well hold the key to a lot of alleged ghostly sounds and sightings.

One could go on and on reciting the ghost tales and legends of this ancient city but the fact is despite all my visits there, there simply wasn't enough time for me to investigate all the ghost stories concerned. As mentioned at the beginning of this chapter there are said to be 140 ghosts that reside inside the walled city of York. Many fabulous narratives have been excluded from this chapter simply because I have no room to detail them in the way I wish. For example, on a visit to Trinity Church yard in Goodramgate I found out that inside there is a spectre of lady, who by all accounts is looking for her child, and outside in the graveyard there is the ghost of a headless phantom who wanders around aimlessly. Then we have the ghost of the weeping girl at number five-college street. She is believed to be a victim of the plague. The Roman Bath House pub is said to be haunted by a Roman soldier who has been seen down underneath the pub in the old ruined Roman baths. It is said he vanishes into thin air not long after he is spotted; the list goes on and on.

There are however many books on the market that does detail massive amounts of ghost tales of York and I highly recommend the ghost enthusiast to seek them out. One of my favourites is a tome entitled 'Ghosts of an Ancient City' by John V. Mitchell. A local man that has collated many first hand accounts over the years. There is no one better to tell you the stories of haunted York. Packed with spine chilling accounts this book is guaranteed to enchant the reader (as did with me) with true tales of the paranormal.

CHAPTER FOURTEEN

THE CITY OF LEEDS

The city of Leeds is a city in West Yorkshire, is situated on the River Aire, and was awarded the city status in 1893. The Romans settled in Leeds for a while, and after their departure the Normans occupied it. The first reliable record of this area was recorded in the Domesday Book of 1086 when it was known as 'Ledes'or 'Ledis'. In 1068 we know that Leeds was primarily an undeveloped farming province of about one thousand acres or so in scope, and was divided into numerous manors. Ilbert de Lacy built a castle in Leeds in an area known as Mill Hill, which was besieged in 1139 and in 1399 (according to the Hardynge Chronicle) and Richard II was imprisoned there before being transported to another Ilbert de Lacy property in Pontefract, for his execution.

> *The kyng then sent kyng Richard to Ledis,*
> *there to be kepte durely in previtee;*
> *fro thens after to Pykering went he needis,*
> *and to Knaresbro' after led was he*
> *but to pontefrete last where he did dee.*

After the Norman conquest the development of Leeds was slow, but evenually a small town did at last emerge but only after four hundred years or so. There was no military significance and the townsfolk were more intetrested in their agriculture than they were of anything else.

The town itself was small with the streets being very narrow, unpaved, and unlit. The houses, in spite of the fact that stone was in abundance in the district, were made of wood, were whitewashed, and in many cases the roofs were thatched. All around the little town lay the open fields and meadows, cultivated on the principle of strip-farming. Beyond these meadows lay the thick woods of the old forest of Elmet.

The word 'Leeds' originates from the word Loidis, which was the name given to the forest that once covered the kingdom of Elmet. Elmet, during the Middle Ages, was an ancient Celtic kingdom that covered the area that is now known as the West Riding of Yorkshire and the River Sheaf in the south, and the River Wharf to the east bordered it. By the fifteenth century Leeds was a market town and during the Tudor Period (1845-1603), it was visited by one John Leland. John Leland was an English antiquary that had been described as 'the father of local history' and stated that 'it was a pretty market town which stood most by clothing and was as large as Bradford though not as enterprising'.

In 1644 an epedemic of a plague like disease broke out in Leeds resulting in the horrid deaths of over 1300 people. The weekly markets were subsequently ceased in an effort to keep away potential visiors to the area, as people were dying quicker than they could be registered and then disposed of. so servere was this epedemic it was likened to the 'Black Death' of Mediaval England.

By 1715 Leeds was mainly a merchant town, manufacturing woollen cloths and trading with Europe via the Humber Estuary. The population steadily grew from around 8,000 to 10,000 at the end of the seventeenth century, and to 30,000 at the end of the eighteenth. At one point nearly half of England's total export passed through Leeds.

Nowadays Leeds is known for its industrial heritage. There are many art galleries and museums for the more sophistocated culture seeker with locations such as the Leeds art gallery, Leeds City Museum and the Royal Armouries, plus many more places of great interest. The wonderful Abbey ruins at Kirkstall is a wonderful example of a mediaval Cistercian Abbey and is well worth a visit, and I am told that Leeds is also well renowned for shopping, along with its pubs, clubs, and its amazing night life. What Leeds wasn't really known for however, is its population of etheral visitors and phantoms that reside in the historic buildings and parks that festoon this wondeful ancient city. I feel Leeds, like other cities and places such as Newcastle upon Tyne and Sunderland etc, have been hibitually overlooked in regards to their folk legends, tales and ghost stories and (to my knowledge) has never been greatly associated with such things as ghosts and folkloric tales.

Things are beginning to change however with a number of books and publications now becoming available written by personages such as ghost walker and Leeds city guide Ken Goor. Ken released a great book in 2008 detailing the ghosts stories and legends of Leeds and it is simply called 'Haunted Leeds'. From the same series and publisher of my own 'Haunted Newcasltle' book, Haunted leeds is a fascinating glimpse of a world we know very little about and in my opinion, is a very warm welcome to the 'Haunted' series, and of course to the literature of ghosts and hauntings in the north of England. I am privelidged to have corresponded with Mr Goor during the compilation of 'The Supernatural North' and my thanks go to him for the help and assistance that he gave me. A personal story of his will be relayed at the end of this chapter. For the time being however, I have decided to detail only a few venues that are reputedly haunted in the Leeds area so any reader wishing to research the ghosts of this particular city a little further I would suggest they aquire Ken's book.

Our first haunted venue is probabaly one of the most well known haunted properties in the area and is known as *Temple Newsham House*. In 1544 King Henry VIII give the house to his niece, Margeret Countess of Lennox and her husband, Matthew Staurt, and it was there they give birth to their son Henry, Lord Darnley (the famous husband of Mary Queen of Scots). Once known as

Neuhusam, this spendid house has seen many owners come and go until it fell into the hands of the Ingram family in 1622 when it was bought for £12,000. For three hundred years it stayed in the Ingram family until it was sold to Leeds City Council in 1922 by Edward Wood, the first Earl of Halifax. Since then it has been a spectacular museum open to the public. Set in 1500 acres of lush parkland that was landscaped by Capabilty Brown in the eighteenth century, Temple Newsham House is without doubt one of the finest historic estates in England and like other old historic estates, it is of course reputed to be haunted. The most well-known spectre to walk the corridors there is said to be one of the ancestors of the Ingram family, Mary Ingram. She has reportedly been seen meandering around the locale sporting a blue night gown or flowing dress so therefore she has become known as the 'blue lady'. Her treasured jewelry that was given to her by her grandfather, was alledgedly stolen by a highwayman one night when she was on her way home. For weeks after the attack, she continually asked for her jewels in a state of trauma due to the robbery, whereupon she refused to eat or drink. She evenually died aged only fifteen.

Another resident shade is known as the White Lady and by all accounts, she was caught on film there by a local group of ghost investigators. The sighting and recording made BBC news in 2007 and caused quite a bit of a stir within the paranormal communtiy. The ghost is thought to be that of Lady Jane Dudley who has reportedly haunted the house for over half a century. Lady Jane Dudley is said to have hanged herself at the house after falling in love with a man whom she would never be with, Lord Darnley; he, as previously mentioned, married Mary Stuart.

Phantom monks, two to be precise, are also said to reside at Temple Newsham House. One is said to glide silently across the grass in the area of the golf course and disapear without a trace, and without leaving any footprints, and the other was reportedly seen on the south side of the house. Known as the 'hissing monk' this spectre is said to have filled the ears of the unfortunate witness with an awful hissing sound after it was spotted back in 1980. Said by some to be the most haunted house in the north, Temple Newsham House really is a wonderful old stately manor house and is well worth a visit if you are ever in Leeds. I will leave you with one final comment in regards to the ghosts of Temple Newsham House. After being asked if they believed in ghosts, one of the staff there once said to someone 'I have no choice really, as I have seen plenty while working here'.

We move on now to the magnificent ruined Abbey that is Kirkstall Abbey. Kirkstall Abbey is located about three miles from Leeds city centre and is by far one of the best preserved monasteries in the whole of Great Britain. Set in beautiful parklands and aesthetic scenery along by the River Aire, Kirkstall Abbey was founded in around the mid 1100s by the Cistercian order of monks that came from Fountains Abbey near Ripon. It is said that Kirkstall Abbey is one of the most important historic buildings in the Leeds area and if you ever see the place during a visit you would understand why. The Abbey was home to a vast community of monks until its dissolution in 1539 when sadly many parts of the building were stripped and taken away to be used in other newer and more acceptable buildings. This explains why the Abbey looks partially built; nevertheless it is still favoured by the historians as the best-preserved Abbey. There are many buildings housed on this complex so the visitor will have much to do should he or she visit.

The magnificent nave, which is the original church interior is there to be explored with its towering walls and magnificent arches and flanking chapels that were once used by the lay brothers of the order. The nave leads you to the ruined tower that stands majestically soaring into the heavens. Part of the tower collapsed during a great storm in 1779 but was restored to some extent by the Victorians so a further collapse was avoided. There are the Cloisters, the East Range, the monk's former dormitories, the Refectory, the Novices quarters, the Abbots Lodgings and many, many more areas to see and explore.

Kirkstall Abbey is said to be home to a ghost or two and it is no surprise that the resident ghosts are monks. Documented reports of a ghost precession with sad looking spectres dressed in white garb that are seen making their way slowly down the centre of the nave have come in from time to time. The main ghost said to reside here is thought to be that of the former Abbot, who by all accounts, is heard moving around more than he is seen. People are often said to report hearing his footsteps and shuffles as he ponders around museum area of the complex. I was told however, the last known sighting of the monk occurred back in the 1930s, over seventy years ago. Out of interest, during my researching I came across a wonderful photograph of a monk like shape praying in the grounds of the Abbey. The picture, which *does* look remarkably like the *shape* of a monk with bowed head, is unmistakably the sun shining through an aperture (probably another window) onto the wall, a classic example of simulacra if I ever saw one. One just wonders why pictures like these are even submitted for analysis. One has to be so careful when taking pictures on ghost hunts, I bet my bottom dollar if the photographer had just lifted his or her head after taking the frame they would have seen the sunlit shaped figure there on the wall – who knows though, I may indeed be wrong, but I doubt it.

There are many other ghost stories and legends in and around Leeds, and one other particular place that is well reputed to be haunted is a theatre known as the City Varieties Music Hall, which is in Central Leeds. The music hall is owned by Leeds City Council and is run by the Leeds Grand Theatre and Opera House Limited, which is a company that is owned by the council. It was originally built in 1865 as an extension to the White Swan Inn and is well known across the UK for its music, comedy and other types of variety performances.

Upon chatting with ghost walker and historian Ken Goor one night on the telephone, he informed me of a number of ghosts that are said to haunt this wonderful old theatre and subsequently went on to say that there is a ghost there that is said to play on the piano that is housed in the theatre. 'A pretty well known ghost' he said, 'but not the only one'. The other ghost, as there are said to be two, is thought to be the ghost of an unknown woman.

She has been seen on a number of occasions as she meanders around the theatre.

This brings me to Ken's personal account of a ghost at the City Varieties. He told me that on his many ghost tours and walks of Leeds, he often tells people ghost tales and accounts that have been experienced by *other* people. Now he has his own experience to relay after one night in the theatre back in February 2008. He was at the music hall to see the well-known singer Sandi Thom, and it was during the performance when this particular ghost made its appearance, or should I say made itself *heard* in Ken's case, as he didn't actually see anything. As he was inside enjoying the show (at the back and leaning against a barrier), listening to Sandi's hit *Flowers In My Hair*, he suddenly heard a woman's voice very close to him saying, 'Excuse me please'. Thinking it was a paying guest, he moved his body as he was crouched over, and stood up straight to let whomever it was past, only to be very surprised at the fact that no one at was there at all on the isle. He looked around and no one was walking either way, neither was anyone making their way back down to their seats, yet he heard a woman say to him 'excuse me please'. This bewildered Ken somewhat, who seems to be a level headed and sensible man. Could this have been the ghost lady that walks there? From my conversations with Ken on the telephone he give the impression that he is a very open, genuine and honest person and I believe he told me this story in all sincerity.

I for one know for certain, that these things do occur; indeed I have heard similar things myself. I have also spoken to enough witnesses and heard an adequate amount of ghost accounts in my time to work out whether or not these stories may be made up or exaggerated. I think you get a knack of sifting the lies from the truth and if we are all honest, we all know a bullshitter when we hear one! In Ken's story, I heard what I believe to be the truth. So I leave Leeds with Ken's chance ghost encounter. This is a short but very tantalising introduction to some of the ghosts of that wonderful metropolis in West Yorkshire that is Leeds. I re-iterate, should readers want to lean more about this fascinatingly haunted area, you can do no better than purchasing Ken's book detailing in full the ghosts and legends of Ledes (Leeds).

CHAPTER FIFTEEN

WEST YORKSHIRE

In early 2009 Drew Bartley, Fiona Vipond and myself headed of to the quaint little village of Haworth in West Yorkshire to spend a night searching for its alleged ghosts. Haworth is a small but beautiful village situated in the heart of what is known as 'Brontë Country' due to its historic connections to the famous authors Emily, Charlotte and Anne Brontë. The Brontë family moved to the village in 1820 and resided at Haworth Parsonage, which is now the home to their legacy in the form of the Brontë Parsonage museum. This famous trio of sisters were world famous for their poetry, and their novels with books such as the English literary classic *Wuthering Heights* (Emily Brontë 1818-1848), *Jane Eyre* (Charlotte Brontë 1816-1855) and *Agnes Grey* (Anne Brontë 1820-1849). They lived in Haworth most of their lives after being born in Thornton near Bradford. The Brontë sisters also had one other sister that sadly died at the young age of ten, (Elizabeth Brontë 1815-1825) and a brother named Patrick Branwell Brontë (1817-1848).

Patrick Branwell Brontë was a known drug addict and an alcoholic and would often frequent the nearby opium dens. He also spent a lot of his time in the village's charming old public house, the Black Bull. It was these foul habits that led to his untimely death in 1848 aged only 31. The Black Bull was one of our reasons for visiting Haworth village as it is well reputed to be haunted by a number of alleged ghosts.

G.H.O.S.T. co-founder and my good friend and colleague Drew Bartley, was born and raised in Bradford and spent many of his early years frequenting Haworth with many happy memories. Many a time, he and his brothers and friends would get up to mischief (not in a serious way of course) in the local cemetery at night and would often scare themselves silly talking about the villages, and more so the cemeteries alleged ghosts. I asked Drew if he could tell me a little about his adventures in Haworth.

'I love Howarth because of the history it has and because it is like stepping back in time for me. The buildings are well preserved and they have that amazing old world look and feel about them, for me this is Yorkshire at its best. I also enjoyed supping pints (when I was old enough) at the local Inn known as the Black Bull which is situated on Howarth main street. Branwell Brontë used to drink there and his ghost is said to haunt the pub, Howarth also boasts what is probably the creepiest graveyard in the world. It has literally,

Bolling Hall in Bradford. William Tempest saw the ghost lady one night in 1642 and she has not been seen since. Photograph by Drew Bartley.

thousands of bodies in it as in the old days they would often stack coffins on top of each other due to lack of space. I was born in Bradford and would visit the graveyard when I was a young lad. My friends and I would scare each other shitless and it was great. Fiona and I visit when we get the chance and we often do ghost vigils in the graveyard while we're there ... I have a very strange photo taken minutes after Fiona said she felt somebody behind her!'

As mentioned, a few years ago Drew and Fiona began to revisit Drew's old haunts by returning to places such as Bradford and Haworth and the like, in order to rekindle old memories and to see his place of childhood once again. On a number of these trips they would stop off in other areas of interest such, as Bolling Hall, East Riddlesden Hall, Nunnington Hall and the Old Silent Inn public house to name but a few. All these places are of course reputed to be haunted so it was a must for the author to accompany Drew and Fiona on this, one of their latest nostalgic visits to Drew's native Yorkshire.

Our first stop of the day was Bolling Hall, located just one mile from Bradford city centre. Bolling Hall, or at least the Manor of Bolling, originally dates back to around the mid 1080s where it is mentioned in the Domesday Book that was compiled around that time. Occupied by a number of families over the years, such as the *Tempests* and of course the *Bollings*, the hall was

East Riddlesden Hall was built by James Murgatroyd and completed in 1692. It is reputedly haunted by at least five ghosts including a ghost coachman and a grey lady. Photograph by Drew Bartley.

eventually handed over to Bradford Council in 1912 after it fell into a state of serious disrepair. It was subsequently restored to its former glory and turned into a museum that is now owned by Bradford Museums. It is a wonderful reminder of times gone by. The interesting thing about Bolling Hall nowadays is that it is situated precisely in the middle of a normal and everyday council housing estate (which is something you don't see everyday) and like the rest of the Bradford Museums; it is completely free to get in to.

After coming back from one of his trips away Drew told me an interesting story that was told to him during one of his visits by a member of staff. It concerned a family that had turned up to visit the hall for the day. Upon their arrival a fellow whom they presumed was a member of staff met them at the door. He subsequently informed the family that the hall was closed. Bolling Hall is normally closed on Mondays and Tuesdays to the public, so the family in question, albeit disappointed somewhat, decided to return another day.

A few days elapsed and the family returned to the hall for their visit and upon entering, decided to mention the fact that they had been disappointed a few days earlier, as they were unable to get in due to the fact it was closed. They told the guide at the museum about the chap they encountered and were subsequently told that there was no staff at all there on that particular day, or at least there shouldn't have been. The guide then asked what this fellow looked like, so he could perhaps identify him, and when the description of the man was related, the guide seemed somewhat bemused.

It appears that the description they give fitted that of a former caretaker of the house that had died many, many years ago. Drew told me that the guide had taken them in and had showed them a picture of the man he thought it sounded like, and when they saw it, sure enough they identified the long dead man as the person they had seen at the front door on their first visit. Much to my delight after asking one of the museum guides during our visit there, I found out there appears to be another ghost too. This one is, by all accounts, the most infamous 'ghost' in relation to Bolling Hall. The room in question where the ghost is said to reside is appropriately called 'The Ghost Room', and by all accounts, I was told, it has been many years since the phantom had made her last appearance.

It was back in 1642 when the English Civil War was rampant and when William Cavendish, the Earl of Newcastle stayed at Bolling Hall with his comrade, and [then] owner of the hall, Sir Richard Tempest. Bradford was being besieged by the Royalists under the command of the Earl and despite his best efforts he could not take the small town. Angered at this frustrating prospect, it is said he went to his bed one night declaring to defeat the small town once and for all the following day by promising to kill every last man, woman and child that would get in his way.

It was during the night prior to this assault on Bradford when the ghost of Bolling Hall appeared to the Earl. His bedclothes were pulled from him during his slumbers at least three times, and to his horror, upon awakening for the third occasion, he saw a pathetic and dejected ghost of a woman clasping her hands together and saying the words 'Pity Poor Bradford' over and over until the apparition disappeared into the ether. Disturbed by this vision, the Earl was said to have had a change of heart about his vow to kill every last man, woman and child. Instead he decided upon attacking and slaying only those that put up some form of armed defence. In effect, this ghost had had a purpose which it served quite well, resulting in only a dozen deaths during the Earls siege as opposed to the potential massacre that would have occurred had the ghost not paid him a visit. Such a breathtaking old building in which we spent a few hours exploring during my adventures away in West Yorkshire.

After leaving Bolling Hall we set off for the village of Howarth. Time was getting on and we wanted to get to our B&B before it got too late. Our first port of call in Howarth, after booking in to our digs, was of course the Black Bull pub. After a long day on the road with a stop off at Bolling Hall, there was nothing more important at this present moment in time, than relaxing in an old world pub, and sinking a pint of the landlords finest ale – well, ghost hunting is hard work you know. The pub, reputed to be haunted by the aforementioned Branwell Brontë, is a typical old world pub with traditional style wood panelling, low ceilings and heavy beams and a darn good pint. One of the pubs most interesting features however, is the old wooden chair that can be seen half way up the stairwell.

The chair is said to be the very chair that Branwell used during his many visits to the pub, usually under the influence of his beers and his opium. The chair, damaged somewhat over time, stands as a memento for the inn as a reminder of times gone by. On it there is a sign that simply says 'The Branwell Chair - this is the original chair that was occupied by Branwell Brontë on his many visits to this inn'. It is also, for the record, the chair in which his ghost is reported to have been seen sitting on. I must admit I was quite tempted so sit in it – just to be able to say that I have sat in the very chair Branwell did – but I decided that my [now] rather ample frame, combined with my weight, would easily crush the small wooden chair beyond the point of repair. So for this reason (and because I didn't want to risk breaking it full stop) I decided to give it a miss.

During my research for this book I came across a wonderful story in regards to a ghost of another of the Brontë siblings. According to Jack Hallum in his book, *Ghosts of The North* (1976) Anne Brontë spent many an unhappy year as a governess at nearby Blake Hall. After the Second World War, Blake Hall was demolished and reduced to a pile of rubble by the bulldozers. Prior to the hall being demolished it is said that a resident of New York, a Mrs Topping, bought the magnificent wooden staircase from within the hall and had it shipped off to her Long Island home where it was re-assembled and installed. Not long after the stairwell was erected in her home, she is said to have saw the ghost of a sad looking lady with light brown hair and wearing a blue Victorian style dress. As the silent phantom glided up the stairs, Mrs Topping knew almost immediately that this woman *was* the ghost of Anne Brontë. It appears that purchasing the wooden stairwell may have saved the shade of Anne Brontë, a most enchanting narrative, don't you think?

Moving on, and having spent the day meandering around this wonderful little village visiting places such as the Brontë Parsonage Museum, its wonderful little church and Haworth's magnificent graveyard, we decided (after supping another pint) to retire to our B&B for some rest as we had planned to return to the magnificent graveyard to carry out a short vigil there in the hope of discovering any paranormal activity.

On an earlier visit to the graveyard Drew and Fiona ventured around after midnight and attempted some EVP experiments. Nothing odd was recorded during this short stint so they decided to split up. Drew went to one end of the graveyard and Fiona went to the other. They told me that during this stint, Fiona felt she was not alone while standing in the pitch-dark corner of the graveyard. Feeling rather unnerved she made her way back to meet Drew, but said nothing about what she had just felt. They swapped positions and then Drew then stood in the same place *without* knowing what Fiona had felt and subsequently felt the same thing, he felt unnerved and not alone. After a picture was taken in that very area, they discovered an anomalous mist across the frame. Breath? Drew and Fiona don't think so, they think there was indeed someone, something – a denizen of the otherworld perhaps – with them in the graveyard, but who it was they have no idea.

At about 09.00pm we headed out into the village for another meander around. We found a nice coffee shop down one of the side streets and decided to order some tea and warm up a little before we ventured into what Drew described as 'the creepiest graveyard in the world'. I must admit I felt quite apprehensive about going in but looked forward to it nonetheless. At 11.00pm we ventured into the cemetery and after spending an hour or so in there we experienced nothing untoward. No anomalous pictures were taken neither did we have any success with the EVP machines. At 12.30am we headed back to our digs to have some rest.

Morning came and after showering and getting ready we met up in the restaurant area of the B&B for a full English breakfast. I had the works with about half a dozen rounds of toast followed by a gallon of pure orange juice. Drew and Fiona tucked into their breakfasts too as we discussed the plans for our day. On our way home it was decided we should call in at the Old Silent Inn pub before visiting the beautiful East Riddlesden Hall in Keighley.

The Old Silent Inn, formerly 'The Eagle', stands on Hob Lane in Stanbury, which is about a mile or so west of Haworth village and is reputed to be a very quaint little pub indeed. Standing alone and desolate on the country road, this fine 'good grub and real ale pub' is just what you would expect to come across if you were out looking for a traditional style haunted pub. To me, it has 'ghosts' written all over it and with a history dating back over 400 years or so, you won't be disappointed should you visit the place. We certainly won't. Upon venturing inside I was delighted to see one of my favourite attributes in regards to old world pubs, and that is the low ceiling with old-fashioned beams. I ordered myself a pint of Theakstons Old Peculiar and sat down on one of the seats in the bar while waiting for Drew and Fiona to join me. Drew also downed a pint of Theakstons Old Peculiar but poor Fiona, being the driver, settled for a mineral water with ice.

While chatting with the barman about the pub I managed to glean a great story about how the pub became to be named 'The Old Silent Inn'. It appears there are connections with the famous Scot, Bonnie Prince Charlie, as it is said he once stayed there during the 1745 Jacobite uprising. I was told that at that time, the locals of 'The Eagle' were asked to refrain from telling anyone about the pubs 'special guest' and so remained quiet until he departed some weeks later after making a daring escape through a trapdoor in the building when the authorities eventually tracked him down. The locals were loyal and always kept themselves to themselves even when crimes occurred with people being murdered and left on the moors. When the authorities came to question them they were always met with 'silence'. 'No one ever knows anything up at that old and silent Inn,' they would say, and so the name was born.

Absolutely fascinating don't you think? In regards to ghosts I was told about the infamous 'Bell lady', who is said to be a former landlady of the pub that often roamed the moors ringing a small bell in order to attract any stray or wild cats that may have been in the area. She is more often heard than seen, I was told, with the sound of her bell being heard on many occasions much to the bewilderment of those that hear it. After an hour or so in the pub we bid the staff farewell and hit the road.

On our way home we promised ourselves we would stop off somewhere to visit, as we did on the way there with Bolling Hall, and where better to go than the lovely East Riddlesden Hall. The hall, which was built by James Murgatroyd and completed in 1692, is now owned and cared for by the National Trust so entry for me was free. Readers of my other books will know that I am a member of the NT and English Heritage and have been for as long as I can remember. We chose East Riddlesden Hall simply because there are a number of ghosts that are said to reside at this wonderful old Statley abode that is neatly situated on the brow of a hilltop that overlooks the River Aire. The house has been quite famous for its spectral inhabitants for many years now and has been featured in many a good ghost book, this one being the latest in a long line of tomes discussing its ghostly goings on, and I dare say it won't be the last. As we arrived I couldn't help notice the air of magnificence that this building had and I somehow felt I already knew the place, but how? I hadn't been here before! Then, later on, I found out that the building was used as film location for the 1992 adaptation of Emily Brontë's *Wuthering Heights* staring Ralph Fiennes and Juliette Binoche. It was then when I realised where I had seen this building before.

There are at least five ghosts associated to East Riddlesden Hall according to Peter Underwood and in his wonderful book, *This Haunted Isle* (1984), they are detailed quite nicely. After hearing the ghost accounts first hand from the [then] house administrator, Major W.D. Morris-Barker during his many years of research he wrote up the accounts in a thorough and methodical way for us all to enjoy. Through Peter's book I became aware of these ghosts so upon my visit, I knew exactly what I was looking for. The staff and guides relayed two of the five stories that I was aware of and these stories I will relay to you now. The other three stories can be found in Underwood's previously mentioned tome, so I will leave it to you...the dedicated ghost hunter to read them in his book, which of course every serious ghost hunter should already own.

The first story in relation to East Riddlesden Hall is that of a ghost coachman that has been seen in and around the lake area of the complex. It is believed that upon returning back to East Riddlesden Hall the horse he was riding was somehow frightened causing it to react rather violently. It subsequently galloped – taking man and coach with it – into the lake where the horse and coachman drowned. The ghost coachman is thought to be seen at dusk as he searches for his lost horse and coach.

Then there is the famous 'Grey Lady' that is said to wonder the corridors and hallways of the house. She is said to have been locked in a room and left to starve to death after her husband had found her in bed with a lover. He too was dealt with in the same manner being bricked up within the walls of the house, a rather frightening way to die one thinks. The Grey Lady ghost is said to be this woman and has been seen many occasions over the years. In fact, one lady, a former employee of the house, seen the ghost on so many occasions she could describe her in minute detail, and she also began to greet her with a 'hello' when she came across her in the corridors but a reply from the spectre was never forthcoming much to her annoyance.

Such a fascinating place is East Riddlesden Hall with a rich supply of ghost tales and legends and it was indeed a great venue to end our trip with. It certainly was a pleasure visiting all the aforementioned locales in search of these elusive spectres, or at least stories in relation to them, and I dare say my quest for ghosts in this part of the north is far from over. I will inevitably return one day to seek out more of the ghosts and legends of this beautiful area of West Yorkshire, as I am sure there are many more still waiting to be discovered there.

CHAPTER SIXTEEN

LANCASHIRE

The north of England is a very historical and haunted part of the United Kingdom; indeed this is one of the reasons why I wrote this very book. The county of Northumberland in the North East is said to have more castles than any other county alone, with a total of over forty strongholds and ruined fortresses that adorn the magnificent Northumbrian terrain. The amount of battles that have taken place up on the border countries literally number into the hundreds with the land now being saturated in the much spilt blood of the English and Scots. Let us not forget the north was also home to the most harrowing case of witchcraft and murder this country has ever seen with the trial of the infamous Pendle Witches in Lancashire. The Pendle Witch trail was the most notorious witch trials that Great Britain has ever documented ultimately culminating in the execution of ten witches at Lancaster Castle in 1612, and it all happened in the north of England. We will return to the Pendle Witches later in this chapter.

The north of England has another wonderful accolade, an accolade to which the tiny hamlet of Borley on the Essex and Suffolk border once encompassed between 1863 and 1944, and that is, it is home to the most haunted house in Britain, Chingle Hall. Described by ghost hunter James Wentworth Day as 'One of the best authenticated examples of a haunted house', Chingle Hall is a 700 year old manor house that is reputed to house more than ten active spirits inside and outside the premises. The ghosts include a girl named Eleanor, who was allegedly held captive for twelve years in one of the small rooms inside the house, (now known as Eleanor's Room), a monk, a cavalier, a green man, an abundance of children (inside and outside), a hanging man, a number of spirit animals including dogs, a demonic-like entity and a poltergeist. For many years now Chingle Hall has been subjected to paranormal activity and ultimately this has led to the house being subject to paranormal investigators, and plenty of them. Many radio stations have carried out live broadcasts there, as has many, many TV programmes been filmed there. Famous psychic medium, Billy Roberts filmed a TV documentary at Chingle Hall, as has Michael Aspel when they filmed LWT's *Strange but True* series in the 1990s.

Chingle Hall was built around 700 years ago and originally it had a thatched roof and a wooden drawbridge. A moat, that can still be seen

Chingle Hall in Lancashire is reputed to be Britain's most haunted house. Monks, children, a green man, a poltergeist, and former owners are all said to haunt these ancient walls and gardens.

today, runs around the house and was a sign of stature rather than a defence mechanism or a safegaurd during the sieges. When Adam de Singleton first built the house it was named 'Singleton Hall' after the family that lived there. In 1620 John Wall was born there but when he grew up he was sent away to be educated and in 1641, he became a Franciscan Priest and was known to be one of the last English Roman Catholic martyrs. During King Henry VIII reformation it was illegal to practice Catholicism, so priest holes were made at Chingle Hall. If the Kings men raided the house, the practising monks had a place to hide. In 1678, John Wall was subsequently apprehended at Rushock Court near Bromsgrove as he was tendering the oath of supremacy and was taken to Worcester Jail where he was told his life would be spared, if he turned his back on his religion. Needless to say he declined and was subsequently hung, drawn and quartered a year later in 1679. His body was distributed to his friends and his head is said to have been took on a tour of the continent before being smuggled back to the hall and buried within the walls or in the gardens of Chingle hall.

In his book *This Haunted Isle*, Peter Underwood FRSA recalls his many visits to Chingle Hall. He states that,

'Chingle Hall is a fascinatingly hidden house built in the form of a cross that lies at the end of a long drive. I have lost count the number of time I have been there, for the place has an intriguing and puzzling atmosphere and it does seem indisputable that ghostly forms have been seen and heard here many, many times'.

He went on to say'

'I remember the late Mrs Margaret Howarth telling my wife and I unequivocally, 'this house is undoubtedly haunted' And she went on, 'We hear ghostly footsteps constantly in some rooms and passages and sometimes heavy footsteps walk over the bridge across the moat, through the old front door and across the hall...once, eight people heard these footsteps ... door latches move, sometime night after night and then not for a while...doors open by themselves ... dogs hackles rise at something they can see, or sense ... objects are moved, water appears from nowhere, monk like figures have been seen inside the house and in the garden ... Once my brother and I watched a cloaked form for fifteen minutes before it faded and finally disappeared; No, we were not afraid; now I can't think why we weren't but we never slept in that room afterwards'.

Brilliant accounts of paranormal phenomena reported to Peter Underwood by a former owner of the house. It must be stressed that there are a couple of examples previously mentioned, that I could personally verify because I have had the opportunity to spend many a night investigating Chingle Hall. The aforementioned door latches being moved and ghostly footsteps being heard in the rooms and corridors I have witnessed for myself at the house, and have managed to catch them on tape. I was sitting in Eleanor's room late one night with Glenn Hall and Claire Hall (nee Smith) from the North East Ghost Research Team, when we all heard the floorboards begin to creak and groan as though someone was walking on them. Footsteps (although no one was there) made their way along the corridor and into the John Wall room where they ceased.

Drew Bartley and Fiona Vipond of G.H.O.S.T. were downstairs in the Great Hall at the same time carrying out their vigil and they too heard the ghostly footfalls. Drew even yelled up the stairs to us and asked us if we were moving around. We were not, and the video footage can prove this. It felt so strange to be looking through the doorway of the upper corridor knowing no one was there, yet hearing the creaking and groaning of the floorboards with crystal clarity. There was definitely something otherworldly making its way down that corridor that night, maybe John Wall himself and if I have to be honest, it was quite unnerving.

During my many days and nights at Chingle Hall I managed to experience and capture an array of paranormal activity including many wonderful anomalous sound recordings. On one occasion, while carrying out a séance in the Great Hall area we all heard the sound of coins bouncing off the metal fire that stands in the room. No coins could be found and nothing could be identified as the source of the noise. On another occasion we recorded a number of voices that were definitely not any of the investigators present. A male voice can be heard on one recording saying the words, 'Dare come the dead', followed by a female

Pendle Hill near Clitheroe. This is a place of aesthetic beauty, charm and character, but it has a macabre and sinister history due to the famous Pendle Witch trials of 1612.

voice immediately after saying, 'Bring me the Bible'. Another anomalous voice recording was made by Claire Smith and it said, 'Get out, get out my house'. It was said in a whisper and by god it sends shivers down the spine.

As well as hearing strange disembodied breaths or sighs, one of which frightened myself and a colleague of mine somewhat, and many other kinds of strange paranormal phenomena we can now agree with the late Mrs Margaret Howarth when she said 'this house is undoubtedly haunted'. The attention this house has received for over fifty years now is most certainly justified and being able to visit it, and investigate it from top to bottom has to have been one of the highlights of my ghost hunting career.

Because of my excursions to Chingle Hall I have also been able to explore the county of Lancashire a little more than I could have hoped for. Pendle Hill near Clitheroe in the North East of Lancashire was an ideal locale to visit for a number of reasons. For starters, it was on the way to Britain's most haunted house, and as mentioned earlier, the area of Pendle has a macabre and sordid history with the infamous Pendle witch trials. Many times on our visits to Chingle Hall we would drive through Pendle Hill and visit different areas. I recall the first time we visited the area and we stopped off at a beautiful little village called Newchurch.

Newchurch-in-Pendle, as it is known, is situated on the south side of the great hill and offers fabulous views and panoramas of the surrounding countryside. There really isn't much to do in this tiny village but it is part of the Pendle Witches car trail. Of course I knew of two places at Newchurch where I wanted to visit, starting with the fantastic little shop that is open 364 days of the year, come rain or shine, through all four seasons. Witches Galore is a shop that is dedicated to the history of the Pendle Witches and makes its money by trading on the area's history. It is owned by Maureen Stopforth, and inside you will find a whole host of wonderful delights and spooky merchandise ranging from key rings, to cups, to postcards, books, CDs, DVDs, videos, maps, masks, you name it, Witches Galore (the Aladdin's cave of Pendle Hill), will sell it.

During my visit I bought a number or odds and sods including a booklet on the Pendle witches, and a lovely mug for drinking my hot cup of tea. I had seen a video on the ghosts of Lancashire and recognised Maureen from that, so I decided to introduce myself. On the video Maureen claims the shop and building it is housed in was haunted although she didn't really believe in ghosts as a rule. Strange things had occurred in the shop and in the area where she lives above it and this was confirmed to me when I asked her about it. It is wonderful little business and I wish her all the very best of luck with it.

The other place I wanted to visit was the picturesque St Mary's Church. There has been a church or a chapel on this site since around 1250 and is a wonderful example of an old English house of worship. However, it most noticeable feature (to the author) is a great eye on the west side of the church tower that is known as 'the eye of god'. The eye of god is reputed to be a sacred talisman that looks over the small village and keeps it from evil. Ultimately, Newchurch has its connections with the Pendle Witches due the graveyard that is situated next to the church, for it is there where a number of the 'Nutter' family are buried. One certain member of the Nutter family, Alice, played a key role in the whole saga, which we will delve into soon and it was she who was convicted and hanged for being one of the Pendle Witches. Her grave is said to be the one outside the church door, leaning against a wall with a skull and crossbones carved into it.

On 19 August in the year 1612 Alice Nutter, Isobel Robey, Jane and John Bullock, Anne Redfern, Katherine Hewitt, Anne Whittle (known as Chattox) James, Alizon (Alison) and Elizabeth Device were hung by their necks until they were dead at Lancaster Gaol in front of a massive justice hungry crowd. Another of the victims was named 'Demdyke', but she died in prison before her actual trial. James I was then on the throne and had a real hatred for the art known as 'Witchcraft'. He even published a book on demonology called 'Demonology' (or Deamonologie) that was written in 1597 and it included sections detailing his belief in witchcraft, and in demons. The book (which is still in print today) is said by some to be the most interesting yet controversial writing in the history of Christianity.

The story of the Pendle Witches began in the March of 1612 when old Chattox broke into the house of Demdyke. This occurred in the forest of Pendle and at this time the land belonged to the King and was used as his

Witches Galore in Newchurch-in-Pendle owned by Maureen Stopforth, is the Aladdin's Cave of Pendle Hill that sells just about anything you could ask for in relation to the Pendle Witches. It is also reputed to house a ghost.

hunting ground. During the burglary, which occurred at Malkin Tower, it is said that £20 worth of belongings were taken, and in those days that was a lot of money. Alizon Device, who was the granddaughter of old Demdyke (Elizabeth Southerns), saw Chattox wearing a garment of clothing that was stolen from her house and subsequently it was reported to the authorities. An investigation perused and Chattox was arrested for the burglary. In retaliation for her arrest, she accused Device and Demdyke of being witches.

No one knew what to think of this accusation until a while later. One day Alizon Device was out begging when she came across a down and out fellow who she attempted to beg from. He hurled abuse at the beggar woman who in turn was then said to hurl abuse back at him and cursed him on the spot. He dropped to the ground feeling numb and paralysed on one side of his body. Device made her escape and the beggar, known as John Law, was taken into a nearby Inn and helped. Later in that same month, Alizon was questioned by the authorities in regards to the incident on the road, and admitted that it was she that bewitched the pedlar. Not only did she confess to being a witch, she implicated a number of other individuals in the process, including her grandmother, Demdyke, old Chattox and her daughter Anne Redfern. She claimed that they too, caused upset and harm to other people and livestock in the vicinity with the use of witchcraft. They were all rounded up and taken away for questioning at Lancaster Gaol.

Tynedale Farm in the shadow of Pendle Hill.

Rumours then began to circulate that a larger number of witches were at work in Pendle, and it wasn't long before the authorities had arrested all those involved. It was said that a meeting was taking place with the remainder of the witches' coven at Malkin Tower (the house of Demdyke) and all present on that day were captured and carted off. James Device ended up confessing all, which resulted in the imprisonment and then the execution of the individuals (including himself) that were ultimately destined to become known as the Pendle Witches. The story of the Pendle Witches was documented in a book called *The Wonderfull Discoverie of witches in the countie of Lancaster* (1617), by the clerk of the courts, Robert Potts, and the story has been told and re-told over the centuries and is still remembered to this day. It is an absolutely fascinating story, which adds to the charm and character of the Pendle area.

During another visit to the Pendle area, again while journeying to Chingle Hall, we explored the area more. On this occasion we returned to Newchurch for yet another visit (I just love Witches Galore) and also to find and visit Tynedale Farm. Tynedale farm is an old derelict farmhouse that has become quite famous after Living TV's *Most Haunted* team carried out a live investigation at Pendle Hill on Halloween 2004. Over the three-night investigation the MH team went into Tynedale Farm to investigate its ghostly reputation only for each individual to be carried out unconscious one by one, until there was hardly anyone left to carry out the investigation. They say they were targeted and 'picked off' by the evil spirits of the hanged Pendle Witches, but whatever happened on that fateful night, whether it was indeed the spirits of the witches, or as Dr Ciaran O'Keefe put it, 'a psychological hotbed of activity', it made fantastic viewing.

Prior to MH visiting this particular location, ghosts and apparitions seemed to centre on this farmhouse that was built in around the mid 1700s. An apparition of a monk has been seen around the area of the farm and a hooded figure has been seen kneeling on the lonely desolate dirt road that leads to the farmhouse. People often-reported strange occurrences and hear strange noises and laughter coming from inside the empty farmhouse. It is believed by some locals to be the restless spirits of the Pendle witches. To this day descendants of the Nutter family are said to own Tynedale Farm and it was allegedly used as one of the Pendle witch's many covens.

After driving around for a while we thought that we would never find the place, until by chance (I think), we stumbled across a sign that simply said 'Tynedale'. We knew now that we were close, so we crept forwards along the country roads in the Pendle Hill area in the hope we found the farmhouse. Soon we came across a farmhouse but we were not sure if this one was the one so we parked up and got out the car. After a walk around, and discovering this farmhouse was not Tynedale Farm, we headed back to the cars. Suddenly, Fiona and Drew decided to venture over to the brow of the hill on which we were standing to check out the view, and when they reached the top, and looked out across towards Pendle Hill itself, there before them (down the bank) stood the ruined shell that is Tynedale farm, what a stoke of luck!

We ventured down the hill to take a look at the place and we were met by a number of people that were obviously residents of the adjacent farm. We were told by one person that Tynedale farm gets a lot of visitors these days, due to the MH programme, and is available for investigation. This is when we discovered it was still in the hands of the 'Nutter' family who are descended from hanged witch, Alice Nutter. Unfortunately, we were not allowed to stand on the road directly in front of the house, or venture down the garden path as it was private land, but we were allowed to take pictures of the derelict haunt from on the field that stood over the road. This we did, as well as film some video footage for a posterity DVD.

The county of Lancashire is indeed a wonderful place and I have visited it on many occasions. The seaside resort of Blackpool is one of my favourite places on the Lancashire coast, and is a very haunted town indeed. I have decided that Blackpool warrants a chapter on its resident ghosts for itself, rather than include them in this small chapter dedicated to the county of Lancashire. An acquaintance of mine, Julliette Gregson, is an authority on the ghosts of Blackpool and has kindly helped me with the Blackpool section of this book. I *have* travelled to Blackpool in search of ghosts and have also investigated the infamous ghost called 'Cloggy' from the *real* haunted ghost train at the pleasure beach. A summary of that exciting investigation will also feature later in the book.

Samlesbury Hall in Preston is reputedly haunted by Dorothy Southworth who is heard to weep and shout in this, her one time ancestral home.

Moving on, we now head to Preston to the magnificent Samlesbury Hall. Located on Preston New Road in Samlesbury, the hall is one of the most impressive manor houses I have ever had the good fortune to visit. I have been a member of associations such as English Heritage and The National Trust for many years, and have travelled across the UK visiting their magnificent sites, but there is just something about Samlesbury Hall (that is ran by Samlesbury Hall Trust) that makes me literally gasp in wonderment. I cannot believe that this Grade I listed building was going to be demolished and I am so pleased that it wasn't. The building really is a national treasure and its resident ghosts have attracted ghost hunters and TV companies from all over the world including Living TV's *Most Haunted*, and the American paranormal investigators, TAPS to name a few.

The hall was originally built in around 1325 or thereabouts by Gilbert de Southworth, a devout Catholic, and was intended as a gift for his wife. In the same year however, Robert the Bruce set fire to it as part of his advancement from the north. Gilbert de Southworth then decided to rebuild the hall only this time he made a large moat around it to protect it from the marauding Scots and other unwelcome guests. Generations of Southworths were born and died at Samlesbury Hall. John Southworth was murdered in 1654 for refusing to renounce his Catholicism, demonstrating that religious intolerance was even then alive and kicking. John Southworth had a daughter named Dorothy (or Dorethea). Ironically, she was, in a sense, to fall prey to the same fanaticism and intolerance that saw off her father.

Dorothy was, like the other Southworths, Roman Catholic. Her 'crime' was to start courting one of the Houghton family from nearby Houghton Tower. The Houghton's were staunch Protestants. Despite their religious differences, Dorothy and her suitor decided to marry. To do so locally would have caused uproar, and they were told that permission would be refused anyway. Saddened if not surprised, the couple decided to elope. Secrets have a way of outing themselves, of course, and a brother of the bride-to-be uncovered their plans. Enraged, he confronted the couple as they strolled hand-in-hand along a footpath. Within seconds the young Houghton lay dying. Dorothy had now lost both her father and her fiancé to bigotry. Saddened and embittered she lived the life of a recluse and eventually passed away in a local convent. Not long after Dorothy's passing, the sounds of weeping and shouting could be heard at Samlesbury. However, these were not the sounds of her relatives in mourning but, eerily, the sounds of Dorothy herself. Her ghost had come back to haunt her ancestral home.

Apart from hearing the mournful wails, many people claim to have seen Dorothy walk the corridors and rooms of Samlesbury Hall. She apparently dresses in white and looks distressed. Some say she appears confused, or as if she is looking for something. Interestingly, the appearances of Dorothy's ghost are not limited to the hall itself. She has also been seen in the surrounding grounds and even wandering along the road to Blackburn. Numerous motorists, including servicemen from a nearby RAF base, have caught her wispy, spectral form in their headlights, only to see her disappear. Sometimes they see her after stopping, floating towards Samlesbury Hall.

For a while the building was used as a public house, a factory, and a school for girls and in the mid 1850s it was in danger of becoming derelict. The Harrison family then purchased the hall and poured money into its restoration and saved it from its neglect. The hall has seen seven centuries go by and has also seen many deaths. In one room in the hall, it is said that a young monk or catholic priest had his head cut off by soldiers of King Henry VIII. The hall is also reputedly haunted by the 'decapitated man of the cloth' and has been seen in the very room where he lost his life. There has also been a suicide on the premises and it is reported that were two suspicious deaths there during the Second World War.

Truth to tell, the little village of Samlesbury itself lays claim to a number of spooky legends, any one of which would likely unsettle the faint of heart. Take the churchyard of St Leonard the Less, for example. In times gone by less enlightened individuals thought it quite acceptable to put to death anyone whose religious beliefs were in any way unconventional. Tip your hat the wrong way, or miss church on a Sunday, and you could easily be executed for 'witchcraft'. Actually, the body of an alleged witch lies in the aforementioned churchyard, although whether she was guilty of anything at all is highly debatable. This didn't stop the locals worrying about it, of course, and so, for good measure, eight metal spikes were hammered through the horizontal gravestone to stop her from 'rising up'.

We now head off to Bolton in Greater Manchester to the grade I listed building that is Smithills Hall. Smithills Hall is yet another of Lancashire's old original stately homes and airs magnificence and a grandeur like no other. Set in the middle of acres of lush parkland on the outskirts of the city, Smithills Hall is one of Lancashire's oldest houses dating back to the fourteenth century. Over the years many families have come and gone and a lot of people have had the privilege of residing there. From around 1335-1498 the Radcliffe family owned it until it became the seat of the Barton's until the 1660s. It was later occupied by the Belasyse family until the early 1720s and then subsequently purchased by Joseph Byrom whose family occupied the manor until the early 1800s. The Ainsworth family then owned the property until 1938 and during their occupancy the hired the notable architect George Devey (1820-1886) to carry out extensive restoration work. George Devey was a London born architect that also designed Ascott House in Buckinghamshire and other houses and cottages in the county of Buckinghamshire. His work at Smithills Hall greatly improved the original edifice, which subsequently added to its already great worth.

In 1938 the Ainsworth's sold the hall to the Bolton Corporation who then turned it into the magnificent museum that it is today. Still in the hands of the Bolton Corporation, Smithills Hall is classed as a 'scheduled monument' which essentially means it is a protected building against unauthorised change and is one of the finest buildings I have had the pleasure of visiting. You see, many years ago in the early 1990s as a younger lad (early twenties), I used to live in Lancashire and was actually based in Salford in Manchester. With the cult TV programme *The Hitman and Her* hosted by Pete Waterman and Michaela Strachan, I travelled the length and breadth of Lancashire, the North West and beyond visiting nightspots as a dancer. Yes, that's right, you read correctly, your favourite paranormal investigator was once in fact a TV dancer (and quite a good one too).

Anyway, during my time in Lancashire with the Hitman and Her, we would usually record the shows on a Saturday night (sometimes a Thursday) that left the rest of the week free to do, as I wanted. I lot of the time I went back to Newcastle to see family and friends, and the rest of the time I spent exploring Lancashire's heritage. I had always been into ghosts and even back in those days I was actively seeking out the spooks. Indeed it was in 1993-94 when I first contacted UFO and Ghost hunting expert Malcolm Robinson for advice and assistance in researching things such as ghost sightings and UFOs.

My visit to Smithills Hall as I recall was on a wonderful summer's day and I spent quite a lot of time there enjoying its many rooms and locations such as the Chapel. There has allegedly been a chapel on this spot dating back to Saxon times and this is where a ghostly figure has been seen kneeling near the alter. Another ghost that of a woman has also been seen in the chapel area, and sitting in one of the pews.

Many other ghosts inhabit Smithills Hall including the infamous 'George Marsh'. A protestant vicar at the time of Mary Tudor, he was tried for heresy at Smithills Hall and subsequently burnt at the stake. His ghost has allegedly been seen in various areas of the great house such as the shop area, the chapel, and the great hall. It is said that when he was taken downstairs before his execution, he stamped his foot down on the floor leaving an imprint. He then said the foot imprint shall forever remain at Smithills Hall as a reminder of his martyrdom, and it has been there ever since, and it can still be seen to this day.

The Ainsworth family during their residency there, were said to have removed the very slab that the footprint is sunken into and had it removed from the house altogether. From that point on, it was said that poltergeist-like activity tore through the house with such ferocity and strength, it was deemed as unbearable. After a while the family could take no more. Following some advice, they replaced the stone slab back to its original position inside the house and the vicious activity ceased. It appears that George Marsh did not want the stone slab (the sign of his martyrdom) removed from the house and his angry spirit sought vengeance until it was ultimately replaced.

There are many stories similar to the aforementioned narrative and a lot of them are in relation to screaming skulls. Calgarth Hall in Cumbria is one such tale as is the screaming skull of Wadley Hall in Manchester and of course Burton Agnes Hall in Yorkshire. These locations are said to become polt-infested when the skulls are removed from inside the houses. There are many more accounts of screaming skulls in the north of England and we will take a closer look at some of them in one of the closing chapters. But in the meanwhile I will close this chapter by saying that Lancashire is a truly wonderful county to which I have had the utmost pleasure exploring over the years. It is indeed, an historical region of the north of England that warrants further visits and exploration.

CHAPTER SEVENTEEN

THE GHOSTS OF BLACKPOOL

Blackpool is a fun seaside town located on the North West coast of England in the county of Lancashire. It is known for its confectionary known as 'Blackpool Rock', its donkey rides on the sandy shore under the great Blackpool Tower, its 'kiss me quick' summer hats that many an old granny will wear on a day out while singing the old time classic 'Oh I do love to be beside the seaside', and the unmistakable sound of the Wurlitzer Organ. The reader will be aware that I have already included a section on the county of Lancashire (of which Blackpool is a part) as well as the following chapter, which is devoted to the ghost train at the Pleasure Beach, and may ask why I have done this, as surely they should fall under one category. Well...let me tell you, the simple fact is because the ghost train investigation is the *only* overnight investigation I have carried out in Blackpool itself, I felt the book warranted a chapter dedicated to it. The town of Blackpool itself is a ghost-ridden metropolis with phantoms in abundance and haunted locations dotted hither and thither. For this reason I have decided to the town of Blackpool gets a chapter for itself too, simple.

I have been to Blackpool countless times in my life and in my opinion I have seen the place steadily decline in regards to its tourism and holiday resort factor. Don't get me wrong, I am not saying Blackpool is not a nice place anymore; it is.... what I am saying is that it is not the same as it used to be, having said that however, nothing is really is it? My early visits there with my family back in the 1970s and 1980s I remember places like the Golden Mile being cram packed with literally tens of thousands of holidaymakers with no room at all available to sit on, on the beach. Deck chairs, windbreaks and hankies on heads as far as the eye could see. Shops and restaurants were stuffed to the gills with people all wanting their teas, juices, fish and chips, iced creams and toffee apples etc, while the Pleasure Beach, well.... you couldn't get another person in there with a shoehorn!

Nowadays it seems the sunshine we would get in those early days appears to have retired along with the holiday makers and variety shows that once dominated this one time thriving seaside town. Sure, there are theatres and pier-end variety shows that still run to this day but not as many as there used to be. Blackpool, I am afraid, has become redundant and I think this is largely due to holiday makers travelling abroad to places like Corfu, Tenerife, Cyprus and Benidorm, and with so many amazing deals with flights and

Blackpool Tower was officially opened on 14th May 1894 and is haunted by a number of shades from bygone days. One ghost being John Bickerstaff, the Lord Mayor of Blackpool in 1889 and the man behind the great tower itself.

accommodation (due to the many holiday's firms competing against one another), it is no wonder.

Personally, give me Blackpool any day as opposed to cheap, booze filled fag smoking week long drinking sessions in temperatures over 30 Degrees Celsius. Nowadays during my visits there, they are still enjoyable, but like I have already mentioned, they are not the same. I am considerably older (and wiser) now and at one time I would want to ride a donkey along the beach, take a dip in the ice cold Irish Sea, or beat my father and Brother on the Crazy Golf course. But nowadays, or should I say in more recent times, I often spent my time in Blackpool's many pubs and nightclubs bopping the night away in the hope I would meet the perfect lady, I never did, but I had a lot of fun trying!

Blackpool is not the only resort (in my opinion) to have changed or declined over the years either. A perfect example of this is Whitley Bay on the North Tyneside coast. At one time 'Spanish City' was a thriving seaside fairground with Waltzers, Big Wheels, and not to mention the magnificent 'Corkscrew' roller coaster that looped the loop midway through this terrifying white-knuckle ride. Again, things went downhill at 'Spanish City', and it was even worse than Blackpool's decline. Blackpool is still a great place with plenty going on as opposed to Whitley Bay's Spanish City, where the entire complex became literally, a ghost town.

The Ghost Train at the Pleasure Beach is haunted by a man nicknamed 'Cloggy' who is heard clumping around the tracks when the ride is vacant. Drew Bartley, Fiona Vipond, Paul Dixon and myself all heard these phantom footfalls during a specially arranged investigation by a Channel 4 TV crew.

Although times do indeed change and some holiday resorts in Britain do go downhill somewhat, there is always one aspect of the heritage that remains. Nowadays they have become a massive tourist attraction that earns *some* people copious amounts of money, and that is the ghosts. Ghosts have become big business and unfortunately too many people are jumping on the 'ghost hunting bandwagon' in order to line their pockets. If I saw through the eyes of a businessman, this would be good. However, I do not see the world through eyes of the businessman; No, I see the world through the eyes of a serious paranormal investigator and quite frankly I feel these enormously cheesy moneymaking spook nights, tours of terrors and orb observations that are crammed with novelty, tomfoolery and gimmicks can be a bit of a headache. However, if done in the correct way i.e., being respectable, honest, and with ethics, making a few bob I suppose is essentially quite harmless. Anyway, that said, Blackpool is a wonderful place nonetheless with its ghosts and folkloric tales dating back many, many years.

During one particular stay at Blackpool a few years ago when we came to attend the investigation at the infamous ghost train (which can be read about in the following chapter), we stayed over in one of the many hostelries and B&Bs that Blackpool has. This hostelry was different from the norm as it was reputed to be haunted, or at least that is what we were told. Upon arriving we got chatting to our hosts for the few nights that we stayed there, and they confirmed to us that this quaint little seaside hotel was indeed reputed to be haunted. I shall refrain from naming the venue due to the owner's request, and I am sure you can understand why. After we arrived and had settled in, we were surprised to be told there was a 'celebrity medium' staying at the hotel and had already detected the unearthly presence that was said to reside therein.

We were introduced to this spirit medium (who I shall also keep anonymous), who subsequently showed us around the premises while at the same time telling us where *this* presence was and where *that* spirit was. The hotel was only meant to have had one ghost but by the time the medium was finished there was about four...or five, very subjective I must say! The hotel was a long thin building, but went back quite some way, and up at least three or four floors with a small narrow and steep stairwell that led from bottom to top. In all honesty the place wasn't exactly the Ritz in regards to its décor, or its hygiene for that matter, with dozens of crammed box rooms festooning the thin gaunt corridors. There was literally no room whatsoever to swing a cat, not the best place I have ever stayed in. Our room had two bunk beds in it with a gap of about two feet between them. There was only one cupboard in the room so we decided to keep all our equipment in our bags under the beds instead. Regardless, it was our home for the next two nights and it was haunted – that was the main thing.

After a while we had a bit of an explore of the hotel but didn't have much time really as we were headed out to conduct the ghost train investigation. By the time we arrived back at the digs it was far too late to think about conducting any research or partaking in any vigils so we held back until the following night. When the following night came along we set about conducting a séance in the main bar area of the hotel. From what we can gather, it is believed that an unknown spectre is said to walk the upper corridors and stairwells of the building and has been seen mooching around near to a small flight of stairs just off the landing area.

Poltergeist-like activity has also been recorded in the main bar area along with bottles being moving around and glasses being heard to 'chink' and 'clink' when the bar is empty. Many a time the owner has stuck his head in the door to see what was going on only to find the bar area completely still. Our séance in there lasted about 90 minutes and it was quite eventful to say the least with emotions running high, tempers becoming frayed, and an alleged sighting of a shadowy figure that was standing in the corner of the room. For the séance we were joined by a number of guests of the hotel that had an interest in spiritual matters and it *seems* that whatever resided in there, did indeed want to make its presence felt. We made a number of recorded temperature drops during the séance which were quite significant along with seeing (and hearing) the bar table that the sitters were gathered round, being moved about in a rather aggressive manner. No one was touching the table at the time so it remains a mystery as to how the table was actually being moved. This scared our guests somewhat as I don't really think they were expecting anything to happen.

It was also noted that during our time in the main bar area in the early hours, one of the guests 'claims' to have seen the figure of a man standing in the doorway to the room. Again, this scared the witness to the point of hysteria and had to be removed from the room in order to calm down. This particular guest is adamant that the sighting was not down to imagination nor was it down to either being tired, or hallucinations, although how they knew they were not hallucinating eludes me. Nevertheless something odd was indeed occurring down in the bar that night, but what, or who it was we don't know.

Blackpool has many more haunted venues, some are not very well known like our B&B, and some very well known indeed. One of the better-known haunted locations is of course the magnificent Blackpool Tower. I have visited the tower on countless occasions now and I am always impressed with it. Many a time I have took the lift to the top of the tower to check out the splendid views and to walk across the infamous glass floor. The tower at Blackpool is a Grade I listed building that was officially opened on 14 May 1894 and has been providing entertainment for the people of Blackpool, and Britain for nearly 120 years. The idea came about for the tower at Blackpool after one John Bickerstaff – who was the Lord Mayor of Blackpool in 1889 – saw the Eiffel Tower in Paris while holidaying there with his family. Upon his return from Paris, a committee was formed, followed by the Blackpool Tower Company, which ultimately, through hard work and much fund-raising, saw his dreams become a reality. The tower took three years to build using over 2,500 tons of steel and over four million bricks, and cost approximately £300,000, which in today's money is in excess of over £40million. It rises 518 feet over the Lancashire coast and is one of the UK's most recognised landmarks. In fact, I recently read somewhere that even Adolf Hitler had grand designs on Blackpool and the tower, and planned to drapes it with giant swastika flags as his troop's march up the Golden Mile! Of course this was to be done *after* successfully invading Britain, which of course never happened.

The tower at Blackpool is a magnificent piece of Victorian architecture and was so cleverly designed. In the event of it collapsing, it was designed to fall onto the beach and into the sea, and not on town of Blackpool. It was also built to sway in the wind, genius! In 1956 however tragedy struck the tower with a great fire breaking out in the magnificent ballroom that was designed by Frank Matchum. The entire building was nearly lost due to the actions of one careless individual with a discarded cigarette that wasn't extinguished properly causing tens of thousands of pounds worth of damage. Luckily, the ballroom was restored to its former glory after a few of the remaining and original workmen returned to carry out the restoration.

There are many ghosts said to reside at the tower complex starting with the shade of John Bickerstaff himself. Upon enquiring there during my visits, and in my search for ghosts, I have been told by tower staff that Mr Bickerstaff himself has been seen on many occasions as he ambles around the corridors and recesses dressed in his Victorian attire. When I asked why he haunts the place I was simply told 'he loved the place so much he won't leave it'. A cliché if I ever heard one, but very plausible in the same respect. I also managed to speak to a member of staff that worked in the gift shop, or at least one of them. This was many years now and I doubt she still works there, although I could be wrong. As I was perusing the shelves looking for a pamphlet or a book on Blackpool ghosts, I chanced to ask her if the staff had ever witnessed anything for themselves. I was told ever so enthusiastically and with such gusto 'Oh yes indeed'.

The lady went on to explain that it was the end of the day and business was coming to a close. It was time to lock up and vacate the area, but there was just one small job left to do. As she set out to do the job (which was to pay a visit to the little girl's room) she pondered out into one of the corridors and it was then when she had her experience. 'What looked like a shadow seemed to be making its way down the corridor towards me', she said. Thinking it was perhaps another staff member lurking in the corridor, she thought nothing of it, and continued with her journey to the girl's room, until she became closer to it. The figure, which by now took on something resembling a human shape, was described to me as 'not solid, and shimmering'. One thing she did notice about it was that it seemed to be wearing a top hat, or a tall hat. 'There was just something definite about this' she said. Whoever it was, was wearing an old tall hat. She decided to turn away and make a hasty retreat from the ghostly figure and saved her 'visit' for when she left the premises. When I asked if she was scared by the ordeal she said 'at the time I was a little nervous, but on reflection I guess this is what is expected when one works in old historical buildings such as this'.

An acquaintance of mine, Juliette Gregson, is an authority on Blackpool's ghosts and legends and she tells me that there are many, many haunted locations in this area and has very kindly let me modify and utilise a piece of her work that gives the reader a low-down of some of the haunted sites in the Blackpool area. She begins by telling us about the Frenchman's Cove which is in the South King Street area and once housed *Duckworth's Tobacco Warehouse*. Reports from a former owner have said that workmen that were down in the cellar have thought that someone or something had been watching them. The former owner was sent an article and an odd photograph from the time when the warehouse was originally built, and this revealed that the ghost in question came from Scarborough and was apparently called Laura Schoons. To this day, the late at night staff *still* feel that someone or something is watching them.

Moving on to the next location Juliette tells us that Blackpool may owe its early reputation for healing the sick in mind and body, to the priests who once took refuge in the isolated building known as 'The Foxhall' back in the seventeenth century. The original building was far from grand. It was a long, low three-gabled residence, which resembled a farmhouse. Its three storeys each had 4-5 rooms with low ceilings. The ground floor also included a private chapel. There was a small lead tower on top of the house and it could be entered from within, by a staircase. The thick walls contained many hiding places (priest's holes) and secret passages. Over the years this house turned into a hotel and pub, and it is believed that many spirits over the years have been seen and felt there ranging from priests, smugglers and the aristocracy.

The Old Coach House is a former vicarage that is reputed to be the oldest building in South Shore. Guests have told the owner about the spirits that reside there and watch over the visitors. Allegedly, the guests told her that a male figure had been seen staring at them while they were eating a meal and was said to be described as wearing a cap and black cloak. A second spectre is a female and goes by the name of Shirley. She is thought to look after the dinning room.

Blackpool Pleasure Beach has not one but several ghosts that reside in the world famous amusement park. If you dare visit the *Ghost Train* where the footsteps of Cloggy, who was a former ride operator that always wore clogs has been heard. (Of course we will be taking a ride on the ghost train in the next chapter, but for the time being we will let Juliette elaborate), 'My late grandfather worked as a joiner there and at times had to repair the track', when I asked him, he said, 'Oh yes, there was something or someone that watched over us!'

The ghost of a small female child, aged about nine, is said to have been seen at Sir Hiram Maxim's Gift Shop. Sir Hiram Maxim's Flying Machines is the oldest ride at the park, and built in 1904. About three years ago, and overnight, an item moved itself to a completely different spot. Poltergeist-like activity has been recorded there on occasions along with an eerie sense of presence being detected by visitors and staff alike.

At the Star pub on Blackpool's promenade there have been sightings of eerie shadows and a male figure seen in the cellar, the living accommodation and Morgan and Griffin Bars. He is said to bear a resemblance to Karl Marx. A number of years ago now, two workmen claim to have spotted him. More recently, only a couple of years ago, a figure was seen at 3am walking through the bar before disappearing. No one knew who it was or why it should have shown itself that particular night. Other strange goings on include the moving of pictures on the walls of the first floor in the building, the enchanting sound of a woman singing, glasses and bottles being moved and lights being switched on and off.

The local ice rink claims to have several 'ghosts' with various apparitions being seen backstage in the dressing rooms, perhaps previous show skaters of year gone by? Julliette says, 'Late at night I have heard someone or something skating on the ice, when I have gone to look, nobody was there'. Lights and the equipment move of their own accord, and doors have been found wide open after they had closed and locked with padlocks. Staff working late at night, whilst walking across to the tractor bay, have also felt really cold, chilled to the bone in fact, and an 'awful' presence was simultaneously felt.

The Eagle and Child pub claims to have a ghost that goes by the name of Murph or Murphy, apparently, sometimes before midnight, you can hear him moaning at the bar and scaring away the customers. Rumour has it he was an old highway robber from London who came to hide from his previous crimes although why he haunts there is anyone's guess.

In December 1936, the *Blackpool Evening Gazette* carried an article entitled 'Carleton Ghost?' A Layton taxi-driver claims he has seen a ghost with a green face near the gates of Carleton Crematorium where five years previously, a lonely widow had been battered to death in nearby Robins Lane, which is a quiet area near to Carleton. Perhaps the green face had been this poor woman's ghost? The taxi driver, Harry Hodges, picked up a young lady from North Station and took her to the crematorium. He pulled up to the gates and found himself staring into the face of an old man, 'with sunken eyes, long dark hair, a Punch-like nose and prominent chin'. The woman screamed and jumped out of the cab and ran off, Harry watched as the face moved in front of his cab and then disappeared.

The Illuminations Department building on Rigby Road is an old building which has a history as a former donkey stable prior to taking on its current semblance. Due to the nature of the work, involving a lot of nightshifts, staff are often in the building late at night and it is not surprising that reports often come in of them having had what they perceive as supernatural experiences. One of the fitters had often complained of feeling cold and of a presence hanging around when he was working in the fitting shop early in the morning. Other staff have reported strange noises. A visiting medium has identified the spirit as a 'Ted' who had once owned a boat and drowned in a freak accident at sea.

In 1994, Blackpool woman called Jill Cook called in a priest, two psychics and even a Mormon missionary to try to help her get rid of a ghost which she claimed regularly attacked her. The attacks began in early 1994, when she felt something climb into bed beside her and pull off the towel, which she was wearing, wrapped round her head. She felt a 'vile' sensation as it touched her 'like tiny needles trying to pierce my skin'. While she continued her efforts to get rid of the entity, she discovered that placing an ioniser in her room seemed to move the ghost from one room to another.

In the early morning of Christmas Eve 1919 the body of 26-year-old Kathleen (Kitty) Breaks was found among the sand dunes at Lytham St. Anne's near Blackpool. She had been shot three times with a revolver. Frederick Rothwell Holt, who had been her lover, was arrested and charged with her murder. Holt's footprints together with his service revolver and blood stained gloves were found in the sand dunes. Many holiday makers and locals over the years have claimed to see the sad wandering spirit of this woman. Our final ghost takes us to Raikes Hall. Raikes Hall was previously a private dwelling and is now a public house in Blackpool. Once a convent, one of its former inhabitants who drowned herself nearby comes back to visit from beyond the grave and move items around the pub. Late at night regulars have heard strange noises from cellars.

So there you have it, a short, yet fascinating account of some of the haunted locations that Blackpool has to offer the visitor, and of course the ghost hunter. Now, brace yourself for a ride on what is to my knowledge, the *only* haunted ghost train in Britain as we examine the dark and echoic passageways of the Blackpool Ghost Train.

CHAPTER EIGHTEEN

THE
BLACKPOOL GHOST TRAIN

Blackpool pleasure beach was founded in 1896 and attracts about 8 million people every year. One of the most famous and biggest fun parks in Europe with tourist attractions and an abundance of rides Blackpool pleasure beach is home to one of the biggest roller coasters in the world – and I have ridden it!

A few years ago I had the opportunity to visit Blackpool and conduct an investigation at the pleasure beach. The venue was the infamous haunted ghost train, which believe it or not, really is reputed to be haunted. 'Clog's' or 'Cloggy' is the resident spectre that has been seen and heard clumping around the tracks with his big 'Clog' boots on. He is said to have built the ride back in 1930, and after his death, as he loved his fairground attraction so much, it is said that he never left it.

Cloggy is said to follow the staff around the train tracks and is said to touch them and breathe in their faces giving them a shock to say the very least. Visitors to the park have also reported many spooky goings on while being on the ride leading people to believe that there may be more than just one ghost residing there.

In 2002, a well-known TV company and ghost-hunting programme visited the site and conducted an investigation and as far as I am aware, we are the only other investigative team that have been allowed access to investigate the hauntings. We were also being filmed for a Channel Four TV documentary and this is why we think access to the ride was given to us. On the night of our investigation we were escorted to the train ride by a number of the pleasure beach attendants, and by this time the fairground was totally abandoned. We ventured inside and sauntered around the whole ghost train with the lights on, so we could get familiar with it. As we were checking the place over, the Channel Four film crew were shooting some general footage. They told us that they 'were absolutely terrified knowing soon we were to turn off the lights and seek out Cloggy'. Soon we had finished our brief walk around so we decided to get out the entire teams hi-tech ghost hunting equipment.

After splitting up in to two teams, we separated and began the investigation. Our group went to one end of the ghost train while the other group went to the opposite end as to minimise any noise pollution we might be making. The ghost train you see; is a long and winding echoic passageway and the smallest of sounds could have been amplified to a degree whereupon a false or

inaccurate documentation of alleged phenomena may have been noted.
We had to be extra careful not to misinterpret any normal noises for paranormal activity.

10.40pm and the investigation began. Walking through the jet-black tunnel was quite unnerving to say the least, so we were quite startled when suddenly a very loud noise disturbed us. It sounded like a pump or a generator that continued for several minutes before suddenly ceasing. The other group contacted us via their walkie-talkies to say that they heard the noise. An investigator proceeded to call out to the atmosphere in the hope we got a response. A presence was then felt to the right of us, so a photograph was taken and a light anomaly was caught. However, it was nothing to get really excited about. After a short while, we all felt that the presence that we had decided *was* with us was now no longer with us, so we moved to another area.

Our second attempt at a vigil was carried out where we had placed our trigger objects, which was a cross. We settled down and again, called out to the atmosphere in the hope that we made some sort of contact with the resident spook. After what seemed like a few minutes, the same noise that we had heard previously began, only this time it started off faintly and slowly built up until it was quite loud. We all agreed that the noise we heard sounded very much like the actual mechanics of the train ride as if it was being activated. Again, after a while the noise ceased. The pleasure beach staff later informed us that all the rides had indeed been switched off and no power whatsoever could have turned the rides on. So what was the noise we all heard?

In another vigil that was held later on, we experienced more odd activity in the form of a slamming door. There was no draughts, winds or breezes recorded anywhere so that possibility was immediately discounted. This had all the TV crew's hearts racing, as they had no idea what to expect should the investigation 'kick off' so to speak. Looking back it was rather funny; watching the film crew literally shake with fear as we progressed with the evenings work. We continued; I then called out to the atmosphere and we all heard knocks and bumps emanating from the walls and ceiling. Mysterious lights were caught on my digital still camera and a great light in movement was caught on night vision video camera. As previously mentioned, we heard what sounded like the ghost train ride, or its generator starting up and then cutting out again after 2-3 seconds.

After a break, (which was a much needed cigarette break for the Channel Four crew), it was decided we should try a séance. By this time the Channel Four film crew said that they had all the shots and footage they required for the programme and so they departed and then waited for us to finish off our investigation, before taking us back to our accommodation. We found a suitable spot in the ghost train, formed a circle and held hands and proceeded with the séance. After a short while we all noticed a drop in the temperature and one or two of us began to shiver with the cold.

'Cloggy' I said, 'Are you with us tonight?'
The area seemed to become even colder.
'Give us a sign to indicate your presence please'

At this point a door next to us began to shake and rattle as if someone was trying the handle to gain access. There was no one behind the door.

'Thank you, can you give us another sign please'

Nothing…

'Come on Cloggy! We know you are here, give us another sign please'

I then felt a tap on the shoulder and my blood ran cold.

'Let us hear your footsteps please, that is what you are known for isn't it? We are here with the utmost respect for you and we mean no harm. We are just interested in you and we want to prove you are real'

At this moment we were all astounded to hear the clump of footfalls emanating and echoing from along the dark passageway.

'Who is there' someone called out.

No answer…

'Hello! Hello! Is anyone there?'

Still no answer. By now the footfalls had ceased.

We closed down the séance and searched the ride high and low and found no one at all that could have accounted for the footsteps we heard. The TV crew were still outside, the pleasure beach staff were with the TV crew and the ride…. well, it was deserted. Good news in the respect that we know no one could account for the footsteps, but I couldn't help getting a little annoyed too, because had the TV crew been filming at this point, we may have just recorded the phantom footsteps that are so often heard coming from around this infamous haunted theme park ride, for TV.

A short but very rewarding investigation was now coming to an end and some readers may recognise this story from elsewhere. Well, if I am honest to the reader I will admit that these investigation results feature in my other tome, *In Search of Ghosts*, but because it was such a good investigation, and in such a 'prestigious' and 'hard to get into' place, I figured I would re-write the chapter for this book too.

So just you remember, the next time you holiday in Blackpool and decide to go on the ghost train, be cautious! If something touches you, or you hear strange noises, just ask yourself, its just part the ride, isn't it?

CHAPTER NINETEEN

CHESTER

Chester is a marvellous example of an ancient walled town and it is a place that I have visited on a number of occasions, the last occasion I spent most of my time in the zoo which of course houses a number of rare and exotic animals as well as the many of normal varieties, and a great day was had by all. This one time Roman settlement holds a special place in my heart, simply because it is a walled town very similar to Newcastle upon Tyne, which is of course, is where I come from. I have a great interest in the historic aspect of 'walled towns' and cities, with a few examples being featured in this very book (Newcastle, Berwick, and of course Chester, which, I must add, has the finest and most complete city walls in Britain).

Chester is a northerly county town that lies on the River Dee only a few miles from the Welsh border in Cheshire. In 1541, Chester was granted 'city status' and was originally founded as *Castrum* with the Roman fort known as *Deva Victrix* in the year 79 by the famous *Legio II Adiutrix*. This was a Roman legion under the Emperor Vespasian, who supported Septimius Severus and who of course occupied the one time Roman fort that is so close to the author's home in Tyneside, Arbeia Roman Fort. Arbeia Fort stands on the south side of the River Tyne in South Shields, and is only four miles east of Segedunum Roman fort and baths, in what is now Wallsend. The earliest human occupation at Arbeia is thought to date back to 3000 BC. The Roman fort at Arbeia, when it was originally built in around AD 158, would have had a spectacular and commanding view across the estuary of the River Tyne, making it a very secure and well defended settlement. It was home to approximately 600 Romans and its principal function was to act as a main gateway to the Roman Empire in Britain. It was also a garrison and military supply base for the aforementioned Emperor Septimius Severus between AD 208 and AD 210.

Chester's four main roads, Northgate, Eastgate, Bridge and Watergate, were first laid down back in Roman times over 2,000 years ago with *Deva Victrix* becoming one of the principal settlements in the Roman province of Britannia. In the fifth century, after the Romans departed, the Saxons moved in on the area and made this place their home. It was the Saxons that fortified the ancient town by building the magnificent walls in an effort to keep the Danes at bay and it was the Saxons that gave Chester its name. During the Norman Conquest, which began in 1066 with the Battle of Hastings, (the first step of William the Conqueror's infamous invasion of Britain), William ordered the construction of a castle to be built that would dominate the city, and the neighbouring lands of North Wales, and in 1071 he created the 1st Earl of Chester, Hugh d' Avranches. Hugh was the son of Richard Goz, who was the Viscount of Avranches in South West Normandy and gave over sixty of his ships to the Duke of Normandy for the invasion of England. However he never fought in the Battle of Hastings himself, but stayed in Normandy to assist in its governing.

The great castle in Chester was built by Hugh d' Avranches (also known as Hugh Lupus) in 1070 and is thought to be on the site of a much older construction, probably a Saxon fort, but not yet confirmed. In the twelfth century the wooden tower would have been replaced with a stone one. In the same century, what is known as the Agricola Tower was also built. This is the old stone gateway to the inner bailey. In the thirteenth century, during the reign of King Henry VIII, more additions were made to the castle with the outer bailey being constructed along with other features such as a Great Hall and other residential accommodations. Parts of the castle nowadays are used as Crown Courts and a museum dedicated to the military, with the rest of these remains being a tourist attraction.

In the North West of England during the eighteenth and nineteenth centuries, major changes began to occur in manufacturing, engineering, haulage, transport, farming and cultivation etc. These changes had a profound effect on the North West, Great Britain and ultimately the rest of the world. This was known as the industrial revolution and it marked a key turning point within its societies with almost every aspect of it being influenced in some way. Chester, being in the North West, played a huge part in this revolution with the building of two railway stations, a network of canals and creating vital sources of employment which ultimately provided the area with much needed work and economic prospect.

The city of Chester nowadays is festooned with olde world buildings that date back to the Victorian era with the vast majority of the edifices being modelled on the Jacobean half-timbered style. Black and white buildings that look old and unsound are in fact as solid as the newest of tower blocks, and there are many of them giving Chester a fantastic and historic feel. This is what I like about places like Chester; the historical factor, the ambient feel that you get when you walk the ancient cobbled streets, the old inns and taverns still stand and pull in the punters just like they did hundreds of years ago, and of course echoes and shades of yesteryear still frequent the areas and stalk the buildings in search of eternal rest, haunting this one time Roman Settlement and Saxon walled town.

Of course with Chester being primarily known historically as a Roman town, or at least a one-time settlement, you would expect to hear ghosts of Roman soldiers that still pace the streets and frequent rooms and cellars of buildings tending to their duties, and you would be right. The George and Dragon Pub on Liverpool Street has a ghost just like this and it was after a chance visit to the pub for a spot of late lunch when I managed to glean a little information from bar-staff. After visiting Chester for the day we began to head home and decided to leave the city via the north gate. As we had missed lunch and felt rather peckish, we decided to grab something to eat before we made our journey home. As we were driving out the city we went past this magnificent old world Tudor style public house and decided this was where we were stopping for a bite, and I am so glad we did.

I soon found out to my excitement that the pub was reputed to be haunted. By chance we had stumbled across one of Chester's more well-known haunted establishments and it was allegedly haunted by a Roman Legionnaire. I was informed, over a pint of ale, that the pub was built on an ancient Roman burial ground and although the pub was re-built in the 1940's or thereabouts, it means that we have an ancient ghost in a relatively new building, which isn't unheard of, but unusual nonetheless. Footfalls, I was told, have been heard clumping and thumping as they make their way across the upper section of the building in the early hours of the morning. The footfalls are remarkably interesting, as they seem to move from one side of the premises to the other, ceasing for a while before making their way back. The remarkable thing is, is that in order for them to do this, they would have to go through a number of walls as the area up there is partitioned into many guest rooms.

The ghost, thought to be that of Roman Legionnaire, has frequented the George and Dragon since it was built. I think people presume this ghost is a Roman soldier on sentry duty for two reasons. One, the sound of the footfalls as they pace back and forth with measured tread indicates that it *could* be someone that is indeed on guard duty. Guards do indeed walk back and forth as they patrol their outposts. Two, the fact that the pub was built on a Roman cemetery would almost immediately make one think that if any ghosts resided there, they would have to be Roman. I am going to throw a spanner in the works here and suggest that the ghost may *not* be a Roman soldier after all. Due to the fact there have been no bone-fide or credible sightings of a Roman soldier at the pub I am inclined to think the ghost, whoever it is, may be someone from far more recent times. Maybe a tenant from a former building that once stood on this spot or a former landlord of the pub, maybe it is a staff member who loved the place so much they don't want to leave, who knows.

Having said that it could be a Roman soldier couldn't it? I mean that's what Chester ghostlore says it is and who I am I to suggest otherwise? Regardless of whom it is or what is responsible for the ghostly phenomena there is one thing however we have to take into account. At a recent talk that I attended on the haunting of Borley Rectory at the Society for Psychical Research in London, Peter Underwood commented quite correctly that at the end of the day, it doesn't matter whether a ghost is wearing this type of attire or that type of attire, or if it dated from 1899 or 1910, what is more important, is verifying the fact something anomalous was happening in the first place!

That is what good ghost hunting is about, trying to verify and prove the existence of anomalous phenomena. Details such as types of clothing and dates and timelines can of course come later as a secondary undertaking so please don't think that Peter Underwood (or the author for that matter) is suggesting details like dates and timelines are not important. They are indeed important, and very much so, but you have to get your priorities right if any progress is to be made in serious psychical research. In effect, what Peter Underwood is saying, and what I am saying about this pub, is that it doesn't matter *what* is haunting the George and Dragon in Chester's Liverpool Street, the fact remains that something is.

Another pub in Chester noted for its ghostly inhabitant is Ye Old Kings Head on Lower Bridge Street. It is yet another pub with spirits of the more ethereal kind as well as the medicinal kind too. In my opinion you always find more haunted boozers than any other type of venue and all the savvy ghost hunters out there will indeed know why. The happy memories people have of their local drinking den, the fact that alehouses are a place of meeting, a place of social bonding, of solitude and reflection, a place for letting down your hair and getting pleasantly inebriated after a hard weeks work, no wonder people love pubs.

Pubs and inns also have that air of danger about them too. Drunken brawls have taken place for hundreds of years and countless fights spill out into the streets where sadly, many people have breathed their last due to them. Many inns were used for murders after the victims were enticed into the inns with the thought of free ale. Many pubs and inns had guest rooms where vagabonds and highwayman would hide out resulting in these pubs witnessing much action over the years. Pubs you see, have been around and frequented by people for far longer than most other types of buildings and over the years they retain their charm, their character, their olde world feel, their revellers, guests and their ghosts.

Ye Old Kings Head is no different and houses a ghost or two. Built around the early 1620s, Ye Olde Kings Head is located in the heart of Chester close to a wide selection of shops, bars and restaurants and has eight or so guest rooms. Being a traditional timber framed black and white building (like a lot of buildings in Chester), Ye Olde Kings Head retains the character of old Chester with many of its wonderful features including its Elizabethan fireplaces and a timber beam that was taken from one of Lord Admiral Nelson's ships that sank off the north west coast of England. The ghost there is known as (I am told) 'the boy of room four'. In this room, guests have seen the spectre of the young lad after they are awoken during their slumbers at night. Other rooms are said to be haunted too, with ghostly messages appearing on the mirrors on room six, and on one occasion a woman woke up to see a shadowy figure sitting at the bottom of the bed, that was also in room six.

On Eastgate Street there is a ghost known as Moaning Sarah. She is supposed to be the ghost of a woman that hanged herself many years ago. Sarah was the name given to the ghost by the shop staff in an attempt to come to terms with the frightening shenanigans of the spectre. Naming the ghost in effect, give the shop staff a sense of knowing her and thus made them feel a little easier in regards to her actual presence. The fact that she is called 'Moaning Sarah' is simply because she has been heard to moan from time to time. In *Ghosts of the North* by Jack Hallum (1976) he states that the manageress informed a local newspaper reporter in 1969 that several of the shop girls regularly heard the sound of someone coming into the shop, and when they ventured out to meet and serve whoever it was, they found the shop completely empty, which unnerved the girls somewhat. As did the thumps and bumps that were also heard on many occasions coming from the upper (and empty) room above the shop.

During my research into haunted Chester I came across a very interesting website that claims Chester could well be the most haunted city in England. A lot of cities lay claim to this accolade including York, Derby, London and many others for that matter but after looking at the site for a while, giving it the once over, I decided that Chester may well indeed be a good contender for the title so to speak. Listed on their site is a catalogue of haunted venues in the city of Chester and if all these venues are *really* spooked out, and there *have* been bona-fide sightings and experiences recorded there, then the only conclusion we can come to is that Chester really is a very spiritually troubled city that is abundant with paranormal activity and tales of legend and folklore. Claimed to have between 120-160 haunted sites, those at Haunted Chester claim that one day soon, the city will be known as the most haunted in England.

I contacted the 'Haunted Chester' website and asked permission to list a few of the locations mentioned on their enormous catalogue so without further to do here is an abridged version of haunted venues that this magnificent ancient city has to offer.

132 Watergate Street is said to be haunted by something that creates unexplained thumps and bumps and mysterious cold draughts to the point where no one will live there, a house in Dee Hills Park is home to a ghost monk that is said to wake up the sleeping occupants of this large gothic mansion house, on Bridge Street there is a ghost nicknamed 'George' that haunts the cellar of a shop there, Poltergeist disturbances are said to happen at a house on Abbey Green with objects going missing and re-appearing again with doors being mysteriously locked by an unseen force, a disgruntled former landlord is said to moan and groan about the state of his former pub at a shop on Bridge Street, Chester cathedral is allegedly haunted by the Devil's footprint. It is reported in the 1906 records that the footprint (or hoof print) was found in one of the flagstones inside the cathedral so it was subsequently removed only to have been found again the following morning. In Curzon Park, it is said that a woman in Elizabethan dress can be seen and heard sobbing as the shade of a hanged man swings gently in the breeze.

Would you like me to go on? It is said that in the old abandoned psychiatric hospital there is the ghost of what is described as 'a dark form' that flits from room to room and along the old corridors accompanied by eerie footsteps, at a pub on Watergate Row there is the ghostly scene replayed once in a while of a boy falling into a fire, at Greyfriars it is said that a Chester news reporter saw a ghost standing in the doorway while he was out on a job, on Pepper Street two hooded monks have been observed, the face of an old-fashioned sailor has reputedly been seen at Leche House on Watergate Street, the ghost of a Cavalier has been spotted on the city walls at Morgan's Mount, on Nicholas street a spectral coachman has reputedly been seen dressed to the hilt as he makes his way down a flight of stairs coming from an old Georgian house, in the old fire station (now a restaurant) it is said that the shade of a former fire fighter called Jack is often seen in the old engine rooms, at St John's Church there is the ghost of a monk on the spiral staircase that was once seen by a number of schoolboys; and in the churchyard, there is the spectre of beautiful nun dressed in a blue habit. Her ghost has been seen on many occasions.

So...there you have it, these are just a few of the alleged ghosts of Chester. You can understand now why those at Haunted Chester believe their city is the most haunted city in England. In one respect, I wish I lived in Chester as many of these ghost sightings and reports would be a dream to fully investigate. To be able to track down the old witnesses and collate their statements would indeed be a task within itself but a task well worth undertaking. Of course some ghost hunting vigils of my own would be at the top of my priority list too. We must bear in mind however, that a lot of these accounts *could* well have normal explanations due to one reason or another; perhaps misinterpretation or over active imaginations? Who knows? One thing is for certain though, and that is I have experienced enough paranormal activity during my lifetime to safely say a lot of these things do indeed happen and can safely say hand on heart ghosts and poltergeist are real – its defining them and explaining them where we have the trouble.

So, is Haunted Chester justified in saying they have the most haunted city in England, maybe they are, but I guess we will never know for sure as there will always be another city or another area that will refute the claim, and another counter claim to refute theirs. I guess until we can objectively count the ghosts in each and every city in the UK (which will certainly not happen) we will never know for sure which city is the most haunted city in the UK. The Haunted Chester website can be viewed at www.hauntedchester.com and my thanks go to them for the help with this chapter.

CHAPTER TWENTY

OTHER NORTHERN HAUNTS

As mentioned early on in this volume, the author states that *In Search of Ghosts* (Amberley Publishing 2008) and of course this particular work, barely scratches the surface when it comes to writing up and discussing ghostlore in the north of England, and indeed the whole of the UK itself. What you have read in the preceding pages are my adventures and my efforts to investigate ghost sightings in places and areas that I have been able to spend a certain degree of time in over the years.

Working forty plus hours a week as a Civil Servant, along with being a full-time father to my beautiful daughter, one doesn't get much of a chance to travel around at will visiting and researching the sites as much as I would like to. That's not to say I don't do it, I do. If you have a passion or a love for something then you will find time to pursue your dreams and ambitions like I have. I usually find time at weekends to carryout my overnight investigations and through the week, well, I write up my reports and book manuscripts during my lunch breaks at work and in the evenings I often work through from 8pm to the early hours.

Having a very patient and understanding partner also helps considerably although I do get the impression that she sometimes prefers it if I work upstairs in my office rather than sit downstairs with her, constantly interrupting her while she is trying to watch her telly programmes such as the soaps and reality TV. Seriously though, she knows how important my ghost work is and as long as I find some time for her she is just fine.

Anyway, due to these factors I have not been able to get to, and visit half of the places I would like to, but in the future, well you never know. For the time being however, I have decided to select a small number of haunted locales from across the north that have been researched in various other ways and include them herein to give the reader a little more in the way of information regarding the haunted the north of England. We begin in Cumbria and work our way south through Merseyside and into Lancashire. From Lancashire we go Yorkshire and across to the east coast of England where we visit County Durham. From this point, we will head north up the east coast to Sunderland, Newcastle and then finish off in beautiful Northumberland. Remember, we have seen all these counties, (but not the haunted buildings or particular areas) earlier on in the book, so what now follows is a *further* enchanting look at some of the haunted north.

Levens Hall in Cumbria is a beautiful Elizabethan family home that is haunted by a Pink Lady and a phantom black hound. Picture courtesy of Mullen Design and Levens Hall.

LEVENS HALL, CUMBRIA

Levens Hall is about five miles south of Kendall. It is a beautiful and picturesque privately owned Elizabethan family home that was originally built around a medieval Pele tower, which was built by the de Redman family in the thirteenth century. A local family of rich landowners, named the Bellingham family, chose Levens Hall as the seat of their family and subsequently built around the Pele tower incorporating it into their new residence, this was sometime in or around 1580 with James Bellingham completing the work around 1640. New sections of the house were added with the hall boasting oak-panelled rooms, intricate plasterwork ceilings and a dining room draped with embossed leather wall hangings from Cordova. Also included in the 'make over' was the topiary garden in 1694 by one Colonel James Grahme who acquired the house after the Bellingham owner's betting debts led to the loss of the hall. The Howard family subsequently added a new tower in 1820 when they inherited the house. Tour Levens Hall today and you'll see memorabilia accumulated over generations; snuff boxes, tapestries, paintings by van Dyck, Lely and Rubens, the personal effects of Wellington and Nelson.... all of them carefully preserved and cared for by the Bagot family who have lived at the hall for many, many years now.

Interestingly, it is said that all the aforementioned occupants of the house were somehow related in some way, so we can presume that if this is correct, the house has remained in the same family for over 700 years.

More interestingly, although the house itself is well known for its aesthetic beauty along with its Jacobean furniture and wonderful old paintings, the halls magnificent topiary gardens are actually *more* famous. Essentially, topiary gardens show the intricate art of fashioning sculptures using clipped yew trees and different types of bushes and shrubbery. Plants that are used in topiary gardens are usually evergreens, and have small leaves and needles that produce dense foliage. The garden at Levens Hall was designed by Monsieur Guillaume Beaumont and is a grade I listed garden that dates back to 1694, as previously mentioned. With its tall and perfectly cut yew trees along with its triangular bushes and hedges, the gardens at Levens Hall compare with the finest topiary gardens in the land such as Burton Agnes Hall in Yorkshire, Alnwick Gardens in Northumberland, Athelhampton House in Dorset, Chillingham Castle in Northumberland and Abbey House in Wiltshire to name a few.

Not only is Levens Hall a beautiful old manor house with an historic past that greets you like a warm breeze, it is of course haunted. It is a house that has not one ghost, but a number of them. Most prominent of all is the Grey Lady, a well-attested apparition who appears – regularly if not exactly frequently – to this very day.

The Grey Lady is thought to be a Romany woman who, centuries ago, knocked at the door of Levens Hall to beg for food. Even though the poor woman was starving she was scolded and turned away. However, before she went she laid a curse upon the house.

To my knowledge, the curse does not seem to have unduly affected either the house or its residents, although the Grey Lady has often been seen in the vicinity of the driveway wearing a print dress and headscarf or cap. Curiously, she only seems to appear to children.

Another spectral visitor is said to be that of a black hound that, every now and again, darts down the flight of stairs much to the astonishment of visitors that are about to climb them. Then there is the Pink Lady. It is said that she is often seen gliding across the hall and occasionally walking in the garden. On one occasion the pink lady made her appearance in front of dozens of startled witnesses during a tour of the house one afternoon.

The road coming into the Levens Hall area is reputed to be haunted too. Another ghostly woman is said to frequent 'Levens Bridge' and is said to suddenly move into the middle of the road startling drivers that are coming over the bridge. No one knows who she is or why she haunts the area, but a clearance of the area may indeed be required as one motorist almost killed himself one day as he tried to avoid her spectre as it stood in the middle of the road.

MUNCASTER CASTLE, CUMBRIA

Standing majestically overlooking the River Esk in Ravenglass, Muncaster Castle is reputed to be one of the most haunted castles in the whole of the UK. Standing on what is believed to be Roman ruins, Muncaster Castle played a

The morning sun casts a radiant glow of the magnificent bastion that is Muncaster castle in Cumbria. Home to the Pennington family, Muncaster Castle is haunted by a former jester named Tom Skelton. Photograph courtesy of Brian Sherwen and Muncaster Castle.

key role in the regions history. The castle was built on the north west coast of England and since 1325 its primary role was to guard the area from invasions from the Irish, and protect the many trade routes that came south from Carlisle. It became home to the Pennington family in the thirteenth century when King John granted Alan de Pennington the lands of Muncaster.

In more recent years the Pennington family and their friends have been plagued with some very strange goings on within the castle walls. Doors open and close on their own, ghostly footsteps pace along its many long corridors in the dead of night, and many people refuse to stay overnight at the castle more than once. The ghost is said to be that of a former jester of the castle from the sixteenth century called Tom Skelton, otherwise known as Tom Fool. Legend has it that Tom Fool committed a horrid murder on the grounds of Muncaster Castle by bludgeoning a carpenter to death with a hammer and chisel. He is also reputed to have stood under the Chestnut tree outside the castle (that still stands today) and wait for lost travellers on their way to London to pass by. If he didn't like the look of them, he would send them to their deaths by deliberately pointing them in the wrong direction towards the nearby quick sands where they would soon be in trouble, ultimately sinking to their sandy and murky graves.

The castle has been subject to many overnight paranormal investigations and research, indeed London Weekend Television (LWT) visited the castle in the 1980s and filmed an episode of *Strange But True*. A friend of mine at one time, quite often visited the castle when she was younger and she once told me that she had experienced odd activity there for herself. Standing in the corridor looking at the giant portrait of Tom Fool, she felt an unnerving presence behind her. When she turned around no one was there. Indeed, this happened on another occasion when a visitor to the castle was looking at the same portrait of 'the jester' when she suddenly heard footsteps coming along the corridor behind her. She too, turned around and found no one there.

The Tapestry Room at the castle is also said to be haunted but not, it seems, by Tom Fool. One friend of the Pennington family that was staying in the room swears blind he woke up to the sounds of talking, or murmuring *inside* the room. Described as 'a child crying and a woman talking to her' he searched high and low for these people but found no one. No explanation was ever found for it, and as he found out the next morning after a poor nights sleep, he was the only person residing in that wing of the castle. Other people have experienced the same phenomena too while staying in this one time guest bedroom. An interesting postscript to this tale tells the story of some old plans or blueprints of the castle that were found, and upon studying the documents it was discovered that part of the Tapestry Room was once used as a nursery. Could this account for the crying child?

Nowadays the castle offers the public the opportunity to carry out 'all night sit ins' in the haunted Tapestry Room for ghost hunters and all those that love to be chilled to the bone. I might book in one night soon and hope to hear for myself the ghosts of Muncaster Castle.

KIRKSTONE PASS INN, CUMBRIA

'Who comes not hither ne'er shall know how beautiful the world below'.
William Wordsworth penned these very words after visiting Kirkstone Pass, which is situated near the junction of two roads, one of which leads to Windermere and the other to Ambleside in the beautiful Lake District. The Kirkstone Pass Inn, which sits on the lonely desolate windswept road, is one of the highest pubs in England standing at 1489 feet in the Lakeland fells. Dating from the seventeenth century, the Kirkstone Pass Inn was formerly known as the 'Traveller's Inn' and many cold and weary traveller did indeed stop there for food and shelter during the ice-cold winters. The buildings original structure is said to date back to the 1490s but after 1847-48 after the building lay derelict for a while; it began to decay due to the elements. However, the building was restored so this one time 'monks retreat' was rescued.

There are many ghost stories associated with this seventeenth-century Inn with many of the visitors reporting 'strange occurrences'. Stories persist of a terrifying spectre that has been seen near to a tree known as the hangman's tree. She is believed to have murdered a child in the inn many years ago. Another ghost, said to be that of a traveller, also haunts the area in and around the pub after becoming lost on one winters night during a blizzard, she is said to have frozen to death. Inside the pub there are the ghosts of another lost hiker and a grey lady that are said to be responsible for a number of poltergeist-like activity that has been witnessed inside the premises. Doors are said to open and close on their own, glasses are thrown from behind the bar and staff and visitors alike often feel an eerie sense of presence.

By far the strangest tale concerns a phantom coachman that is dressed in seventeenth-century attire. This spectral being is said to have appeared on a photograph that was taken outside the inn by a family and subsequently followed them home where he now haunts their house! I have travelled through the Lake District on many occasions and have passed through Kirkstone Pass on a few of those occasions but have yet to stop there and sup a pint of their finest ale. Maybe sometime soon this will be rectified.

SPEKE HALL, MERSEYSIDE

From the Lake District in Cumbria we now head south and visit one of the north's finest counties in the north west, Merseyside. I have been to Liverpool only a few times in my life with the majority of these occasions being a competitor at Judo tournaments that were held in St Helens. Another occasion was when we got lost on-route to North Wales, and ended up going the rough the Mersey Tunnel (those roads are dreadful). The Mersey Tunnel itself is said to be haunted by a ghostly hitchhiker that has been seen on a number of occasions at the turn of the new millennium. One motorist is said to have pulled over to assist this lost young lady only for her to disappear into thin air when he approached her. No one knows who she is.

Being a member of the National Trust however, brought me to Merseyside for my most recent occasion (2004), and that was to visit the wonderful Tudor house that is Speke Hall. We could have chosen any of the wonderful National Trust properties to visit on our day out, but chose Speke Hall simply because of its sheer magnificence and its aesthetic beauty.

Located in an area of Liverpool noted for its timber-framed buildings, Speke Hall is without a doubt one of the most exceptional buildings of this nature, by far. The building dates from around the late 1400s but it is believed that a far older house once stood on the actual site. The Norris family first occupied Speke Hall after they acquired the manor of Speke (*Spec* – which means brushwood in Old English) in or around the fourteenth century and resided there until the eighteenth century. The Norris family built most of the present house we see today and like many of the family's in that area at that time, they were staunch Catholics. Needless to say that many priest holes were built into the walls of Speke Hall, which shows people of today the families dedication to the old faith.

After the Norris's came the Beauclerks and this family let the manor go in a big way. Lack of care and much needed repairs saw the hall decline to the point of total disrepair. Three generations of this family almost saw the end of Speke Hall.

In 1795, a local sugar merchant named Richard Watt bought the house and spent many hours and hundreds of pounds restoring the ramshackle of the manor house. Upon his death, he bequeathed the hall to his ten-year-old nephew, Richard. When he was old enough, he spent considerable time refurbishing the house, which was eventually completed by around 1880. In 1878 a certain Miss Adelaide Watt came of age and took over the house and devoted the rest of her life to looking after it. However, in 1943 the house became the property of the National Trust and has been looked after and cared for by them to this day.

I was told during my visit there that the house does indeed have a resident spectre or three! During the tenancy of the Beauclerks it is said that the family became financially ruined. Hearing this news the lady of the house, Lady Beauclerk lost her mind and was said to have murdered her young baby in despair and then took her own life. The cries of her dead baby have been heard echoing throughout the long corridors of Speke Hall, as has the restless ghost of Lady Beauclerk herself. The third ghost is thought to be that of a monk that walks into a wall in one of the rooms. A recent discovery of a bricked up door has been found at the point where the monk disappears, so one presumes this wall could have housed a secret passage, or an escape tunnel for these monks that were so cruelly hunted down and killed for their beliefs during the reformation. Speke Hall really is a house of many mysteries.

LEASOWE CASTLE, MERSEYSIDE

This one time castle and family home is now a thriving hotel that is said to be very haunted indeed. With over fifty en-suite rooms this one time stately home that was built for the 5th Earl of Derby dates from 1593 is said to be the home to a number of ghosts. A priest hole is hidden behind a giant mirrors that is on the wall on the grand staircase indicating that monks or priests may have resided there at some point during the reformation. The hotel is now one of many haunted locations that have opened its doors to paranormal research teams throughout the UK and ghost nights and overnight vigils can be held there.

It is said that the ghosts are that of a father and his son that tragically died on the premises many years ago. Similar to the story at Speke Hall, the tale tells of a father and son that were incarcerated at the castle after a family dispute. The father is said to have killed his son and then killed himself rather than face the horrendous suffering due to torture they were inevitably facing in the hands of their captors. The room in which they died was converted into a bedroom and many paying guests have reported seeing two ghosts in that room. One is of an adult male and the other is that of a young boy. Without question, it has to be the ghosts of the sad and tormented father and son.

CROXTETH HALL, MERSEYSIDE

Standing in the centre of the 500-acre Croxteth country park, Croxteth Hall is a magnificent quadrangular Edwardian home on the fringes of Liverpool and is one of the most historic houses in Merseyside, it is the ancestral home to the Molyneux family that once lived in Sefton. Richard Molyneux built the original house in 1575 and parts of it can still be seen in the south wing. In 1702 the 4th Viscount Molyneux added the west wing to the house, which is undoubtedly the most extravagant piece of the residence. Over the next two hundred years or so, new sections were added which subsequently added to the size and the actual building, and of course it's monetary worth. Nowadays, it is in the hands of Liverpool city council and is a museum that is open to the public.

The ghosts that are said to reside there are many and include the phantom of a boy that has been seen in the dinning room next to the fireplace. In the billiard room a strange dark shadow has been observed and it is believed that the 6th Countess of Sefton, actually saw the ghost of her deceased husband in one of the bedrooms. His ghost has also reputedly been spotted gliding through the tearooms. In the attic, phantom footfalls have been heard when no one else is around to account for them, and in another corridor, disembodied voices have been heard along with doors being slammed closed as if something is in a vile temper.

Ghost Hunter and paranormal historian Richard Felix was chased from a vigil there at Croxteth Hall during one of his investigations. It was in an area known as the kitchen corridor where he heard footsteps coming his way. He knew there was no one else in the vicinity and made a hasty retreat. If any of the readers have read my other books they will be aware that I faced the exact same phenomenon at the Schooner Hotel in Alnmouth. On a solo vigil in a corridor also known as the kitchen corridor, I too heard ghostly footsteps coming towards me, and well.... to be honest, legged it! Richard seems to have got out in one piece from his ordeal; I on the other hand ran into a wall that I thought was a door (it was dark), resulting in a bumped head, stubbed toe, gashed wrist and a smashed clipboard – ghost hunting eh!

ALSTON HALL, LANCASHIRE

Into the county of Lancashire now and we visit Alston Hall. Alston Hall is in Longridge near Preston and overlooks the beautiful Ribble Valley. It is a centre for adult learning and has been for many years now. The house was built in the late Victorian period and has many architectural features that are gothic in style. Surrounded by beautiful lush countryside, Alston Hall is a wonderful place of learning that almost any student should want to enhance their education in.

A friend of mine from the Lancashire area spent some time at Alston Hall and had an experience of the paranormal for herself. Julliette Gregson, now an authority on the paranormal in the North West said, 'About two years ago

I attended a counselling weekend as part of course there. On the first night I did explore and had a walk round. On the first floor I saw a young boy in a period outfit, perhaps Victorian or Edwardian. Later when I asked a member of staff about this it was indeed confirmed that a young boy had been seen by the staff and other people visiting'.

Another story concerns a former pottery teacher called David Summerville that once worked at hall many years ago. It is said that while he was working late into the early hours one night he heard heavy footfalls coming from a downstairs area in the building that led to the wooden flight of steps to where he was situated. Thinking it was one of his 'mature' students he approached the top of the stairs to greet him. To his surprise, the footfalls continued up the stairs towards him one by one, getting closer with every second that elapsed, only there was nobody there. Almost thirty years on David can still remember the experience like it was yesterday and is convinced that what he heard at Alston Hall was genuine ghostly footfalls.

WHALLEY ABBEY, LANCASHIRE

The village of Whalley is a typical and attractive Lancashire village with a good range of galleries, pubs and shops where olde world buildings sit side by side with the newer, more modern buildings. It lies not far from the ancient market town of Clitheroe, and the magnificent Yorkshire Dales, and is easy accessible by all form of transport. Standing on the banks of the River Calder, Whalley Abbey is a fourteenth century edifice that is now in ruin, but started its long history as an Abbey for the Cistercian order of monks. In 1537, during the dissolution of the monasteries Whalley Abbey was transferred into private hands of Ralph Assheton and was subsequently converted into an Elizabethan manor house. It remained a private residence until the early 1920s when it was taken over by the Church of England.

Gaunt and enchanting these ruins are, it is a well known fact that it is not just aesthetic beauty, charm and history that these ruined walls retain, for it is said that the Abbey is haunted by a procession of phantom monks that have been seen on many occasions. With their hands clasped together as in prayer, and with their heads bowed, they walk silently from one end of the grounds to the other. The ghost of John Paslew is also said to haunt the Abbey with poltergeist-like activity being experienced preceding his impending materialization. John Paslew was the Abbot at the time of King Henry VIII and when the Abbey was ceased during the dissolution of the monasteries, Paslew was tired for treason and subsequently executed.

MARSTON MOOR, YORKSHIRE

The Battle of Marston Moor took place in Long Marston on 2 July 1644 during Britain's first civil war that lasted from 1642-1646. Under The Marquess of

Newcastle and Prince Rupert of the Rhine, the Royalists battled against the combined forces of the Scottish Covenanters and the Parliamentarians (under the Earl of Leven, Earl of Manchester and Lord Fairfax) after the Scottish Covenanters and the Parliamentarians had been besieging York City. An army led by Oliver Cromwell on this cold and barren wasteland that stands in central Yorkshire, just seven miles west of York, annihilated the Royalists.

Prince Rupert had been assembling his growing army as he advanced through the North West, and his aim was to relieve the city of York of its enemy. On 1 July 1644, Prince Rupert sought battle with the Scottish Covenanters and the Parliamentarians although he was seriously outnumbered at the time. Soon, both forces began to gather on different sides of nearby Marston Moor to do battle. Prince Rupert's prior efforts to build and unite his forces, combined with numbers of the Scottish Covenanters and the Parliamentarians, made the Battle of Marston Moor the largest of the civil wars with tens of thousands of men fighting, ultimately, for the city of York.

Prince Rupert and the Marquess of Newcastle were convinced the Scottish Covenanters and the Parliamentarians would not attack until first light and therefore retired to rest. However, the element of surprise seemed to give the Scottish Covenanters and the Parliamentarians the upper hand because at around dusk, just as the sun was setting, they advanced forth and attacked the Royalist army. The battle lasted two long hours with the scene being eerily lit by the low harvest moon. The roar of thousands of men and the clash of steel on steel reverberated around the fields as the blood spilt and saturated the land until there was only one army left standing, the combined army of the Scottish Covenanters and the Parliamentarians. Oliver Cromwell had defeated the Royalists and it was the battle of Marston Moor that made him. York was ultimately forced to admit defeat to Parliament, and subsequently the north of England was lost to the King.

It comes as no surprise then, that for many years the site of the battle is very well-reputed to be haunted with many ghost sightings of dazed and injured soldiers being seen in various parts of the fields, and the paths and lanes surrounding them. They say powerful and traumatic events can be somehow recorded into the fabric of buildings, an area of land or even time itself and is then somehow played back *after* the actual event to those fortunate enough to be able to witness them and the Marston Moor spectres could essentially be the best example of a haunting of this kind.

The ghost sightings date back to just after the battle itself and reports of ghosts in the vicinity have been reported as late as the 1970s. The late Andrew Green (1927-2004) tells in one of his many tomes (*Our Haunted Kingdom*) the story of a ghost sighting that occurred in 1968 on a road between the A59 and B1224 – which isn't far from Long Marston – by a group of lost tourists that were looking for their lodgings at Wetherby.

A number of people were spotted as they drove slowly along the road and were thought to be tramps, or homeless people. The strange thing was, was that if they were tramps; they were oddly dressed to say the least. They seemed to look like Cavaliers with long cloaks, cockades and wide brimmed hats with shoulder length hair, and long top boots. They now presumed that the group of four or five individuals were making their way home from a fancy dress party and thought no about it until they drove past them. On turning around to view the spectacle one last time before heading off, they were all astonished to find the road completely empty. They only found out later after some research, that the road they saw the silent figures ambling down was actually an unclassified road that was not even on the map. It was a thin winding road than ran right through Marston Moor, the scene of the battle where over 4000 Royalists paid the ultimate price.

The forest of Knaresborough lies about eight to ten miles west of Marston Moor and it was there where a whole legion of phantom soldiers has been seen on a number of occasions. Dressed in white uniforms they are believed to be the famous 'whitecoats' of the Marquess of Newcastle as they march to their impending doom. The whitecoats made a last and desperate stand during the closing stages of the Battle of Marston Moor and were also savagely butchered by the victors.

The spectres of the Battle of Marston Moor, it seems, live on with many of them being seen in this area on many occasions. Indeed, Jack Hallum comments in his book, *Ghosts of the North*, 'there are other less-tangible reminders that this now-peaceful spot was once a field of slaughter, for it is ghosted by many of those who fell that day'.

THE BUSBY STOOP INN. YORKSHIRE

Said by some to be Yorkshire's most haunted pub, the Busby Stoop is an eighteenth-century drinking den located in near Thirsk, and takes its name from a former landlord called Thomas Busby that interestingly, was gibbeted opposite the pub in 1702 after he murdered his father-in-law. His lifeless remains were said to have been hung up and left to rot and decay with the crows picking at his eyes as a deterrent to other would-be criminals. It is said that when Busby was taken from the pub he cursed the very chair that he was dragged from and claimed that 'anyone who dared sit in the chair would suffer a tragic and painful demise'. Why on earth one would curse a chair (of all objects) eludes the author, maybe the building, or perhaps those that dragged him away, but nonetheless the chair was, and still is, reputedly cursed.

Over the years it is said that there are indeed some unfortunate individuals that have came to an untimely demise after taking a pew in the 'haunted chair'. Heart attacks, motorcar crashes, an air crash, a motorbike crash all followed certain people that had reportedly sat in the cursed chair. There is even one person who was ran over and killed on the main road. All the people that had mysteriously died were also said to have died within days of sitting in the chair, some within hours. Because of this the chair was subsequently re-located in 1978 to Thirsk museum where it can be seen mounted on the wall high enough to avoid anyone sitting in it.

But did the removal of the chair from the inn take away any supernatural force that could have been residing there along with it? Apparently not, as it seems the pub is still frequented by the ghost of Thomas Busby. He is said to have been seen on occasions hanging from his neck inside the pub. Pretty harrowing thought, wouldn't you agree?

The author's friend and colleague, Ralph Keeton, spent a night at the pub in search of ghosts and he informed me that he sensed a number of active spirits that resided at the inn. One of them, he said, had trouble with his joints and was unable to walk properly. Although he couldn't quite put his finger on who exactly the spirit people were, he did tell me that one of them was indeed responsible for some of the strange behaviour that had been reported there in the past. While investigating the main bar area he picked upon a burly man and a 'water well' that was in the vicinity. As it turned out the pubs original cellar was in that very spot where he sensed it but it had been closed off for good due to constant flooding. He rounded up by saying that an interesting night was had by the team of investigators he had attended with some very odd occurrences being reported.

THE PLOUGH INN, YORKSHIRE

The Plough Inn is an eighteenth-century former coaching inn that is situated in the luxuriant countryside of the Yorkshire Dales. It is a two-star rated building that contains a wonderful oak panelled dinning room, a lounge and bar, a large conservatory and has nine en-suite guest rooms available for hire. It was built in the early 1700s and was once a farmhouse that belonged to the Wigglesworth estate and it was back then when the owner's wife began selling her own home made special brews. In 1750 as the farming industry began to decline, a drinking establishment was made and thus it became known as the Plough Inn.

Since that point the inn has went from strength to strength, and has progressed into what we see today, which is a beautiful ran friendly old pub. However, the inn's history hasn't always been a happy and prosperous one. In March 1945 a fire broke out in the pub resulting in the deaths of two people. A servant girl along with a former landlady sadly perished in the flames and it is said that the ghost of the servant girl haunts the inn. The owners told me that she could still be seen and sensed to this day as she panics in an attempt to escape the burning building. People have reported seeing a girl dressed in 40s style clothes as she hurries along one of the corridors on the upper level of the inn. Staff and visitors have also reported a strange sense of presence within certain parts of the building, along with the unexpected feeling of being totally out of breath. The strange thing about this 'out of breath' phenomenon is the fact that it is often reported by people that don't know the buildings history, and, more oddly, reported in the very spot where the servant girls body was found at the top of the stairwell.

I spent a night there a few years ago now and was part of a team that investigated alleged haunted properties just like this one. We were the first team to be allowed access to investigate the Plough Inn and some interesting

The Plough Inn at Wigglesworth in Yorkshire. A phantom horse and cart has been heard making its way down the old country lane next to the inn.

'odd activity' was documented. It was a great privilege to be able to seek out the spooks at the Plough Inn, and my results and investigation report can be found in, *In Search of Ghosts* (Amberley Publishing 2008).

During my visit, the pub owners also informed me that it is not just the old pub that is home to a ghost. Reports have come in of a phantom horse and cart that has been seen and heard clip clopping and rumbling down this once lonely country road that runs past the inn.

NORTH ROAD STATION, DARLINGTON, CO. DURHAM

The railway station at Darlington known as North Road Station has long reputed to be haunted. The station, which is now a museum, dates back to the 1840s and once served the Stockton to Darlington rail service. By all accounts a suicide took place there inbetween the late 1840s and 1890 and it is the individual that killed himself that is said to be the ghost that inhabits at the station. Upon discovering the dead man's body, he was taken to the station cellars where he was kept for a period of time until they were able to transfer him to the local mortuary.

OTHER NORTHERN HAUNTS

In December of 1890 the [then] night watchman was on duty when he spotted a man coming out of the cellars wearing old-fashioned attire including an old style hat and coat and with him, was a black dog. The night watchman approached the figure thinking he must be an intruder. No one knows for sure what happened next but it believed that the mysterious figure took a swing at the night watchman as he approached him subsequently knocking him to the ground. After he got back up, he took a counter swing at the mysterious figure but to his utter shock, his punch went straight *through* the man resulting in scrapped knuckles on the wall and fireplace that stood behind him. At this point the mystery visitors dog attacked the night watchman by biting him rather savagely, and only ceased in attacking him when the mystery figure called off the animal. It is said as they walked away from the ruckus, silently...and through the cellar wall.

No one believed the night watchman and everyone presumed that he must have been drunk, until they found out that the night watchman was a good honest citizen, not prone to an over-active imagination, and a committed teetotaller. The Incorporated Society for Psychical Research (SPR) were convinced the story held some validity so much so, they sent an investigator up from London to document the case. After interviewing the witness and conducting his research, he left the North East convinced that what went on that cold and dark night was a bone-fife paranormal incident. They say to this day the phantom dog can sometimes be seen scampering around the station; that, along with disembodied human voices, ghostly footsteps, and other inexplicable ghostly phenomena.

THE GRANGE AT HURWORTH, CO. DURHAM

Hurworth on Tees near Darlington is where the magnificent one time Victorian mansion now known as the Grange is located. The building work for this Victorian home was completed in 1875 by the famous architect Alfred Waterhouse, and it was built as a wedding present for Waterhouse's nephew, James Edward Backhouse when he married Elizabeth Barclay Fowler in 1873. They had fourteen children, and upon James death in 1897, the house was left to their oldest son, Edward.

The Backhouse family residence came to an end in 1912 and between 1912 and 1950 the house was occupied by a number of other families. The Rogerson family, and the Spielman family to name a few but in 1955 it went to the Reverend William Donnegan and the Hospitaller order of Saint John of God. The nearby Holy family school of Saint John of God was relocated into the Grange and was used as a school for boys. The Grange was sold in 1967 by the Hospitaller order of Saint John of God and subsequently closed down the school whereupon in 1968 it fell into the hands of Durham County Council who in turn gave the building to Hurworth church parish council, and on 20 September 1969 opened this former beautiful stately home as a community centre, which is still being used today by the locals and the community of Hurworth-On-Tees.

The Grange at Hurworth on Tees is thought to be inhabited by a shade of a woman said to be one of the Backhouse family daughters. A wonderful old Victorian mansion that is now used as a community centre.

Over the years the Grange has reputedly been subject to paranormal activity and ghost are often seen wondering aimlessly along the corridors and then suddenly disappearing. Doors are said to open and close on their own, and often, cold spots and unexplained temperature drops have been reported, giving the Grange a reputation with the locals as a very haunted building.

Colin and Cindy Nunn, along with their research team, Anomalous Phenomena Investigations (API) continually investigated the Grange for over six years before moving back home to California in the United States of America. Over the years API accumulated an abundance of anomalous sound recordings, photographs, and other evidence to suggest the Grange really is haunted. I had the privilege to join API on many of their overnight studies of this spectacular one-time Victorian mansion and I was not disappointed. However, if you wish to read up on what happened, I must once again refer the reader to, *In Search of Ghosts*, that details the whole affair. In the meanwhile, all I will say is that the building that was once home to over fifteen Victorians is *still* home to at least one or two of them.

THE CAULD LAD OF HYLTON CASTLE, SUNDERLAND

One of Sunderland's more famous legends is that of 'The Cauld Lad of Hylton'. Hylton Castle stands disused and ruined in an area of parkland in the Hylton area of Sunderland (hence the name) and is a shadow of its former glory. The impressive gatehouse to the castle is all that is left of this one time fortress with its great hall, its bedrooms and other appendages of the Hylton establishment, including the workshops and stables now being long gone.

It is said that William de Hylton originally built the castle in the early 1500s because of his love of extravagance…and his tremendous fear of the marauding Scots. A young servant boy by the name of Roger Skelton was employed at the castle but was prone to malinger off from work from time to time and had sly sleeps in the stables. One day, his master stumbled upon him sound asleep while he was on duty and duly ran him through with a pitchfork in one of his rages that he was known for. The boy didn't really stand a chance against the brutal force of this fully-grown man and died a horrible and painful death.

The Baron was said to have been sent away in order to get a pardon from the local bishop, William Jameson, for this brutal act and when he came back he was frowned upon and despised by the locals. By all accounts it wasn't just the locals that caused him problems upon his return, but the ghost of the young boy was literally coming back to haunt him. His sad ghost was reported to walk the castle and its grounds rubbing his hands together and muttering the words 'I am cold'. This presumably is where the spectral inhabitant of the castle gets his name. Other incidences occurred too when staff at the castle saw what appeared to be a young boy sitting by the fire in the great hall getting warm. When they approached the boy to help him, he is said to have disappeared into thin air.

My good friend and colleague Mike Hallowell has covered this story in his 'WraithScape' column for the *Shields Gazette* and with him being a leading expert on the hauntings on the south side of the Tyne, I thought I would consult him to see if I could glean any more information.

'You know there was a lot more to the haunting than this' he said to me.

'Did you know there was a lot of aggravation and upset in the castle's kitchens on many occasions believed to be caused by a poltergeist that infested the castle around about the same time as the cauld lad was haunting it. Sometimes, the poltergeist would throw around kitchen utensils and such like making a terrible din in the process. Other times staff would come into the kitchen and find all the equipment that they had just gotten out to use all put away nice and neat in the cupboards. I don't know for sure if the polt activity and the cauld lad were linked, but some seem to think they were'.

I never knew this and I am glad I consulted Mike. I also found out that the hauntings came to an end after the Hylton family were advised by a local wise woman to leave out warm clothing for the boy, and every now and again leave the roaring fire burning through the night. This appears to have done the trick and the ghost of the boy has allegedly, never been seen again. However, the legend of the 'Cauld lad of Hylton' still lives on in the traditions and the folktales of Sunderland's populace. Perhaps they keep the story alive because they have an empathy with the poor young boy in some way, and for whatever reason don't want to think that he has indeed moved on. Or perhaps maybe the ghost of the cauld lad has been seen once more in recent times, perhaps in

All that remains of Hylton Castle in Sunderland is the gatehouse. The Cauld Lad, or Cowed Lad, is thought to remain in the area after being killed by his master after being found asleep in the barn.

and around the gatehouse, or indeed inside the ruin of St Catherine's chapel that stands next to the castle, who knows.

THE SUNDERLAND EMPIRE THEATRE, SUNDERLAND

The Sunderland Empire Theatre stands on High Street West in the centre of Sunderland and is reportedly haunted by a number of ghosts. One, believe it or not, is thought by some to be that of comic legend and *Carry On* star Sid James (1913-1976). Sid James did indeed perform there on many occasions and unfortunately for him, he died on stage there too. On 26 April 1976 Sid walked on to the stage for the last time and suffered a fatal heart attack in front of the 2,000 strong audience, who all thought it was part of the act. He was starring in *The Mating Game* with his co-star Audrey Jeans on its opening night when he collapsed. It was a sad and tragic end to one of the world's funniest movie stars.

It is said that not long after his death, people visiting the theatre began to get an eerie sense of his presence especially actors and actresses that just happened to be using his old dressing room. I have learned recently that one or two big stars that have appeared there, have indeed claimed to see the ghost of Sid himself in the theatre. Although none of them will openly admit to it, much to the relief of the theatres management. They it seems, deny the stories of Sid's ghost – perhaps out of respect for his family. Also, a theatre group laying claim to having a ghost such as Sid James may be seen by some as a bad publicity stunt to attract punters regardless of whether it is true or not. Whatever reasons, the theatre categorically denies the ghost and who can blame them?

Fellow comedian Les Dawson (1931-1993) was however, one of the famous stars that claimed to have experienced something very strange while attending the Empire Theatre in 1992 but never told anyone exactly what it was he saw. He never returned to appear there again after revealing 'what I saw was the worst experience of my life'. One wonders just what it was he saw. Some say it could have been Sid's ghost, but I guess we will never know for sure as he took his secret to the grave.

More recently in 2006, Mike Hallowell was invited into the theatre to cover the 30th anniversary of Sid James's death for his 'WraithScape' column. A three-part feature was written up, telling the history, the alleged ghosts of the Empire, and of course the death of Sid James. During his visit to the theatre he was shown all around the premises by one of the staff while conducting his interviews. With him he had his EVP machine and while explaining to the staff just what EVPs were, he made a recording that astonished both the member of staff he was with, and himself. On it you can hear Mike talking to the member of staff while faintly, and in the background (inbetween Mike's voice and the member of staff) you can hear another woman's voice saying 'shall we tell him'. This was followed by a short chuckle, or a laugh. Considering there were only two people in that part of the theatre (the Gods) at the time it really is a hard one to explain.

The theatres other ghost is said to be a woman who was a former stage manager called Molly that was reported to have disappeared without a trace during the Second World War. No one knew where Molly really went, although some suggest she ran away with a Russian sailor. She has allegedly been seen by a few staff up in the 'Gods' area of the theatre, the exact same area where Mike made his amazing recording.

DOXFORD HOUSE, SUNDERLAND

Doxford House is a breathtaking privately owned stately home in the Silksworth area of Sunderland that was once home to the famous 'ship building Doxford's' of the northeast. It is built on land that was once known as the 'Silksworth memorial Lands' and was constructed between 1775-1780 by William Johnson. This eighteenth-century mansion is said to house an underground medieval chapel, which adds a little mystery somewhat to the history of the house. In 1783 William Johnson leased out Doxford House, but after his death in 1792 the house fell into the hands of Mr H. Hopper of Durham. Mr Hopper was the Johnson family lawyer and must have also been a great friend.

Mr Hopper left the house to his nephew, Thomas, and it was his daughter, Pricilla Marie Hopper that eventually married General Beckwith and moved into the house. The front entrance to the house was then built which carried the Beckwith coat of arms. It is a magnificent piece of stonemasonry that can still be seen to this day.

The Beckwith's moved to Shropshire in 1890 and the house was then leased to a man called John Craven and after his death in 1902, Charles Doxford took up the lease to the house. Charles Doxford married Kathleen Vasey Storey but as that marriage didn't work out, he went on to marry his cousin, Agnes Vera Headley. But it was to his first wife that their daughter was born, Aline Sylvia Doxford on the 8 December 1922. Aline Doxford went on to live at the house after Charles's death in 1935. The house is said to be haunted by the ghost of General Charles Beckwith with his phantom being spotted by students on many occasions in the 1980s when the house was used for student accommodation. He has also been seen in the main house area on the grand staircase and in the large bedroom upstairs many times since the 1930s. It is also believed (but not substantiated) that the ghost of Aline Doxford may still reside in the property too.

Doxford House's present owner, Phil Jeffries has confirmed to G.H.O.S.T., that he thinks his property is indeed haunted. He told us that his two large and very fierce Alsatian dogs will not venture upstairs in the house. They do say dogs have a 'sixth sense' and they are more in tune with the spirit world than us humans think, and can see and sense things that we can't. If this were indeed the case, well, it would seem that there is something lurking on the upper floors that ultimately keeps these huge and fierce guard dogs at bay.

It must be said that Doxford House had always been an 'unearthed gem' in regards to haunted locations in the UK, until Fiona Vipond and Drew Bartley

Doxford House in Sunderland (formerly Silksworth Hall) is said to be haunted by General Charles Beckwith with his spectre being seen on the main stairwell in the house, and also in the master bedroom.

of G.H.O.S.T. discovered it. With hidden details of its resident phantoms going back to the 1930s this not so well known haunted property had *never* seen any paranormal investigators or ghost teams carrying out their investigations. Since the discovery of Doxford House, G.H.O.S.T. (of which the author is one of the founding members) has been instrumental in running paranormal investigations and generally documenting the strange phenomena that this house generates.

THE ARMSTRONG PARK JOGGER, NEWCASTLE UPON TYNE

In Newcastle upon Tyne east there is a wonderful area of parkland that houses not one, but three natural areas of outstanding beauty. Festooned with paths and trails these parks, namely Heaton park, Armstrong Park and Jesmond Dene are wonderful retreats for those that like to spend time surrounded by the natural world. They are very popular with walkers, cyclists, and families that like to meander through them. The English industrialist and engineer, Lord Armstrong, after which one of these parks is named, donated the land in 1883 to the city of Newcastle upon Tyne. It is also this particular park that is said to be haunted.

On many a crisp and cold autumn day, I have slowly meandered my way through the quite often desolate and lonely pathways that snake their way through these serene and wonderful areas of natural beauty, for whatever reasons. Sometimes it would be a Sunday morning stroll to get some of the wonderful fresh air into my lungs. At other times I would be out cycling, and when I felt really active I would jog through all three parks and beyond.

It never occurred to me that those lonely paths that intertwine around the acres of land through miles of dense forests and woodland could indeed be haunted. I don't know why, I just didn't. The clues are there; old desolate ruins can be found in all three parks that obviously date back hundreds of years or so. In Jesmond Dene there is the famous old water mill that is now a Grade II listed building, the wonderful old ruin that was St Mary's Chapel that dates from the twelfth century, among others. In Heaton Park there is an old shell of a ruin with only two sides left standing and a wonderful arched doorway leading into what may have been the old Heaton Hall.

Going back to Armstrong Park, there is yet another old derelict tower that stands adjacent to the tennis courts. It rises to about twenty feet at the top of a wooded embankment to which at the other side, and at the foot of the bank is one of the old trails. It is on this old trail where the phantom jogger is said to run.

This particular ghost story was told to me a few years ago and it was one haunting that had never been documented in a book of this kind until early 2009. (*Haunted Newcastle*, by Darren W. Ritson – The History Press) although according to witnesses it did feature in the local newspapers prior to that.

The individual that passed on the story to me is an honest, reliable person that I know for certain wouldn't lie to me. I know this for a fact because it was my *father* that saw the ghost in Armstrong Park and told me all about it. Here in his words is his account of what he saw one Tuesday night back in 1986.

'One Tuesday night in September 1986, on the way home from Shiremoor, the Metro train I was on broke down and we had to wait for the replacement bus service. Since the train had came to a standstill at Jesmond Metro Station and I was in close vicinity to Jesmond Dene, I decided to walk and pick up my bus at Heaton instead, which would take me home. It was not far to walk, so I headed off on my short journey, which took me past the River Ouseburn and then into Armstrong Park and onto the path down from the old tower.

It was getting dark by this time and I was in a hurry to get out at the other end where Armstrong Park joins Heaton Park. As I continued along the path, a figure ran past me from behind. He was tall, thin and in silhouette due to the light levels being so poor. It was not until the runner had gone by that I realised he had made no noises whatsoever; no footfalls, no heavy breathing, nothing. I also thought it was strange how he was so tall.

After that I thought nothing more of it, until about 12 months later when I read about someone else's account in a newspaper concerning a ghost story in and around the same area. It brought all my memories back to me from that night when I had heard that that stretch of pathway was allegedly haunted. The story I heard concerned a phantom runner, who was seen in shadow form, and ran 12 inches from the ground'.

BAMBURGH CASTLE, NORTHUMBERLAND

One of the north's most impressive fortresses, Bamburgh Castle nestles nicely on the Northumberland coast about 40 miles north of Newcastle upon Tyne and 20 miles south of Berwick upon Tweed. Perched on what is known as a basalt crag and almost on beach level, Bamburgh Castle most certainly dominates this area. Spectacular views for miles around can be seen from its battlements and on clear days one can easily view the township of Berwick upon Tweed, the impressive yet rather small Lyndisfarne Castle (that is sat on a hill on Holy Island), and into the Cheviot Hills. There are many visitor attractions at Bamburgh Castle including the Armstrong Museum, detailing the life and times of Lord Baron Armstrong whose family still own the castle, and the Bamburgh Castle Aviation Artefacts Museum, (BCAAM). Here, displayed are many relics and artefacts that have been found and preserved after surviving the first two World Wars. A very impressive collection if I do say so myself.

Having visited the castle on dozens of occasions I can say with all sincerity that this superb bastion is indeed one of my all time favourites. Not just for the ghosts too (which we will touch upon soon) but for its sheer magnificence, its grandeur, and it's all round opulence. Bamburgh itself is a wonderful little village too, with its Grace Darling Museum (which stands opposite her final resting place at St Aidans Church on King Street), its traditional olde world public houses, and its quaint little row of shops and accommodation that line the high street. Many a time I have meandered out from my glorious little B&B or hotel at first light to be greeted by the imposing fortress that stands towering before you.

Bamburgh really does live in the shadow of the great castle and I can't emphasise enough just what a wonderful place I think this is. The castle is said to date back to the first century BC with one of the oldest sections remaining being the impressive lofty Norman keep. Built by Henry II and played a huge and vital part in the infamous War of the Roses in 1464, the castle was the first castle in history to be subjected to cannon fire. All but the keep was damaged during the siege but in the eighteenth and nineteenth centuries, work began to restore the castle. It wasn't until 1894 when it fell into the hands of the Armstrong family when the first Lord Armstrong bought it and subsequently continued restoring the castle.

As far as I know there are only two ghosts that reside at Bamburgh Castle however I may stand corrected. The first is a phantom known as the 'Pink Lady'. I remember going away with my junior school; I must have been about eight years old and we stayed in a little building that housed a dormitory, and a few rooms for the necessary amenities. It was in Seahouses, just a mile or so down the road from Bamburgh. One day we were taken to Bamburgh for the

Bamburgh Castle on the Northumberland coast dominates the surrounding area perched high on rocky crags. It is haunted by a distraught woman known as the Pink Lady, and a knight of old that walks in the great keep.

day and we were told all about the Pink Lady that was said to haunt the castle, its battlements and the surrounding sand dunes that cloak the area.

Believed to be a Northumbrian princess that once lived at the castle, the pink lady fell in love with another that she was never to be with, as her father sent him overseas. Eventually, after waiting many years for his return from sea, her father told her he had met another and fell in love. It was all a lie to get her to forget about him but alas, this backfired in the most horrendous way. After becoming even more depressed she took herself to the top of the castle wearing her favourite pink gown, and threw herself to her death onto the rocks below. This ghost is said to be seen every so many years or so standing in the dunes with her gown blowing in the breeze still waiting for her long lost love.

During my trip to Seahouses with my junior school we were allowed to stay up until after dark on the sand dunes in the hope of catching a glimpse of the elusive pink lady – fully supervised of course – I guess I have Mr Horrocks and Mrs Saint to thank for my first ever ghost vigil all those years ago, we never saw her.

The other well-known ghost that haunts the castle is a spectral inhabitant of the great keep. Said to be a knight in full armour, this phantom has been seen, and heard on many occasions as he rattles and clatters his way throughout the echoic chambers that stand at the foot of this Norman edifice.

YE OLD CROSS INN. ALNWICK. NORTHUMBERLAND

There isn't another pub in the north of England with such a fine legend like that of the dirty bottles of Alnwick. Tucked away just around the corner from the magnificent Alnwick Castle, on 'Narrowgate', Ye Olde Cross Inn is a splendorous drinking den that houses no ghosts, but an eerie and macabre tale of death and prophecy. In its window facing the front street, there is a collection of old dirty and dusty bottles that are standing on shelves made of old, and now very much decaying wood. It is this display of old bottles that the pub is famous for, as they have stood untouched for over two hundred years or so.

It is believed that the owner of the inn, at that time was making a display of bottles for his window in order to tempt locals in to purchase his goods. Many shops and businesses practice this method everyday in order to achieve good sales, and it's as common now as it was two hundred years ago. Nevertheless, as he was stacking up his window display, the [then] owner of the property is said to have dropped down dead with a fatal heart attack. The window display, almost finished, was subsequently closed and locked up with the display being left exactly how it was.

There is a local legend at Alnwick that suggests if the bottle display is touched or altered in anyway, the person that touches them will suffer the same fate as the old owner, and will die instantly on the very spot. Now, thanks to tourist information centres and the Internet, these and other folkloric tales of the supernatural are known the across the globe and many thousands of people visit Alnwick in their droves to see the 'cursed bottles' of Ye Olde Cross Inn.

It's amazing to think that at one time the belief in such 'supernatural matters' were looked upon with scorn and ridicule, indeed ghosts and poltergeists are still widely rejected by the scientific community et al. Yet, over two hundred years have gone by since the window was locked up and no one to this day has dared to move the bottles...I think that tells us quite a lot about what people really think in regards to curses and old wives tales, with the lack of actions in this case, speaking louder than the words!

The Dirty Bottles in the windows of Ye Olde Cross Inn in Alnwick are said to be cursed – move them, if you dare!

The most haunted castle in England? Chillingham Castle lays claim to having an abundance of ghosts including Lady Mary Berkeley, a Blue Boy, the former castle torturer John Sage, and a monk to name a few.

CHILLINGHAM CASTLE, NORTHUMBERLAND

Chillingham Castle lies situated in the wonderful windswept Cheviot Hills of Northumberland 12-15 miles north-west of Alnwick. It is right on the borders of England and Scotland and is reputed to be one of the most haunted castles in Europe. It is said to be haunted by Lady Mary Berkeley who roams the castle looking for her long lost love, who had ran of with her sister and never returned. Indeed on dark cold nights they say you can hear the cries of anguish emanating from within the castle walls.

Another spectre seen in the castle is that of the 'Radiant Boy' or 'Blue Boy'. During renovations of the castle a wall was knocked down and a skeleton of a young boy was found along with some blue fabric. It is said that the phantom of this ghost is often seen around midnight glowing blue. The grey lady is said to haunt the Topiary gardens, which are situated to the side of the castle, and disembodied muttering is often heard coming from the empty library. On many occasions the author has visited the castle and spoken to the owner – Sir Humphrey Wakefield – and he assures me that although his ghosts are friendly, yet somewhat mischievous, they are most certainly welcome at his home.

CHAPTER TWENTY—ONE

SCREAMING SKULLS OF THE NORTH

I will close the book with a final chapter on what has to be one of my favourite types of hauntings. I have always been fascinated with stories that are centred on human skulls and their gruesome legends. The north of England has an abundance of skull legends and there are many haunted houses that to this day, display their sinister relics that are said to cause much psychic disturbance. For me, there is something distinctly hideous about the remains of the decapitated human head, with its grinning teeth and large eyeless sockets that seem to stare at you from the glass case that it is usually kept in.

As we all know, the skull contains the brain which, in the average human, weighs something close to 14½ ounces. The skull, then has for centuries been seen as the seat of the emotions and the home of the personality. Because of this it is not surprising that after death the skull has a reputation for being haunted more than any other part of the human body.

Back in Roman times skulls were venerated, and some believed that the spirit of the previous 'owner' could still live inside. It isn't hard to see why skulls have gained such an eerie reputation – you just have to look at one to figure that out.

Over the centuries many haunted locations have had 'skull connections' which often involve eerie tales of screams being heard and horrendous poltergeist-like activity erupting whenever the skull in question is moved from its proper resting place. Such accounts might sound like romantic old ghost tales of yesteryear, but the truth is that many of them were well witnessed. What follows is just a small handful of my favourite 'skull legends' from the north of England.

CALGARTH HALL, CUMBRIA

Some time ago, during a trip to Lake Windermere, I happened to be staying in a traditional B&B which commanded a spectacular view of the distant Lakeland Fells. As I gazed out of the window in my room, the vista was so serene that you could almost touch the tranquillity. *A place of peace*, I thought.

Although the Lakes are indeed beautiful, the whole area is renowned for being subjected to a variety of paranormal phenomena. During my stay I was told about one such incident, which I'll relate to you now; the story of the Cursed Skulls of Calgarth Hall.

Calgarth Hall actually stands on the shore of Lake Windermere, and is one of the oldest buildings in the vicinity. Allegedly, the manor house is subject to a curse connected to the aforementioned Calgarth Skulls.

Kraster and Dorothy Cook lived on a plot of land which was seemingly coveted by a chap called Myles Phillipson, a local man of both wealth and influence. It seems that Phillipson had designs to build a grandiose mansion, but the farm dwelling owned by the Cooks was in the way. He'd tried everything – even offers of cash – but the Cooks, as was their right, decided to stay put.

Just before Christmas, Phillipson turned up at the Cooks' home and attempted to make peace. He regretted the bad feeling between them, he said, and wished to make amends. Not only was he happy to let the Cooks stay in their home, but he'd also like to invite them to his own house for Christmas lunch. Not convinced of Phillipson's nigh-miraculous change of heart, the couple hesitated before reluctantly agreeing.

Kraster and Dorothy turned up on Christmas Day and seem to have been treated courteously by their hosts and their friends. They did not join in the revelry and dancing, however, as they felt somewhat out of place amongst so many well-to-do people. Eventually they said their thanks and left.

If the legends that have come down to us are true, Kraster and Dorothy Cook were actually being set-up by the Phillipsons. The following day a troop of soldiers arrived at their cottage and promptly arrested them after carrying out a 'search of the premises'. Who would have guessed it; they just happened to 'find' a silver bowl that had been on display in the Phillipson household the previous day. The obvious intimation was that the Cooks had stolen the bowl during the time they were there for Christmas lunch. The flabbergasted couple were imprisoned for a week before being tried. A huge array of witnesses was called forth to testify on behalf of the Phillipsons – and against the Cooks. The elderly farm couple never had a cat's chance, and they were duly hung. However, before their execution Dorothy Cook made a chilling prediction to Myles Phillipson:

> 'Watch out for yourself, Master Phillipson! You might think you have done a fine thing, but that tiny scrap of land you lust for will prove to be the dearest a Phillipson has ever bought or pinched. Neither you nor your breed will ever prosper on it, and whatever plan or scheme you take up will wither in your hand. Whatever cause you set your arm to will always a loser be. The time will come when no Phillipson will own so much as an inch of land, and while Calgarth walls stand, we will haunt them night and day. You will never be rid of us!'

Even before the bodies of Kraster and Dorothy Cook had been taken down from the gibbet, the Phillipsons had already begun to tear down their dilapidated cottage and commence building a magnificent a new dwelling of infinitely grander proportions. It took almost a year to finish building the new hall, and it wasn't long before the words of Dorothy Cook came back to haunt the Phillipsons, if you'll excuse the pun. To their horror, two grinning skulls were found resting on the banister rail by Mrs, Phillipson, who staggered into the ballroom where she had guests, to announce her grim find. The irony was that the skulls were found on Christmas Day – exactly one year since the Phillipsons had set up the Cooks so that they could claim their land.

Philipson was horrified and ordered these skulls to be destroyed, only to no avail as the skulls were found back in the house after being destroyed time and time again. The hall, night after night, was then disturbed by howls, shrieks and terrible screams. Philipson knew the Cooks had indeed come back to haunt him, and with a vengeance, and so they did for many years after. The skulls remained in Calgarth Hall, staring at Phillipson with their evil grins every time he walked past and never again did he get a good night's rest - until his dying day. It was a grim reminder of the evil deed Phillipson so unjustly carried out. The Phillipsons had no luck upon the land and their fortune dissipated just as Dorothy Cook had predicted.

A guide on the Windermere cruise relayed this great tale to me as we sailed past and viewed Calgarth Hall from the lake.

WARDLEY HALL. MANCHESTER

The skull that resides at Wardley Hall is another cranium with differing legends to account for its existence. By tradition the skull, which was kept behind a recessed panel, was said to be that of the profligate (and morally corrupt) Royalist supporter Roger Downs.

According to legend, Downs believed himself to be above the law to such an extent that he once got away with murder. Not that, being a toff, he got others to do his dirty work for him, mind you. He may have been a bully and a cad, but he was no coward and had so much faith in his own pugilistic abilities that he would take on anyone who was foolhardy enough to accept his challenge.

There is an old saying that 'what goes around comes around', and eventually Downs ended up biting off more than he could chew. On one occasion he provoked a boat watchman near the Tower of London, and no doubt thought that like everyone else he'd ever fought his foe would collapse under the weight of his punches. It was not to be. Somehow, the watchman managed to grab a sword and decapitated Downs with one swipe. His body was pushed into the Thames and was never seen again. Bizarrely, though, his head was packed in to a small crate and sent back to his home.

At least, that's the official story. It is a great yarn, but alas it simply isn't true. In the latter half of the eighteenth century the coffin of Roger Downs was exhumed and opened up. His body was inside – still firmly attached to the head.

The truth about the Wardley Hall skull is radically different. In reality it belonged to Father Ambrose Barlow, who was hung, drawn and quartered because of his religious affiliations in 1641. Gruesomely, his head was then displayed for all to see at Lancaster Castle. The skull found its way into Wardley Hall when it was purchased by a Roman Catholic sympathiser. Due to the climate of the day, ecclesiastically speaking, the man who now owned the skull preferred to keep his purchase hidden, as to declare it would have given strong hints to his Papist leanings. It was hidden away in Wardley Hall, only to be rediscovered by the owners of the house in the eighteenth century.

Things seemed to go pretty well for a time and there were no reports of skull-related spookiness in Wardley Hall. One day, however, an over-officious servant decided to poke his nose into matters that really didn't concern him. He found the skull and, without so much as checking with his employees, took it upon himself to throw it in the nearby moat.

This might have seemed like a great idea at the time, but it wasn't. Almost immediately a terrible thunderstorm broke out, and it was so severe that the residents of Wardley Hall were in no doubt the two incidents were connected. The skull, they concluded, was displaying its wrath at being forcefully removed from its resting place. The owner had the moat drained at his own expense (personally I would have taken it out of the servant's wages) and the skull was eventually located. With due solemnity it was returned to its rightful position.

The relocation of the skull back to its former place seems to have done the trick, but over the centuries stories have attached themselves to it. It has allegedly been burned, smashed, ground into dust, shot full of holes and disfigured in other ways, and yet it always returns miraculously (and in one piece) within hours and is normally found resting upon the doorstep, grinning.

The notion that the skull, whether or not it is haunted, is a screaming skull seems to date back to the 1930s and was apparently the product of some over-zealous journalism. It is also rumoured that a former Bishop of Salford was in the habit of removing the skull from Wardley Hall – I'm not sure why – but by all accounts nothing spooky happened.

BURTON AGNES HALL

In East Yorkshire there stands a delightful Elizabethan mansion known as Burton Agnes Hall. It was built for one Sir Henry Griffith at the beginning of the seventeenth century, but before the mortar was dry the premises was already accruing a gloomy reputation.

While Burton Agnes Hall was under construction, Anne Griffith, a daughter of Sir Henry, was waylaid by several thieves who beat her severely. She lay at the spot where she was attacked for some time, semi-conscious, until she was discovered by two of her sisters. It didn't take them long to work out that Anne's injuries were so severe that she wasn't going to recover. As the story goes, with her dying breath she informed her siblings that she had an unusual request to make. Fully aware that the remainder of her life was to be measured in minutes, she made them promise her that, after her passing, her skull would be located in Burton Agnes Hall, a place of which she had so many fond memories.

Although Anne's sisters dearly wanted to fulfil their sister's dying wish they felt that it was both macabre and inappropriate. Hence, the woman was at first interred in the village churchyard. However, within days the household at Burton Agnes Hall became severely disturbed by eerie noises, including rattling, thumps and pitiful screams. The family and retinue of servants suffered this as long as they could, but eventually concluded that it was their failure to honour their sister's dying wish that was at the heart of the problem. With some reluctance they had the body disinterred. The skull was carefully separated from the torso and then buried behind one of the walls of the great hall. Almost immediately the haunting activity ceased. The skull is still there to this day, and peace reigns over Burton Agnes Hall. Should the skull be removed, however … well, let's just hope that never happens.

BOWLAND HALL, YORKSHIRE

There is a 'screaming skull' story attached to Bowland Hall, although relatively little is known about it. Like the Burton Agnes Hall skull, however, it seems to have an affinity with the building in which it is housed and gets distinctly upset if it is moved.

One twist on the Bowland Hall skull story is that relocating the skull not only sparks off paranormal activity, including bangs and wails, but also allegedly brings about an increase in deaths of the owner's family. Best leave it where it is, then!

BROUGHAM HALL, CUMBRIA

The location of Brougham Hall has played host to a fortified outpost since at least the latter half of the fifteenth century and was, with tongue placed firmly in cheek, called the Windsor of the North by Victorians. The hall is the traditional seat of the Brougham family, which unfortunately became extinct in 1608-09.

Brougham was a favourite of the Royal Family, with both King George V and King Edward VII both enjoying the hospitality of its owners. In the 1950s the structure of the hall began to decline and it was almost demolished in the mid-1980s. However, a restoration programme was enacted and with every passing year the hall inches closer to something akin to its former glory.

As one might expect with an edifice of this nature, ghosts – or at least, ghost stories – abound. Spectral soldiers have been seen wandering around its hallways, objects and artefacts have been seen to move of their own accord and loud, anomalous noises – including bangs and screeches – have been heard.

There is also said to be a cursed skull at Brougham Hall, and it has been alleged that bad things will indeed happen should it ever be removed. To prevent such a circumstance it has been secretly hidden in a wall within the building, and long may it stay there.

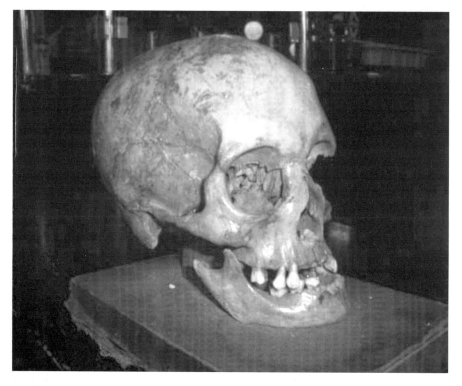

A grim relic stands encased at Ye Olde White Harte Pub in Hull. A constant reminder of the troubled times that this pub has seen. No one knows how the head came to be at the tavern, but it is thought that it was found in the pub, in 1881.

YE OLDE WHITE HARTE PUB, HULL

Ye Olde White Harte is one of the most popular pubs in Hull, despite the fact that to access it one has to slip into a narrow alley that runs between Silver Street and Bowlalley Lane. Since the mid-sixteenth century it has provided refreshment for a wide range of clientele, including travelling minstrels and travelling salesmen.

From early days, the pub and its patrons were not bothered about avoiding controversy. There is a room upstairs, commonly referred to as the Plotting Parlour, where in 1642 Sir John Hotham made known his desire that King Charles should be banned from the town. Anyway, it all got a bit out of hand and ended in the Civil War. Sir John, presumably after being allowed a last drink in the pub where the hullabaloo all started, then had his head lopped off.

There is a skull in the pub which is – don't look surprised – allegedly haunted. It is supposedly that of a young lad who was hit over the head with a flintlock by a drunken sea captain determined to show off his strength. For some reason the remains of the victim were placed in a recess under the stairwell, and there they remained until a fire occurred in the nineteenth century.

Another story regarding the origin of the skull is that it was found in the upper reaches of the inn, under the eaves, when renovations were being carried out in 1881. The skull, and other remains, were said to belong to a young servant girl who had at one time enjoyed an affair with the landlord. Afraid that their relationship was about to be made public, the man killed the girl, dumped her body in the roof and walled it up in the belief that it would never be found.

Obviously showing signs of wear and tear after all those centuries, the skull was given a bit of a wash and brush up and now takes pride of place in the bar where it is housed in a plastic case.

THE KNARESBOROUGH SKULL

Back in 1905 there stood in Knaresborough, North Yorkshire, an old Manor House. The beautiful edifice looked directly down upon the banks of the meandering River Nidd, and had done so without interruption since the thirteenth century.

Back then the manor was in the possession of a Mr. A.W. Bowes, who delighted in showing guests the authentic oak panelling and other original features. Bowes, to his credit, had the interior of the mansion completely renovated, and it was at that point where workmen in his employ made a strange discovery; the skeleton (or some say just the skull) of a woman buried underneath the staircase, just like the lad buried under the stairs in Ye Olde White Hart in Hull. Some reports at the time hinted that the woman's death (whoever she was) had been concealed due the manor's close proximity to a local church, although no one seems to know exactly what the motivating factor was here.

At some point, Mr. Bowes and his spouse took to sleeping in what was then known rather poetically as the 'Blue Bedroom'. The Bowes, both of whom disavowed any belief in ghosts or the supernatural, were forced to have a rethink after experiencing some extremely strange episodes themselves.

'During the night we keep hearing the sound of footsteps outside on the landing', Bowes admitted, and both he and Mrs. Bowes saw with their own eyes the door leading into the Blue Bedroom opening of its own accord no matter what precautions they took to prevent it.

Now at first the couple believed that the door was being blown open by a draught, but this was ruled out by a process of elimination. Bowes even tried placing a chair against the door with the back-rest underneath the door handle. There was no way in such a circumstance that the door could open naturally, but by the following dawn open it was, and they were both left scratching their heads in perplexity. On another occasion they heard a loud 'bump' against the door when no one was on the other side.

Just who the ghost of the Manor House might be is something that has never been resolved satisfactorily, although both Chaucer and Oliver Cromwell are believed to have slept there. Cromwell, in fact, slept in the Blue Bedroom used by the Bowes. There is certainly something odd about the Blue Room; it contains a secret cupboard operated by a hidden spring which at one time served as a Priest Hole. Initially Mr. Bowes tended towards the idea that the ghost of the Blue Room was Cromwell, but later came to think that it was connected with the woman whose skull was found buried at the foot of the stairs.

THE HEXHAM HEADS

In 1972, the two young Robson brothers from Hexham, Northumberland, had a rather curious experience whilst digging in the family garden of their home. What later hit the national headlines is not, strictly speaking, a 'skull' story, but as it involves two stone heads and something akin to a ghost I think it deserves a mention.

Whilst working in the garden the brothers uncovered two stone spheres each about the size of a grapefruit. On closer examination they were found to be crudely carved heads, although where they had originated – and when – was never satisfactorily resolved. Several nights later, a neighbour called Ellen Dodd was sitting watching TV with her daughter when they both saw what was later described as a 'half-man, half-beast' enter the bedroom. The women screamed – quite naturally, under the circumstances, I think – as the creature turned around almost nonchalantly and headed back down the stairs. When they plucked up the courage to go downstairs themselves they found their front door open, as if the beast had exited there.

All of this was interesting enough, but it was to get better. Academic Dr Anne Ross took possession of the artefacts, which by now were starting to develop their own pedigree. Whether it was true or not I don't know, but rumours were circulating that the heads were of ancient Celtic origin.

Several nights after taking the heads home, the good Doctor awoke at 2am and admitted to feeling 'cold and frightened', though for no particular reason. Then she looked towards her bedroom doorway, and saw something truly disturbing:

> 'It was about six feet high, slightly stooping, and it was black, against the white door, and it was half animal and half man. The upper part, I would have said, was a wolf, and the lower part was human and, I would have again said, that it was covered with a kind of black, very dark fur. It went out and I just saw it clearly, and then it disappeared, and something made me run after it, a thing I wouldn't normally have done, but I felt compelled to run after it. I got out of bed and I ran, and I could hear it going down the stairs, then it disappeared towards the back of the house.'

Dr Ross seemingly put the entire episode down to a nightmare, but some time later she arrived home with her husband, the archaeologist Richard Feacham, and found their teenage daughter Berenice in a condition of great distress.

Anne Ross's daughter told her parents that she had entered the family home through the front door, using her key, only to see a huge, black shape dashing down the stairwell.

Half way down the beast effortlessly vaulted over the banister rail and landed in the hallway on its padded feet. Perhaps wisely, Ross passed on custodianship of the heads to others and they eventually found their way to the British Museum. Here also, however, they were said to be responsible for some rather disturbing events of a paranormal nature and they were taken off show. The enigma of the Hexham Heads was never solved, although there have long been rumours that the beast-like apparition that seemed to accompany them was connected to an enigmatic creature known as the Allendale Wolf.

In 1904, farmers in Allendale, near Hexham, became extremely concerned when their livestock started to get killed at an alarming rate. Something was attacking the sheep and killing them with chilling efficiency. Initially the attacks were always perpetrated at night, and in all cases the damage done to the carcasses was horrific. Entrails would be left hanging out and internal organs would be mangled or ripped to shreds. The bulk of the bite marks seemed to be concentrated around the head, neck and feet areas, leading farmers to speculate that the predator was actually a wolf, although at that time there were – at least to my knowledge – no wolves roaming free through our countryside.

Eventually the killings stopped, although the presumably canine perpetrator was never found. It is difficult to say why skulls seem to be so symbolic of ghosts and haunting. I mentioned earlier that the skull is the home of the personality and intellect during life, but this cannot be the whole story. Nor can it simply be the fact that skulls look eerie. Sometimes, the fascination with skulls goes one step further.

APPLEY BRIDGE, WIGAN

At Appley Bridge, near Wigan, Greater Manchester, there is a rather oddly-named dwelling known as Skull House. Although it sounds like a fictional location from a 1970s Hammer Horror film, or one of Charles Dickens' novels, Skull House really does exist.

Before we examine why Skull House received its strange name, we need to point out that there is an air of mysticism which hangs over the entire area. There are a number of Bronze Age settlements nearby, and being in close proximity to such ancient sites can often be enough to trigger off different kinds of paranormal activity. Sometimes nearby dwellings of more modern origin can become 'infected' by the strange aura present at the ancient sites and householders will report seeing and hearing strange things.

Mind you, there is certainly something strange about Skull House. It contains numerous strange cupboards and recesses, seemingly superfluous rooms (some boarded up) oddly-shaped passageways and even a Priest Hole. If the architectural design isn't jarring enough, then there's also the skull.

Between Appley Lane North and Miles Lane there is a long pathway called Skull House Lane which was named – no prizes for guessing – after the aforementioned cottage. During the time of the Civil War, when persecution of Roman Catholics was most intense, a local priest from a nearby monastery was forced to flee. The only place that offered any potential for avoiding his pursuers was the cottage. Whether with the aid of the householders or not we do not know, but the priest hid in a secret recess half way up the chimney stack.

Madman Cromwell's soldiers tore the place apart, as they knew that the priest was in there somewhere – they just didn't know where. Eventually, through a process of deduction, they realised that the poor man was in the chimney breast. They tried numerous techniques to dislodge him, but the priest, knowing full well what his fate would be, refused to budge. It wasn't long before the Roundheads hit upon a sure-fire way to dislodge him; with flames. They lit a fire in the hearth with dry kindling and watched in amusement as the flames licked up the chimney and towards the priest. As the smoke billowed, the cleric could take no more and jumped down from his hiding place. As predicted, he was killed.

Not afforded a proper burial, the remains of the priest's skull somehow found their way into the house. Since that day the skull has been displayed on the mantelpiece in the lounge of the cottage which is now, predictably, called Skull House.

But there is more. The skull, you see, is said to be haunted. Over the centuries, many past residents have attempted to get rid of the skull. Firstly, this is entirely useless as it always comes back. Secondly, to even remove the skull outdoors is to invite calamity. One owner threw the skull into the nearby River Douglas, only for it to be sitting on the shelf waiting for him when he returned home. But if he thought that was the end of the matter, he was wrong. He drowned in the same river days later.

Another account speaks of a householder taking the skull several miles away, in the naïve belief that the greater the distance between the skull and the house the less likelihood there was of it finding its way home. When he returned he found that the skull had gotten there before him, and shortly thereafter he fell down the stairs and was badly injured.

It seems that any attempt to remove the skull is doomed to end in failure. The only guarantee is that bad luck will befall the residents, who will suffer from financial misfortune, sickness, broken relationships and untimely death forever after.

Could the strange phenomena witnessed by residents – including the alleged curses – be purely psychological? Could it be that they are so aware of the skull's terrible reputation that, after attempting to move it, they simply sit back and wait for the inevitable, having convinced themselves that the curse will now be activated? The answer to this has to be an emphatic *no*; and for one, simple reason. Anyone who was that scared of the skull's reputation would be highly unlikely to try and remove it in the first place? What sort of numbskull (pardon the pun) would attempt to move the skull from its resting place if they really believed that disaster and probably death would be snapping at their heels within hours? No; those who have attempted to move the skull were likely those who didn't believe in the relic's supernatural powers and probably scoffed at the idea. They soon learned that disbelieving in something is not a guarantee that it won't happen.

I think we must accept that some of the stories associated with haunted skulls are much more than 'old wives' tales', but this brings us no closer to understanding why.

It could be that, after death, the spirits of the deceased still have an affinity with their former bodies. Of course, the flesh rots away and eventually only the bones are left. Now think about it; it probably seems crazy, but if you were a ghost, which bit of your skeletal remains would you feel the greatest affinity with? A toe bone? A bone in your wrist? A rib or two? No; it would be the skull, for during life, that melon-sized bony receptacle held the organ that encapsulated you; your brain, and with it your personality, memories and intellect. I think it is perfectly natural that ghosts retain a fondness for their skulls, and this would also explain why they don't like to see them moved from the place where they perhaps spent many happy times or, just possibly, ended their earthly sojourn like the poor priest at Skull House.

Haunted skulls, screaming skull and tele-porting skulls – they are all true enigmas. We will probably never come to understand them fully, but what we can say is that they teach us something about this strange world we live in; that there will always be mysteries out there to solve, and that despite our best efforts the solutions to some will always elude us.

Haunted skulls should be left where they are, I reckon. It seems reasonable that their 'previous owners' should have the first – and last – say in what happens to them. Anyway; what harm are they doing just sitting there on the mantelpiece?

AFTERWORD

The north of England is without question – in my opinion – one of the most beautiful and enchanting areas the UK has to offer. I have been fortunate enough over the years, to travel the length and breadth of this magnificent collection of counties for one reason or another and in all honesty I can say, hand on heart, that I can not name one particular area as my all time favourite place.

Of course being a Tynesider through and through I can say that the North East of England, Northumbria and the like, does hold a special place in my heart. With areas such as Hadrian's Wall country, the magnificent and picturesque North East coastline with its dramatic cliff tops festooned with its gaunt and ruined castles, the beautiful Scottish Borders where many a battle and siege has taken place, and one of the highest and most remarkable waterfalls in the UK High Force, it is hard to imagine anywhere else so beautiful and so aesthetically pleasing to the eye – but there is.

From the tip of Northumberland on the borders to foot of the Yorkshire Dales, this small yet empowering mid-section section of the UK has an abundance of locales that in my opinion, competes with some of the world's most beautiful and exotic places. I ask myself this question, why travel anywhere else to holiday or visit? There are hundreds upon hundreds of places to experience such as the Lake District in Cumbria, the Yorkshire Dales, York, Chester, Leeds, Hadrian's Wall country and the Borders to name but a few. The list just goes on and on, and with all the aforementioned places and more having dozens of cities, villages, towns and wonderful areas of great interest, each with their aesthetic beauty, fascinating histories, and amazing stories to tell, one wonders why anyone would want to leave the north of England at all.

I think by now the reader will have gathered that the author is clearly a lover of his native north of England, and with good reason, for the north of England, I believe, is not just the most attractive group of districts in the UK for reasons outlined above – but quite possibly, the most haunted.

Ghosts and spirits of the dead have reputedly walked side by side with the living for as far back as historical records show, and from an area with a turbulent and violent past such as the north of England, it is not hard to understand why the author thinks this way. But it is not just the sad and unhappy ghosts, or the alleged negative energies of bad times gone that are sometimes said to remain there as residual imprints - but pleasant memories, happy times, and delightful apparitions can be 'engrained' into the atmosphere or the 'ether' too.

Stately homes and castles, old historic public houses and theatres, Abbeys, old churches, ancient hotels and hostelries all adorn the land and have been standing proudly for many centuries simply taking in and absorbing the times past and in a way, experiencing history in the making. Some say history itself, as it occurs, can imprint itself into the fabric of these buildings and on occasions when the atmospheric circumstances or conditions are right, or perhaps when certain gifted individuals come along, traces or images of these bygone days can be relived, re-experienced and played again like a 'recording' and seen once again. A theory called 'the stone tape' and it is rather odd to think that if this theory does indeed hold some validity, maybe one day a residual image of you or I may be seen by someone 200 years from now!

It is thought by some that the properties that are found in old stone bricks, such as the ones used to make these old English castles, fortresses and stately homes, are the same properties that are used in audio and videocassettes. If true it would certainly gives the whole image and sound playback theory a lot more credibility and is certainly tantalising food for thought regardless of the fact the actual concept come from a play. But if this *is* the case, and *some* of the ghostly apparitions one day become explained, then one mystery would have been solved thus reducing the possibility that after our physical deaths there may be an afterlife.

Or does it? I used the word '*some*' indicating that not all residual imprints or stone tape ghosts are just psychic recordings picked up by those fortunate enough to witness them. Records show that on occasion these types of manifestations, or similar ones, have been known to interact with our world to the point of manipulating the actions of those that witnessed them. Some ghosts have acknowledged themselves by nodding their heads or waving their hands to attract the attention of the witness. Some ghosts have spoken and even engaged in conversations with the living, and more interestingly, some ghosts been known to save lives – directly and indirectly.

Of course the north of England has an abundance of haunted locales and historic sites in which both stone tape apparitional spectres *and* invisible spiritual entities are said reside that are *not* just place memory or stone tape. Conscious, sentient spirits with the will to move around and interact with the modern day world by touching you, pushing you, breathing on you with ice-cold breath when you least expect it. They can toy with your belongings (and emotions) and slam the heaviest of doors in your face! This is where the authors' contemplation of an afterlife comes in and it is these entities spirits or souls that are believed to have stayed behind with us after the loss of their physical life, to either right a wrong or to look after somebody. Are they somehow trapped between the two worlds? Or do they stay simply because they loved the place so much. There are so many theories and ideas as to why they may still remain, but as of yet there are no definite answers.

Let us also not forget our highways and by-ways that adorn the land and have been known to the weary travellers and explorers since they were the ancient and earliest of dirt tracks. These roads are now alleged to be swarming with spectral coaches, phantom soldiers, wandering ghosts, highwaymen, headless horsemen, hooded monks, nuns, black dogs, mysterious cryptozoological animals, goblins, fairies, pixies, demons and witches but until one has seen or felt a paranormal presence or a ghost for themselves, I suppose it is rather hard to believe that they can exist.

Yet time and time again corroborated reports of such experiences and sightings are indeed reported and still they are looked upon as myths. The witnesses are deemed as crackpots, storytellers, they are either deluded or have been hallucinating, sometimes even called barefaced liars. Indeed, looking for a rational explanation is the best way forward and I believe that looking for a logical cause to an occurrence rather than a paranormal one is the first step in understanding what has really been going on. It is said that ninety-five percent of ghost sightings and paranormal phenomena *can* be explained normally, well.... at least to the sensible and levelheaded folk. It's that remaining five percent that fascinates the true paranormal investigator as these are the accounts that we cannot explain so easily.

Our history is rich and varied and you will find a ghost lurking in almost every corner. Of course it is not just the ancient ghosts of Roman legionnaires, soldiers from the Scottish invasions, monks and knights of olde that I have attempted to track down and investigate although I do admit the thought of coming face to face with history, or an historic figure is indeed an exciting one, but normal modern and everyday hauntings too. I feel that these ghosts from recent history are habitually overlooked more often than not and I feel this is a great shame as some of our best ghosts are indeed modern ones.

Think about this question, 'Have you ever seen a ghost?'. Think long and hard and the good percentage of you will probably say 'No'. But how do you know you have not seen a ghost? Is it because they never stood out like a knight in shining armour would? Or perhaps like a Roman soldier or a hooded monk?

Although a rather obvious statement, people have been dying throughout history since the beginning of man and people are dying today and will still be dying for as long as humans are in existence. It's a fact of life; in actual fact, as cliché as it sounds, death for everyone is the only certainty in life, so why should it be only the ghosts of Romans, ancient knights, King Henry VIII and the likes of Oliver Cromwell that haunt our wonderful buildings, land and heritage? Well to answer this question, its not.

The vast majority of ghosts are seen in solid form like you or I and are indistinguishable to other people who are alive and in the physical. If you walk down a busy street in a busy town, how do you know who is dead and who is not? Who is real and who is an actual shade or echo from the past? It may sound like an absurd question but give it some thought. Mr Smith who you have just walked past and said hello to may very well have passed on a month ago. Or Mrs Jones, who you have just seen in the grocers, is presently lying in the morgue at the local hospital.

AFTERWORD

I was told a story from a relative of mine some years ago about a woman he knew from down the street from where he once lived. In his early adulthood he was walking down Shields Road, Byker, in Newcastle's east end when he saw this woman who we shall call Margo, walking towards him.

'Hi Margo' He said to her.

'Oh hello there, is your family well?' she replied to him; as she smiled and walked straight past complete with walking stick and shopping trolley.

Nothing more of this was thought about until that evening's teatime when he was sitting around the table enjoying his evening meal.

'Mother' he said 'I saw old Margo this morning, she asked how we all were.

'Margo?' she said, 'Margo...you sure son?'

'Yes, it was her, she asked how we were.'

'It couldn't have been' His mother said, 'You are mistaken.'

'No I am not' he said, 'It was Margo alright!'

'Well son' she said in a confused manner, 'Margo from down the street died last week'.

My relative tells me he was one hundred percent certain then, and still is to this day that who he saw making her way up Shields Road all those years ago was that of Margo, the friendly old lady from down the street. So it is not just old-fashioned ghosts that haunt us, there are quite a lot of modern ghosts too, if you are prepared seek them out.

What the author enjoys about the thought of ghosts existing is that perhaps there may indeed be a life after this one – after all it would be dreadful to think that after we depart or 'shuffle off this mortal coil' there is absolutely nothing. Nothing except party time for all those little worms anyway! I suppose in a way that is why some people are so desperate to believe in the afterlife and the survival of the soul. To know or to think there is nothing, a cessation of our existence after we die in the authors' opinion would drive us all insane with fear and dread. Let us also not forget those who have passed before us – loved ones, family members, and friends. We all would like to think that they have moved on to a better place and are happy in their new and improved existence – wouldn't we?

In Victorian times, following the Great War, millions of people devoted their lives to spiritualism in the hope that they could one day be re-united with their lost loved ones or at least get messages from them after their deaths, and before their own, for it was believed that *communication* could indeed be made between the two worlds. Today nothing has changed and belief in the afterlife is still as prominent as it was all those years ago and yet scientifically, we have not progressed much in proving this is so.

In this volume the reader will have read accounts of ghosts and hauntings, spectres and spirits from all around my north of England that are just as mysterious now as they were hundreds of years ago. A lot of the ghosts reported and talked about herein may have only ever made one single appearance while others are seen and felt (allegedly) almost on a daily basis. Over the years in my research I have had the privilege of visiting the vast majority of these wonderful establishments contained herein and I have relished these wonderful opportunities with the utmost pleasure.

The fact of the matter is, is that all the venues featured in this work have indeed a good reputation for being reputedly haunted and have somehow managed to capture and retain perhaps a single poignant moment in time. Do souls and spirits really stalk the corridors and rooms of pubs and hotels, houses and castles, lost between the two worlds? Why do ancient battlefields replay the action that once took place there? Who knows for certain? But the human testimony and anecdotal evidence is overwhelming to say the least. Maybe one day we will begin to move forwards scientifically and furthermore, objectively a little quicker to discover the real truth but alas, although we are making slow progress I feel we will not ascertain all the answers – well, maybe not in my lifetime.

RELATED WEBSITES

www.mikehallowell.com/wraithscape

www.ghost-team.net

CONTACT DETAILS

Email the author with your ghost stories and other enquiries at:

darren.ritson@blueyonder.co.uk

Also available from Amberley Publishing

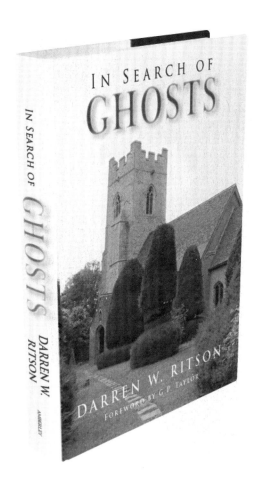

In Search of Ghosts
by Darren W. Ritson

Price: £20
ISBN: 978-1-84868-121-7

Available from all good bookshops or from our website
www.amberleybooks.com

Also available from Amberley Publishing

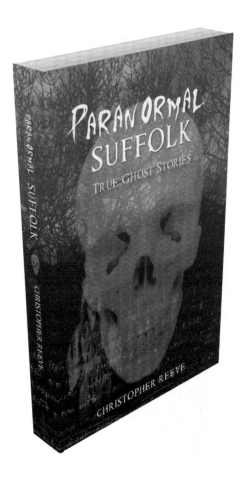

Paranormal Suffolk
by Christopher Reeve

Price: £12.99
ISBN: 978-1-84868-375-4

Available from all good bookshops or from our website
www.amberleybooks.com

Also available from Amberley Publishing

Paranormal North East
by Darren W. Ritson

Price: £12.99
ISBN: 978-1-84868-196-5

Available from all good bookshops or from our website
www.amberleybooks.com

DEATH IS AN ILLUSION